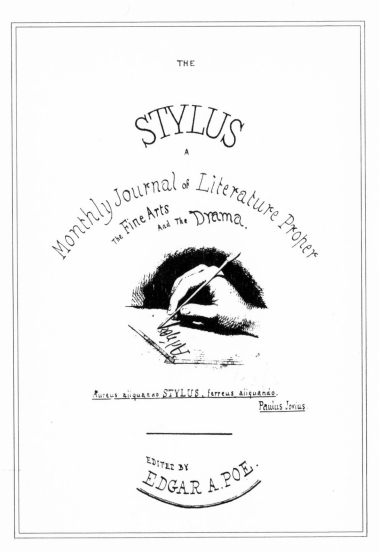

THE

STYLUS

A

Monthly Journal of Literature Proher
The Fine Arts And The Drama.

Aureus aliquando STYLUS, ferreus aliquando.

Paulus Jovius.

EDITED BY

EDGAR A. POE.

Design sketched by Poe for *The Stylus*. Photo courtesy
of the New York Public Library, Rare Book Division.

DISCOVERIES IN POE

BURTON R. POLLIN

UNIVERSITY OF NOTRE DAME PRESS
Notre Dame   London

Library of Congress Catalog Card Number: 76–75149
Manufactured in the United States of America
by NAPCO Graphic Arts, Inc.

CONTENTS

PREFACE

Discoveries in Poe presents a basic theme—that there is much for any reasonably curious reader still to discover about the works and therefore about the life of Poe. I have had to forego, however, attempting to convey much of the excitement or mere *sense* of discovery, so gratifying to the curiosity. That was inevitable, I suppose, in the process of validating guesses, of tracing the chain of circumstances which led Poe from one author to another or from one borrowed allusion to a second from the same source, of demonstrating connections between his life, his reading, and his creative conceptions. These procedures of mine are very different from the intuitive and instantly perceptive processes in Poe. The thrill of my own discovery was too often inexpressible, in ordinary terms, and required a summation in "slow time" that could not possibly represent either my own flash of apprehension or Poe's much faster insights and his ingenious dexterity in handling resources.

I should have liked to recapture here my feelings of shock and fascination, as a child, in discovering "The Black Cat" and "The Tell-Tale Heart." Both were read in the dim, somewhat eerie room that we called "the library," high up in a large house perched on a steep hill in Massachusetts. The winds that howled around that building and seemed to sweep in through the French doors of the room, at times, came directly out of "The Fall of the House of Usher." My imagination supplied the long ascent of Lady Madeleine from the deep cellar of my home, as the floorboards creaked occasionally. I never rambled in the woods or slogged through the swamps without expecting to find some traces of the buried treasure of "The Gold Bug," far as I was from pirate country.

When I moved to New York City, I was able to discover
the "very man" himself who stalked through the streets of
"The Man of the Crowd," although I soon guessed that it was
London, not New York, that Poe intended. Walking around
Poe's cottage in Fordham, near the Grand Concourse and then
over toward High Bridge and the polluted river, I was able
to reconstruct in my mind the countryside in "Landor's Cottage" in its rustic purity. I must admit, however, the imaginative effort needed for transmuting Poe's special atmospheres
into internal reality dwindled with my youth, except on a few
rare occasions when a new scene would suddenly bring back
the intensity of that first vision. Thus, I recently sought out
the catacombs in Paris to check on Poe's accuracy in elaborating a short magazine sketch into the detailed views of eerie
caverns and passageways in "The Cask of Amontillado" and
"The Pit and the Pendulum." The macabre corridors were
amazingly suggestive of Poe's descriptions, and those tales
reassumed for me all their grim life and emotional intensity.
I also sought out the port of Irvine in Ayrshire, Scotland, hop-
ing to enjoy some of the special flavor of the sea which went
into Poe's "Ms. Found in a Bottle," the *Narrative* of Pym, and
other works. There I found only a sand-filled harbor, dis-
appointingly quiet but appropriately melancholy, with an old
rusty dredge at the one dock that still seemed to function. But
the gray day and the blackened old buildings of the town
itself, which one biographer identifies with "The Devil in the
Belfry" setting, put me into unexpected touch with another
phase of Poe, that of the "Sonnet—Silence," and all the other
works that speak of quiet extinction or the faint musings that
spirits hold with each other.

Early in my development of these studies, I knew that I
could not manage to convey the emotional excitement of this
type of recognition and association. Only a poet or master
essayist, like Lamb, could do that properly. But I felt that I
could, at least, share my delight in tracing Poe's materials and
the way he adapted them to his own themes, in showing the

constancy of several of his prepossessions and his combination of the intuitive and the rationalistic, and above all in revealing a glimmer of the brilliant and often sardonic humor with which he buried private jokes—"jeux d'esprit" as he liked to call them. It has been like playing against a powerful opponent who enjoys the sport and yet, half wishing to be downed, grandly throws away the victory with some interesting gesture. Almost every chapter incorporates some of these conjectures, assumptions, and findings of my own.

In the first few chapters I deal with Poe's determination to assume an insouciant familiarity with French literature and culture, without betraying his insecure foundation and the secondary sources of his erudite or flashy allusions. Victor Hugo's *Notre-Dame de Paris,* I found, was a rich quarry from which he could draw the stores for constructing tales and "Marginalia" paragraphs. The poet Béranger served for several sophisticated references in his criticism, although Poe had probably read a very small portion of his writings.

While working on problems in this area I chanced upon new ones involving British writers. For example, concepts and phrases reminiscent of Byron made me return to the British romantic and then to Byron's friend, Mary Shelley. There was nothing surprising in this, since I had previously traced the importance of Godwin, Mary's father, in Poe's criticism. Later, I noticed the extraordinary praise that Poe gave to *Miserrimus,* one of the lurid tales of the Godwin school. This inquiry brought to light a disparaging poem about Poe written by Stoddard, one of Poe's editors; curiously, the poem, too, had the name "Miserrimus." I was then plunged into such fascinating incidental materials as Wordsworth's original misconception of the identity of the man buried under the "Miserrimus" tombstone in Worcester cathedral, a misconception which was carried over into *Miserrimus,* the novel by Reynolds. Finally, it became clear to me that Poe's last distraught word in the Baltimore hospital might well have referred to this novelist.

My attention was shifted to another British novel of the

early Victorian period which was highly praised by Poe but which has since been thoroughly forgotten, the story of *Ellen Wareham*. Here the "chase" led me to examine and ascribe reviews in *Graham's* and the *Broadway Journal* and to a further consideration of Poe as a critic.

The discoveries of the last three chapters were perhaps the most exciting, since they concern the final pages of Poe's life, the dénouement, so to speak, of major plots which had taken many years to unfold. The "Von Kempelen" chapter developed from my interest in Poe as an admirer of Godwin; as a Rosicrucian tale, it could be deemed an epigone of Godwin's *St. Leon*. Most engrossing, I found, was the theme of Poe's *Penn-Stylus* dream, which required me to invoke the aid of Poe as artist, with his graphic illustration of the theme of the iron pen. Here I had the generous aid of two libraries, which allowed me to publish two auxiliary documents, and my acknowledgments will be made to everyone who aided my searches and researches. This dream of having his own magazine, which would serve as a cultural force in benighted America, Poe maintained for at least the last decade of his life.

I have humbly sought, in my *Discoveries,* to tell a little more of the truth about Edgar Allan Poe—unflattering at times, laudatory on occasion—whether it be the truth about themes or ideas that he borrowed or absorbed, about tricks that he played upon the reader, about ideas or propossessions (such as his attitudes toward different types of waterscape which are revealed in his works), or about his relations with a wide range of personalities. I have considered that the pursuit of truth had best be conducted in a mood of dispassionate calmness, my fervid accompanying feelings being muted but not banished, I hope, for who can treat of Poe's varied literary performance without astonishment and admiration?

ACKNOWLEDGMENTS

I wish to express my gratitude for indispensable aid in the writing and production of *Discoveries in Poe* to the following individuals and organizations:

For specific advice from his unequalled store of information and balanced judgment—the late Professor Thomas Ollive Mabbott.

For the encouragement and very practical assistance, permitting travel in this country and in Europe and a term of leisure during 1968—The American Council of Learned Societies and the New York State University Research Foundation, donor of a grant and a Distinguished Research Fellowship.

For providing a wide variety of rare or necessary books and manuscripts, especially through the good offices of the individuals named—the Bronx Community College Library (Professors Jeanne Kolliner and Edwin Terry, with clerical help from Bertha Cohen and Evelyn Schweidel); Columbia University Library (Rita Keckeissen and Eugene P. Sheehy); the British Museum; the Bibliothèque Nationale; the Carl H. Pforzheimer Library (Dr. Donald Reiman); the New York Public Library, including the music collection at Lincoln Center; the Henry E. Huntington Library (Carey S. Bliss); the Alderman Library of the University of Virginia; Dr. William Doyle Hull II of Hofstra University; the Libraries of New York University; the Lilly Library of Indiana University (David A. Randall and Josiah Q. Bennett); and the Library of the University of North Carolina (Dean Walter A. Sedelow and Donna Setzer).

For excellent advice—the University of Notre Dame Press (Emily Schossberger, Dominic Lorenzo, and Ann Rice).

For unfailing good judgment and boundless patience—my wife, Alice M. Pollin.

My gratitude is also due to the editors of various journals for permission to republish, greatly altered, studies which became parts of my book: chapter i, *Revue de Littérature Comparée,* December, 1968; chapter ii, *Revue des Langues Vivantes,* September, 1968; chapter vi, *Comparative Literature Studies,* Winter, 1968; chapter vii, *Nineteenth-Century Fiction,* December, 1965; chapter x, *Etudes Anglaises,* January, 1967; and chapter xi, *Revue des Langues Vivantes,* August, 1967.

VICTOR HUGO AND POE

IN THE MAY, 1842 issue of *Graham's Lady's and Gentlemen's Magazine* of Philadelphia appeared "The Mask of the Red Death: A Fantasy," by Edgar Allan Poe.[1] Written too late to be included in Poe's two-volume *Tales of the Grotesque and Arabesque* (1839; dated 1840), it was a consummate example of his most characteristic style and handling of plot, both in its re-creation of a nightmarish but voluptuous atmosphere and in its grim combination of death by plague with a *bal masqué*. Many sources have been offered for this, one of Poe's most important and widely acclaimed pieces.[2] Yet among the dozen or more suggestions painstakingly and sometimes ingeniously traced, we do not find presented as a major source one which Poe clearly indicates in the tale itself, namely, Victor Hugo's *Hernani*.[3]

Let me recall to the reader the occasion for Poe's reference. Prince Prospero leaves his domain—presumably Florence, if we may equate this Medicean lover of the sumptuous and the artistic with the ruler of Boccaccio's plague-ridden city of 1348 —and shuts up his whole entourage of a thousand courtiers in a "castellated abbey" to defy the plague, called the "Red Death." (The appearance of blood, a reminder of Virginia Clemm's January, 1842 lung hemorrhage, was the motif of the grim tale.) After a half year of seclusion Prospero gives a magnificent masked ball in a suite of seven rooms, illuminated only by lamps directing their rays through variously colored Gothic windows set into the corridor wall. The costumes of all are required to be magnificent and grotesque. "There were much glare and glitter and piquancy and phantasm—much of what has been since seen in 'Hernani.' "[4] The setting is almost everything in this story, which concerns the appearance of a masker among the "mad revellers" who has "assumed the type of the Red Death. His vesture was dabbled in *blood*. . . . When the eyes of Prince Prospero fell upon this spectral image (which, with a slow and solemn movement, as if more fully to sustain its *rôle*, stalked to and fro among the waltzers) he was seen to be convulsed. . . ." He then accosts the figure with drawn dagger in the last room of the suite, its black draperies lighted by a blood red window.[5] As the ebony clock sounds midnight he discovers that the cloak of the figure is "untenanted by any tangible form," and all the guests drop in "the despairing posture" of their instantaneous death by plague, leaving the stage of Prospero's castle strewn with corpses.

This scene is strongly reminiscent of the masqued ball at the end of Act V of *Hernani*. Earlier in the drama, Hernani has courted Doña Sol, the niece of the great nobleman Don Ruy Gomez de Silva; the lovely girl is also being sought by Don Carlos, just before his accession to power as Charles V. The unrecognized nobleman Hernani is saved through Don Ruy's Castilian sense of the courtesy due a guest, even though he is a notorious bandit. Moreover, Hernani is seeking to snatch Doña Sol from both her aged uncle-suitor and Don Carlos. In return for asylum from Don Carlos and his soldiers, Hernani vows to sacrifice himself, even to his very life, at the sound of Don Ruy's horn. In Act IV Don Carlos has a complete change of personality and intention upon gaining the empire; he restores Hernani to his lands and title and gives him Doña Sol in matrimony. The last act consists of the seemingly extraneous episode of the masked ball, presented as part of the wedding ceremonies and attended by Don Ruy in the disguise of a spectral figure in a black domino. In his jealousy, he cuts short all festivities and life itself for Hernani and his bride by sounding his horn and demanding the sacrifice. Hernani is allowed to choose the manner of his death and accepts poison in a goblet, half of which Doña Sol snatches for herself. As the two lovers lie dead, Don Ruy, stricken with remorse, drops also in a "despairing posture."

The points of similarity with Poe's "Mask of the Red Death" are so many that I must conjecture that French critics, reading the reference to *Hernani,* must have nodded in agreement and then gone on to some more esoteric comparison.[6] Even in critical studies and biographies such as those of Celestin Pierre Cambiaire, Emile Lauvrière, and Alfred Colling, there seems to be no treatment of the *Hernani* theme in this tale or of the influence of Hugo in general upon Poe.[7] Neither do I find reference to this subject in the contemporary French reviews of Poe's tales.[8] Even Baudelaire, Poe's major translator and French commentator, whose "artistic parent" Victor Hugo was said to be,[9] limits himself to a very allusive comparison at the end of his preface to the 1857 *Nouvelles Histoires Extraordinaires:* "Our preferences are easy to guess, and every person captivated by pure poetry will understand me when I say that among our antipoetic race, Victor Hugo would be less admired if he were perfect and also that he could have had himself pardoned for his lyric genius only by introducing into his poetry forcibly and brutally what Poe would consider as the major modern heresy—*instruction.*"[10] The uniform silence on the subject of the Hugo-Poe relationship is especially remarkable, since Poe refers not only to *Hernani* but also to Hugo himself and to *Notre-Dame de Paris* elsewhere.

Both "The Mask of the Red Death" and *Hernani* are conspicuous examples of the use of the grotesque, which entered so much into the admiration of Baudelaire and his contemporaries. It seems possible that either through the text itself or indirectly through a British review, Poe absorbed ideas from the famous preface to *Cromwell;* this embodied Hugo's early aesthetic credo and presented a challenge to concepts of classical beauty in literature. Usually Poe's use of the terms *grotesque* and *arabesque,* as in his preface to the *Tales of the Grotesque and Arabesque* of 1839, is ascribed to Sir Walter Scott's long article reviewing the works of E. T. A. Hoffmann.[11] The two words of Poe's book title may have come from Scott's piece "On the Supernatural in Fictitious Composition," but in that case Poe would have had to ignore Scott's strong disapproval of Hoffmann's style.[12] How much more in tune with Poe's preface and practice was Hugo's statement in the preface to *Cromwell* of 1827, here briefly excerpted: "Here is a principle alien to antiquity, a new type introduced into poetry; and, as one factor more in a being modifies the entire being, here is a new form which is developing in art. This type is the grotesque. . . . You make out of the *ugly* a type for imitation, out of the *grotesque* an element for art. . . . In the thinking of contemporaries . . . the grotesque plays a great role. . . . It creates the deformed and the horrible, . . . the comic and the buffoon. . . . The grotesque is, in our opinion, the richest source that nature can open to art. . . . The beautiful has only one type; the ugly has a thousand."[13] These are, of course, only apothegms and principles which are successively elaborated by Hugo in a reasoned, if not entirely reasonable, fashion. When one considers the many representations of horror and deformity in Poe's tales, such as "Hop-Frog," "The Pit and the Pendulum," "The Tell-Tale Heart," and "The Black Cat," one would be inclined to regard Hugo as an ideal spokesman for Poe's practice, whether or not Poe had read this widely discussed and extensively publicized document. In actual fact, *The Foreign Quarterly Review* of the next year (June, 1828) presented a review of *Cromwell* with a convenient summary of Hugo's history of literature—the ages of the ode, the epos, and the drama—with this statement:

> The burlesque is the just and distinguishing feature of the third or present age; it is born of inevitable circumstance, and the overthrow of the unities, and the jumbling of tragedy and comedy, terror and buffoonery, were not the consequences of the decline of poetry, but of the march of time and the progress of human society. . . . The burlesque . . . is natural to the moderns and will come, whether we do call on it or not.

There is little question of Poe's interest in the past and current issues of this journal.[14]

One aspect of Hugo's theory of the grotesque in art, the union of "les qualités les plus opposées" (*Cromwell*, p. 27) was especially developed in *Hernani*, which he wrote in 1829 and which produced such an uproar upon its performance, February 25, 1830. Julleville declares that the leading characteristic of his dramas is "l'absurdité" which springs from the fact that "his personages say the opposite of what they ought to say and do the opposite of what they ought to do." Concerning *Hernani*, he declares that antithesis is the fundamental trait: "He insistently contrasts black and white, the grotesque and the sublime . . . the young man and the old, the bandit and the king."[15] In Poe this principle is always used effectively, as in "The Mask of the Red Death" where the music, dancing, and decoration are brilliantly counterpoised to the ugliness of the plague and the terror of the grave. It is particularly this contrast which Hugo has caught in the last act of *Hernani*; it is this which provides Poe with a general *mise-en-scène* for his whole story and also with specific ideas and even phrases. Paul Henry Láng well summarizes the quality which must have attracted Poe and given him inspiration in the fifth act: "Hugo brings about this state of intoxication by the lavish use of stagecraft, costumes, crowds, the brilliant, though often false application of local color. Most of all, however, by his language, his verse, and his lyric rhetoric."[16]

Even the stage directions for the fifth act of *Hernani* show a parallel with Poe's tale: "Trumpets afar off are heard. Masks and dominoes, either singly or in groups, cross the terrace here and there. At the foot of the stage a group of young lords, their masks in their hands, laugh and chat noisily."[17] This direction, which, I believe, must have been followed in the performance that Poe saw, explains a puzzling circumstance in the story, the fact that, despite the masks, the faces of the human beings can be seen: "While the chimes of the clock yet rang, it was observed that the giddiest grew pale" and "when the eyes of Prince Prospero fell upon this spectral image . . . he was seen to be convulsed in the first moment, with a strong

shudder of terror or distaste; but, in the next, his brow red-
dened with rage." Hugo makes it clear that the dramatis personae have "les masques à la main," probably on a short stick
for ease in raising and lowering their disguise. In Poe's tale
it is only the Red Death whose mask is fixed, and so it is with
Don Ruy in *Hernani*, as he engages in many actions such as
handing the poison to Hernani. The correspondence of these
two spectral figures in appearance and movements is close;
one of the lords at the nuptial ball says:

> Have you not seen
> Among the flowers and women, and dresses gay
> Of many hues, a figure specter-like,
> Whose domino all black, upright against
> A balustrade, seems like a spot upon
> The festival?

> [*Hernani*, V, i]

Poe uses three paragraphs to show how the gay revellers
become increasingly conscious of the intruder in their midst
in the "habiliments of the grave," an intruder who "with a
slow and solemn movement, as if more fully to sustain its *rôle*,
stalked to and fro among the waltzers." Of Don Ruy, Don
Sancho says: "If the dead walk, that is their step," and "if he's
the devil, he'll find one he can address. / Ho, Demon! Comest
thou from Hell?" To this query the masked figure replies: "I
come not thence—'tis thither that I go." Another lord observes:
"Sepulchral is his voice, as can be heard." Poe certainly catches
up the stage directions and actions of Hugo's characters in his
own "dance of death" tale. After the Red Death has extin-
guished all life in the castle, it is as though Poe is envisioning
the play that he had recently seen, with its three corpses giving him his own stage set where "Darkness and decay and
the Red Death held illimitable dominion over all."[18]

A question arises, of course, as to whether Poe did in reality
see a performance of *Hernani* early in 1842 when he was probably writing the tale. I say "probably" because it was very
rare for Poe to retain any unpublished work for long; he was

always in desperate need of funds for his family, especially now that Virginia had been stricken. The tale was to appear in *Graham's Magazine* in May, 1842, a month after Poe left the magazine and was in dire circumstances; he continued to contribute to *Graham's Magazine* for several more years. To deal with the question of performances in America I must give a brief history of the early English-language translations and British productions of *Hernani*. One is a bit handicapped by the lack of any study of Victor Hugo's popularity in America equivalent to Kenneth W. Hooker's *The Fortunes of Victor Hugo in England*. Early in 1831 *Hernani* was played at the Royal Theatre of Drury Lane, London, for a few nights. James Kenney, well known as a writer of farces and light comedies (*DNB*), had offered what Kenneth Hooker calls his "neat, well-made version, entitled *The Pledge: or Castilian Honour*" as early as October, 1830.[19] I quarrel with Hooker's adjectives, for the translation strips the play entirely of Hugo's flashing poetry and brilliant phrasing. It uses a peculiar kind of popular stage diction, a pseudo-English that was never spoken in life. Specific speeches are sometimes quite literally translated, but Kenney veers sharply away from the wording of Hugo whenever he wishes; the episodes of the plot follow closely those of *Hernani*.[20] His poor version of Hugo's eloquent lines was almost immediately put into print in two separate editions of 1831.[21] The names of the uncle and his niece were altered to "Don Leo" and "Donna Zanthe." The play was produced in London on April 8, 1831, with minor success despite the brilliance of the cast, which included Wallack, Cooper, and Macready. In general the British thought the theme of Castilian honor overstrained and found no compensating poetry in their stage version to warrant its being repeated often.[22]

In the Drury Lane company was an actor named William Barrymore, who had made his debut there in 1827.[23] Like many British actors he also indulged in dramatic composition, his forte being farces, pantomimes, and melodramas. Barrymore apparently felt that he had sufficiently exploited the

British stage, and at the end of the year of the showing of *Hernani,* he left the Drury Lane theater for New York, where the Park Theatre announced that it had engaged him and his wife. The 1831–32 season of the Park also included a production of *Hernani,* said to be adapted from the French, the author of the adaptation unnamed. The cast of characters lists Don Leo and Donna Zanthe for April 12, 1832, and it may be assumed that this was Kenney's version of the play, although possibly not so attributed. I feel rather certain that Barrymore imported it, in the light of later events in Philadelphia.[24] There is no further record of a New York performance of the work until 1837, and our pursuit of the matter must take us to Philadelphia, where we shall again meet Mr. Barrymore.

One of the chief theatrical personages of that city was Francis Courtney Wemyss, author of a very particularized account entitled *Theatrical Biography: or, The Life of an Actor and Manager.* He tells of his failures and successes, chronologically, with different productions at the theaters that he successively operated. In reading his self-explanatory account for January, 1835, please remember that a performance of the work described was given also in January, 1842, while Poe was writing his tale in Philadelphia.

> On the following evening I produced "Zanthe," founded upon Kenney's tragedy of "Hernani," which had failed at the Chesnut Street theatre with Mr. Charles Kean for the hero. The secret of this splendid drama, which is now vivid in the recollection of the audience, was simply this: I was preparing "Gustavus," with a Ball Masque, when by some means Maywood and Co. were apprised of my movements, and endeavored to forestal them. Much to my annoyance, they announced "Gustavus," and produced it on the night of my benefit. Barrymore, whose fertile genius in the theatre was never at a loss, came in, and . . . said . . . 'We will give them a coronation as well as a ball masque, and not lose an hour either. Io triumphe!' . . . Wednesday (the night of the performance) did see us triumphantly successful. For eighteen nights "Zanthe" crowded the theatre.[25]

Gustavus III, or the Masqued Ball was Auber's opera, using
Scribe's drama; it had opened at the Paris Opera as recently
as February 27, 1833. Since the beginning of the season, Francis Wemyss had had his whole wardrobe staff working inces-
santly on the costumes of the masqued ball. This kind of
spectacle, a dramatic fad in Paris,[26] was becoming increasingly
popular in the American theater and helps to explain some of
the theatrical effects in the poems and tales of Poe, an invet-
erate theater-goer.

The play script quickly produced by William Barrymore was,
of course, no adaptation of *Zanthe* but Kenney's play itself.
There was never any need to worry about royalties to the
writer at that time for works that were "borrowed" from England or France before the establishment of international copy-
right agreements. One doubts that Barrymore did more than
change a few lines, especially in view of the very different
type of drama for which he was known.[27]

A further account of the early performances of *Zanthe*, given
by Wemyss, explains the impression that the play would make
upon the imagination of the "histrionic Mr. Poe," as M. Bryllion Fagin called him in his study.[28] Wemyss speaks of the
unusually large cost of the play requiring a "brass band, four
drummers," 125 supernumeraries, "many pounds of wax candles," "red fire" (cf. the red illumination of the room of death
in Poe's tale), and lavish dresses and properties, all of which
made it a great success.[29] When Wemyss moved out of Philadelphia to Baltimore, he produced *Zanthe* on November 1,
1841. A small circumstance indicated for that performance
helps us to understand a detail in Poe's tale: "A celebrated
slack wire dancer, Madame Romanini, added to the attractions
of the Bal Masque, in 'Zanthe,' astonishing the good people
of Baltimore by the agility of her movements" (Wemyss, p.
360). This feature is certainly very far from the fifth act of
Hernani with its lyric quality, but, probably added to the
Philadelphia version of *Zanthe*, it helps us to understand why
Poe wrote: "There were buffoons, there were improvisatori,

there were ballet-dancers, there were musicians, there was Beauty, there was wine." One might add that the music of Prospero's ball was not that of the early Renaissance or late Gothic, to match the windows of the "castellated abbey." It was rather the "voluptuous" strains of the relatively new dance, the waltz, which had been imported from Austria via Paris.[30]

The performance of the drama that Poe did see, I feel certain, was one of two given at the Walnut Street Theatre, on January 10 and January 11, 1842. There is every reason to believe that Poe was involved with the theatrical circles of Philadelphia at the time. Quinn speaks of the tradition that he attended "meetings of artists, actors, and writers in the old Falstaff Hotel" of Philadelphia.[31] His first employer there, William Burton, actor and manager as well as proprietor of *Burton's Gentleman's Magazine,* could have made free tickets available to him at the Walnut Street Theatre, at least during 1839–40. Francis Wemyss had employed Burton as a star during 1839 and would thus have known Poe. Moreover, Poe was friendly with the Philadelphian Richard Penn Smith, fifteen of whose twenty plays were performed on the stage and several of which were adaptations of French works.[32] It can be assumed that in January, 1842, Poe was likely to see the Walnut Street Theatre production of *Hernani* or *Zanthe* and to use its atmosphere in developing "The Mask of the Red Death."

There is little likelihood that Poe could have been referring to the printed version of *Hernani.* He is very clear about its being "seen" on the stage; he would not have sought out the French text. Régis Messac declares that the domain of French verse was basically closed to him, despite his quotations from Béranger, for example. He rather tellingly proves Poe's ineptitude in recognizing the rules of French versification. Woodberry earlier makes rather caustic but well-documented attacks upon the solidity of Poe's knowledge of French and comes to the reasonable conclusion that although Poe had started out with a good schoolboy's knowledge of French, enabling him to read fluently a text such as *Gil Blas,* he lost much of it through lack of time for practice and lack of a good supply of French works.[33] Edith Philips subsequently provided more evidence against the firmness of Poe's knowledge of the tongue.[34] Even his most devoted commentators are inclined to suspect the thoroughness of his knowledge of the refinements of French, while insisting upon the fluency of his reading skill.[35] I surmise that Poe used the name of *Hernani* for its prestigious effect, when he had witnessed in reality an inferior version in *Zanthe*.[36] An essential source lies in Hugo's contrast between the *bal masqué* and the spectral figure of Don Ruy, who brings death. Since this contrast was conveyed in Kenney's version and represented on the Philadelphia stage lavishly, we may be confident of its effect upon Poe's creative imagination.

Poe's other references to Hugo and his writings are also of great interest with respect to his critical methods and theories as well as his creative works. The first item is very extensive, occurring in his review of R. M. Walsh's *Sketches of Conspicuous Living Characters of France,* which appeared in *Graham's Magazine* of April, 1841 (Harrison, 10.133–139). This is about one year before "The Mask of the Red Death" and also before all his other markedly favorable references to Hugo. Walsh's book, however, includes a grossly severe critique of Hugo written originally by Louis Léonard de Loménie, although Loménie is not named by Walsh nor known to Poe. The *Sketches* was a book compiled and translated from the individual studies in Loménie's *Galerie Populaire des Contemporains,* a series, says Walsh, published "in weekly number" in Paris and then in volumes by "un homme de rien." Walsh seems to have translated, for his American publication, the whole of Vol. 1 plus the first three numbers or "livraisons" of the second set, before Vol. 2 came out. Hugo is treated in the first set along with Béranger and André-Marie-Jean-Jacques Dupin, the original of the sleuth in Poe's three "detective" tales, which he was to begin later in 1842.[37] Poe is impressed by Loménie's "vigorous and vivacious" style (Harrison, 10.133). The sketch of Hugo, he says, is one of those which he finds most interesting; his review, therefore, comments on Hugo, whom he calls "that absurd antithesis-hunter." The phrase is derived directly from the words of Loménie, via Walsh: "By dint of hunting after this perpetual antithesis of two contrary elements, Hugo . . ." (p. 202).[38]

The most flagrant instance of borrowing by Poe occurs in a sentence which combines a strong condemnation of Loménie's praise of Hugo as a poet with unacknowledged approval of Loménie's criticism of Hugo's fiction. "What can we do but laugh outright at such phrases as the 'sympathetic swan-like cries' and the 'singular lyric precocity of the crystal soul'—of such an ass as the author of 'Bug-Jargal'?" (10.137). In reality this is a pastiche of widely scattered observations in the book reviewed. Loménie had written that "Lamartine has just delighted for the first time the ears of the world with his swan-like voice. To this melodious song, Victor Hugo answers with a sympathetic cry" (p. 194). Earlier in the chapter is this statement: "Born almost beneath a tent, in the most brilliant days of the empire, Victor Hugo had one of those erratic, adventurous childhoods, so fruitful in emotions of every kind, which explains the singular lyric precocity of his *crystal soul*" (pp. 190–191). The apparent reason for Poe's combining this last phrase, italicized by Walsh, with the epithet "ass" for the author of *Bug-Jargal* is Loménie's condemnation of that book, of which Poe unquestionably had no firsthand knowledge. The *Sketches* speaks of its "deformed, odious, cruel dwarf, named Habibrah . . . a worthy brother of Han d'Islande," who is a "kind of ogre," eating "raw flesh" and drinking "human blood." Worst of all, in the eyes of the courtly and chivalrous Poe, "by the side of these hideous creatures, the young novelist placed some beautiful and poetic figures—Ethel, Ordener and Marie . . . who resemble the virgins of Raphael" (p. 195).

This is the only adverse comment on Hugo in all of Poe's works, and it springs entirely, I think, from his need to write quickly a lengthy review of a book which, for the most part, presents Hugo unfavorably. It illustrates Poe's frequently irre-

sponsible critical method but not his underlying opinion of
Hugo; when he read—or reread—*Notre Dame de Paris,* probably not long after this review, he felt it necessary to exempt
Hugo from his generally unfavorable view of novels, which
lack the virtues of the short story. Harrison records an apparently unfavorable reference to Hugo in the "Marginalia"
of Poe, presented as a reprint from *Graham's Magazine* of
March, 1846 and indexed as "a sarcastic allusion to Hugo."[39]
The text seems to say that "one of Hugo's progenitors" was
the man "who had the blood of an ass" and of an "astrological
quack" in his veins. In reality, the original item in *Graham's
Magazine* prints the name as "Hague" and has nothing to do
with Hugo. The allusion there was to Thomas Hague, a char-
latan of Philadelphia, whom Poe had mockingly attacked in
one of his articles of 1840 in *Alexander's Weekly Messenger,*
uncollected by Harrison.[40]

In the creative writings of Poe one slight consequence of his
perusing the pages of Walsh's *Sketches* for the review may
have come from the article on Hugo. The book spoke of Hugo
as author of *Hernani* and *Marion Delorme* (*sic* for *de Lorme;*
p. 189). This name, slightly transformed, was inserted into
Poe's poem "Bridal Ballad" when he republished it in the *Saturday Evening Post* on July 31, 1841, a few months after his
review of *Sketches.* When first printed in the *Southern Literary
Messenger* of January, 1837, the poem lacked a parenthetical
line now inserted into the third stanza: "(Thinking him dead
D'Elormie)." I suggest that Poe used Hugo's title *Marion de
Lorme,* varied of course, only for the phonic effect of its rhyme
with "before me." Killis Campbell has observed that Poe's 1839
review of one of G. P. R. James's books mentions his earlier
work, the novel *De L'Orme* (1836); and in the next number
of *Burton's Gentleman's Magazine* (August, 1839), Poe has
a passing reference to a business establishment named "De
L'Orme's" in his story "The Man That Was Used Up."[41] However, the change in the form of the name in the poem and
the deliberate insertion of the line only three months after his

review of Walsh's *Sketches* points to the chapter on Hugo as
stimulating his revision of the poem.

More significantly, Poe was now about to become familiar
with one of Hugo's major masterpieces. *Notre-Dame de Paris*
very soon was to furnish Poe with a large number of quotations and references. In February, 1842, during the genesis or
writing of "The Mask of the Red Death," in two reviews in
Graham's Magazine Poe makes three allusions to the novel;
these are important in their placement and in their form, for
two are in Poe's own French—very different from Hugo's. First,
in a review of *Wakondah* by Cornelius Mathews, editor of the
magazine *Arcturus*, Poe speaks of the poem as having been
"set forth" in the preceding December issue of *Arcturus* "*avec
l'air d'un homme qui sauve sa patrie*" (Harrison, 11.25). He
places quotation marks around this italicized phrase without
indicating the source. It is actually taken from *Notre-Dame*
with several variations that betray Poe as translating it from
an English edition. Hugo wrote:

> Jehan répondit froidement:—Voilà les cailloux dont je cail-
> loute mon gousset.
> Et, sans ajouter une parole, il vida l'escarcelle sur un borne
> voisine, de l'air d'un romain sauvant la patrie.[42]

A standard English version translates the last phrase: "with
the air of a Roman saving his country."[43] Poe must have felt it
better to reduce the specific "Roman" to a generalized type
of hero. He misses the idiom in *de l'air* by using *avec* and
introduces a clumsy construction in *qui sauve*. English translations, of course, were available to Poe; he knew Frederic
Shoberl's version, published in 1833 as no. 32 in Bentley's
popular "Standard Novels" and promptly pirated in Philadelphia by a publishing firm familiar to Poe.[44]

The second paragraph of Poe's *Wakondah* review reveals
why he neglected to identify the first quotation as coming from
Hugo—his desire to use another phrase from *Notre-Dame*
with Hugo's name added. Here he is dismissing *Wakondah* as

almost beneath criticism, but he promises to do his duty as a
reviewer. "And *very* distinctly shall we speak. In fact this effu-
sion is a dilemma whose horns *goad* us into frankness and
candor—*'c'est un malheur,'* to use the words of Victor Hugo,
*'d'où on ne pourrait se tirer par des périphrases, par des quem-
admodums et des verumenimveros'* " (Harrison, 11.26). The
original in Hugo is to be found at the end of the paragraph
which begins the discussion of Claude Frollo's young brother,
Jehan, as usual out of purse and luck.[45] Hugo wrote thus about
the penury of Jehan: "O consul Cicero! ce n'est pas là une
calamité dont on se tire avec des périphrases, des *quemadmodum* et des *verum enim vero!*" Now it must be observed that
every English translator would be inclined to pluralize the
Latin construction, unless he wished to avoid a plural by a cir-
cumlocution such as "instances of *quemadmodum* expressions."
Thus the Dent translation says: "O Consul Cicero! This is not
a calamity from which one can extricate one's self by a peri-
phrasis—by *quemadmodums* and *verumenimveros!*" (p. 245).
Poe slavishly follows his English edition in preserving the
plural form for both Latin constructions and ignoring the fact
that French conveys plurality here in the article alone. Note
the difference in idiom between Poe's *d'où* and Hugo's *dont.*
Poe wished to have the credit for reading Hugo's novel in
French and also for disparaging the poor poet, Mathews, in
three tongues, so to speak. The sentence of Hugo's perhaps
caught his eye because of its italicized prominence at the end
of the paragraph.

Poe's third reference to Hugo at this time seems to indicate
a more intensive reading. It occurs in the important review
of Dickens's *Barnaby Rudge,* of February, 1842, and demonstrates clearly that he now admires Hugo. He writes: "The
effect of the present narrative might have been materially increased by confining the action within the limits of London.
The 'Notre Dame' of Hugo affords a fine example of the force
which can be gained by concentration, or unity of place" (Harrison, 11.59). The preservation of unity became such a keynote

of Poe's criticism that it inevitably led him into the practice of
writing only short stories, despite the promising lead of his
long *Narrative of Arthur Gordon Pym* in 1837.

In 1845 Poe repeated a previous borrowing from *Notre-
Dame*. He had been engaged in one of his notorious charges
of plagiarism against Longfellow. This chapter in Poe's attack
was especially unsavory since his chief aim was probably to
stimulate publicity for the *Broadway Journal* on which he was
serving. In five successive issues of the weekly magazine, he
replied to a very reasonable defense of Longfellow by "Outis,"
presenting articles which were totally intemperate, contradic-
tory, and illogical. There is no need to retell what many commentators have handled very well. The second of the series, in
the *Broadway Journal* of March 15, 1845 (1.161–163), included
the quotation from Hugo which he had used in 1842 in a
slightly different form:

> "What is plagiarism?" demands Outis at the outset, *avec l'air
> d'un Romain qui sauve sa patrie* [Poe's italics]–"what is
> plagiarism, and what constitutes a good ground for the
> charge?" [Harrison, 12.61]

This time Poe has preserved the nationality of Hugo's meta-
phorical patriot, but he still misses the idiomatic *de l'air* and
the participle in *sauvant* as in the review of *Wakondah*. Perhaps there is a little ironic jesting in Poe's twice using an unacknowledged quotation—one of many—from Hugo, as though
shaking a bit of the spice of learning into the gallimaufry of
petty charges and self-defenses of the "Outis" series.

Out of Poe's notebook must have come another of his
recorded allusions to Hugo's *Notre-Dame,* the first of several
in 1844–45. It is used twice, initially in the sixth of the "Letters" or articles that Poe was writing from New York City for
the *Columbia Spy* of Pottsville, Pennsylvania. In the June 29,
1844 issue, in the course of literary chitchat about the sketch of
his friend N. P. Willis which had appeared in *Graham's Magazine,* Poe observes that it was being attributed to Longfellow,

"whose manner it about as much resembles as a virgin of Mas-
saccio [*sic*] does a virgin of Raphael."[46] A year later Poe uses
the same comparison of the work of the two painters in his
"Fifty Suggestions," which appeared in *Graham's Magazine*
of May and June, 1845. He gives it a significant place at the
end as "Suggestion L." As with other items from *Notre-Dame*,
he seems to favor an association between Hugo and critical
judgment or refinement of taste:

> Painting their faces to look like Macaulay, some of our
> critics manage to resemble him, at length, as a Massaccian
> [*sic*] does a Raffaellian Virgin; and, except that the former
> is feebler and thinner than the other—suggesting the idea
> of its being the ghost of the other—not one connoisseur in ten
> can perceive any difference. But then, unhappily, even the
> street lazzaroni can feel the distinction. [Harrison 14.185]

Poe derived the comparison of Masaccio and Raphael paintings from Hugo's description of Esmeralda: "Elle ressemblait
à ce q'elle-avait été comme une Vierge du Masaccio res-
semble à une Vierge de Raphaël: plus faible, plus mince, plus
maigre" (VIII, vi, 396). In the Dent edition it is given as "She
resembled what she had been just in the degree that one of
Masaccio's Virgins resembles one of Raphael's—looking weaker,
slenderer, thinner" (p. 322). The similarity of idea and of
wording is undeniable. Poe probably liked the comparison
because it demonstrated a refined artistic judgment, especially
since he had marked proclivities for the art of sketching. Both
his criticism and his creative work are full of references to the
graphic arts. Characteristically this concluding "Suggestion"
combines a slashing reference to his fellow-critics with an
instance of epicurean taste.

Notice that this excerpt from *Notre-Dame* refers to Esmeralda after her condemnation as a witch by the holy tribunal
and her imprisonment. It alludes to her "ghostly" appearance
on the tumbril, as she goes to her execution, just before her
rescue by Quasimodo. No one, to my knowledge, has pointed

out how closely the initial situation and details of Poe's "The Pit and the Pendulum" are connected with Esmeralda's sentence by the "Inquisition" and her incarceration in the dungeon of the Palais de Justice (VIII, i–iv, Dent ed., 281–309). The only sources which have been suggested for the tale refer to the events *after* the prisoner of the Inquisition in Toledo awakens from his swoon in the dark dungeon. The details of the pendulum and the closing in of the heated walls of iron suggest Poe's reading of Charles Brockden Brown's *Edgar Huntly,* Llorente's *Critical History of the Spanish Inquisition,* and William Huntley's "The Iron Shroud."[47] To my mind, however, the opening courtroom scene and the well or pit come from *Notre-Dame.* Esmeralda, having been denounced by the frustrated Archdeacon Claude Frollo, is brought into "a hall . . . spacious and gloomy" with "several candles lighted here and there upon the tables." On "a raised platform, were a number of judges, the farther rows just vanishing in the darkness—motionless and sinister visages . . . the *maîtres* in black gowns" (pp. 282–283). Esmeralda denies any dealings with the devil and is led out for torture. She is placed on the fearful apparatus, the "bed of leather," with her foot inserted into the "brodequin or wooden boot" and with "a leathern strap" around her waist. The screw is tightened and her foot is constricted. At the first excruciating pang the delicate dancer screams out her "confession" of all the alleged "practices" (pp. 291–293). She returns to the courtroom: "Night had quite set in. The candles . . . gave so little light that the walls of the spacious room could not be seen. Darkness enveloped every object in a sort of mist. A few apathetic judges' faces were just visible. Opposite to them . . . they could distinguish an ill-defined white point standing out amidst the gloomy background. It was the prisoner" (p. 294).

After her quick condemnation by the judges, Esmeralda is plunged into a dungeon. "She was there lost in darkness, buried, walled up" (p. 298). She loses track of time in the utter blackness, knowing only the dampness of the "mouldy stones of the vault" and the falling of water, which, "drop after drop, thus collected, fell into the pool . . . beside her," and was "the only clock to mark the time"; it was also the only movement "except, indeed, that she also felt from time to time . . . something cold passing here and there over her foot or her arm, and making her shiver." At intervals a turnkey brings her a "loaf of bread and a pitcher of water." Once she saw "a reddish light" in an opened "trap-door made in the vault of the *in pace*" (p. 299). When the Archdeacon finally comes, he prostrates himself before her "on the wet floor" in an agony of desire; his love and his threats spurned, he promises that she will die the next day (p. 307). Esmeralda "fell with her face to the floor; and no other sound was now to be heard . . . save the trickling of the drop of water which ruffled the surface of the pool in the darkness" (p. 309).

In "The Pit and the Pendulum" of 1842 Poe uses a similar situation, although the viewpoint is that of the first person narrator as in most of his tales. He starts at the point in the judgment room after his implied torture by the rack: "I was sick —sick unto death with that long agony; and when they at length unbound me, and I was permitted to sit, I felt that my senses were leaving me." Before he lapses into unconsciousness at the judgment of death, he notes details which are close to those of Hugo: The "black-robed judges" have lips that "appeared to me white. . . . I saw them writhe with a deadly locution. . . . Then my vision fell upon the seven tall candles upon the table" (Harrison, 5.67–68). Next he loses consciousness. "Their flames went out utterly; the blackness of darkness supervened; all sensations appeared swallowed up. . . . Then silence, and stillness, and night were the universe." When he awakes in the damp dungeon he is appalled by "the blackness of eternal night" (p. 71). He has lost track of time, like Esmeralda. He wonders about the exact mode of his death, and begins to explore the walls, "seemingly of stone masonry—very smooth, slimy, and cold" (p. 72). Eventually he proceeds across the floor, "treacherous with slime," trips on his coarse robe and

falls forward, his head over a circular pit, with water far
below. At that point a trap door in the ceiling opens to emit "a
faint gleam of light," as his captors note his accidental escape
from the well. Later he uses the rats of the dungeon to free him
from the frame to which he is ingeniously bound beneath the
slowly descending blade of the pendulum, by rubbing the food
from his dish onto his bonds, which the vermin gnaw away.

There is no need to underscore the many parallels of situation and detail. We know that Poe was paying close attention
to *Notre-Dame* during the early part of 1842, as the citations
in his criticisms in *Graham's Magazine* prove. We also know
that he was writing "The Pit and the Pendulum" during 1842
for its first appearance in *The Gift* for 1843, an annual issued
in the fall of 1842. I conclude that Poe borrowed from Hugo
his prison and courtroom scenes, the pathos of the victim, and
the dream state of Esmeralda. Surely Poe wove in details from
his other reading and his own experience, but Hugo cannot
be ignored as a primary source.

Proceeding in time, we find a treatment of Victor Hugo
entering into the *Broadway Journal* of 1845 in two ways. One
was directly through a review of Hugo's book *Le Rhin*, discussed by Poe in the November 29 issue (2.321) as *The Rhine*
although the correct title was *Tour of the Rhine*.[48] It was characteristic of Poe to change it in his review to one which more
closely approximates the original French title. Many other
examples of Poe's typical methods appearing in the two paragraphs enable us to attribute the item to Poe, although it was
not collected by Harrison or marked as his own by Poe in the
Halsey copy of the magazine.[49] Poe's hand in this review is
easily recognizable:

> This is a reprint of the best of two British translations—
> and is the first American edition. A prefatory discourse on
> European affairs, is properly omitted.
>   The style of this "Tour" is particularly *French*—there is
> no other word for the idea. We find a great deal of point,
> vivacity, wit, humor, archness, novelty—the whole pervaded

and "toned down" by a delicious simplicity.—It is not as a tourist, however, or as a sketcher, that Victor Hugo is most remarkable. His essays in this way are scarcely better than those of fifty other Frenchmen—but as a builder of brief fictions he is unequalled among his countrymen—very far surpassing, we think, Eugène Sue. His "Notre Dâme" [sic] is a work of high genius controlled by consummate art.

The tone of dogmatism and omniscience through the whole is Poe's hallmark, as is his assertion of aptitude for determining the "Frenchness" of the style, even from a translation; he implies that he has read the original in both paragraphs.[50] Poe's contrast of Hugo as essayist and as "builder of brief fictions" is mystifying until one dips into the book itself—very successful in its day, with eight editions in France in 1842 and 1843 according to the English preface. It consisted of twenty-six letters, of which the ninth embodies "A Singular Legend" about the devil and the church at Aix-la-Chapelle and, more important, the twenty-second consists of nineteen separate episodes or brief fictions in "The Legend of Pecopin and the Beautiful Bauldour." These short tales, somewhat in the manner of Washington Irving's *Alhambra,* naturally directed Poe's mind to the greatly admired long fiction *Notre-Dame.* The last sentence accords completely with his other statements about the book, from which he continued to borrow.

In 1845 Poe used another excerpt from *Notre-Dame* in a striking way. Always included among the tales of Poe is a brief essay entitled "The Island of the Fay," based upon an engraving which shows a romantic lake scene with a tiny fairy in a boat. It was one of the regular features of *Graham's Magazine* to open each issue with a "plate" and an accompanying essay or story. Poe pretends to have come upon this scene while rambling through a region reminiscent of the Ragged Mountains near Charlottesville, scene of his brief career at the University of Virginia in 1826. In his reverie he thinks that he glimpses one of the last of the race of fairies, although the creature also becomes symbolic of the course of the year in

her revolution around the island and, by association, also of
death. When it was first published in *Graham's Magazine,*
June, 1841 (18.253–255), it bore no motto. Poe reprinted the
narrative essay in his own *Broadway Journal,* October 4, 1845
(2.188–190), without the engraving. Indeed, most readers are
unaware that it was intended as a description of a picture. In
1845, however, he inserts an epigraph:

> *Nullus enim locus sine genio est.*
> Servius

The phrase owes its origin, indeed, to the *Commentaries* on
Vergil's *Aeneid* by Servius Maurus Honoratus, but it was
transmitted by Victor Hugo, with no acknowledgment from
Poe. Originally it appeared as a gloss on V, 95 of the *Aeneid,*
"Incertus, geniumne loci famulumne parentis," and reads:
"Geniumne loci quia, ut diximus, nullus locus sine genio."[51]
In Servius the words *enim* and *est* are lacking. They are inserted by Hugo in the penultimate paragraph of Book VIII,
chapter v (p. 325); the chapter follows the one which had
already given Poe the double Latin phrase used in the *Wakondah* review of 1842. In this context Hugo is writing about the
noises made by the young brother of Frollo, who is chewing
stale food while in his furnace hiding place. The Archdeacon
has told an unwelcome visitor: "It is a cat of mine . . . who is
enjoying himself beneath it with a rat." The visitor replies to
the reputed alchemist: "All great philosophers have had their
familiar beast. You know what Servius said: *Nullus enim locus
sine genio est.*" The quotation, which was italicized in the
original and, presumably, in all translations, obviously caught
Poe's attention. It is clear that the two Latin words were first
added by Hugo and not by Poe. The American was once again
paying his respect to the classical erudition of Hugo. He must
have thought that the idea of the spirit of the locality thus
underscored by the motto was a good compensation for the
omission of the engraving illustrating "The Island of the Fay."

During the last year of Poe's life he twice makes use of

Hugo material, the first time in a rather indirect although definite way. It occurs in Poe's reference to Du Bartas in the February, 1849 *Messenger* review of Griswold's *Female Poets of
America*.[52] Poe borrows from an English translation of *Notre-
Dame* part of his designation of Du Bartas as "the poet who
was in the habit of styling the sun the 'Grand Duke of Candles.'"[53] Later, for the July, 1849 *Messenger*, in the "Marginalia" section, Poe found himself able once more to use the
Latin garnishing of *Notre-Dame*. He is again vindicating the
role of the severe critic, as he did in the *Wakondah* review.
Poe was often judged abusive, and he apparently felt that he
must justify his candor:

> As for American Letters, plain-speaking about *them* is,
> simply, the one thing needed. They are in a condition of
> absolute quagmire—a quagmire, to use the words of Victor
> Hugo, *d'où on ne peut se tirer par des périphrases—par des
> quemadmodums et des verumenimveros*. [Harrison, 16.172]

This time he varies his own variation of Hugo, in the tense of
the verb—clearly showing his freedom from any slavish reference to his original text. The need for an aggressive criticism
which would reform the condition of the literary art had also
been upheld by Hugo in his preface to *Cromwell*, years before.

The citation shows the considerable respect that Poe had
acquired for the work of Hugo. In view of the significance
of *Hernani* and *Notre-Dame* in Poe's literary development, we
might fairly say that Hugo had played a role in two of Poe's
major tales as well as in his critical concepts.[54] Certainly, without the adaptation of *Hernani* on the Philadelphia stage the
literature of America and, by a curious interaction, that of
France, would be immeasurably poorer.[55] And yet the above
array of citations and themes does not constitute the whole of
Hugo's contributions to Poe's writings. In the following two
chapters I shall indicate how three more of his tales profited
from Hugo's fertile inventiveness and rich vocabulary.

2

NOTRE-DAME DE PARIS
IN TWO OF THE TALES

A SINGLE PARAGRAPH in *Notre-Dame de Paris* by Hugo is the source of several elements of importance in two of Poe's tales: "A Tale of the Ragged Mountains" of April, 1844, and "The Cask of Amontillado" of November, 1846. The elements themselves are varied and the evidence is to be drawn from both internal and circumstantial aspects of the tales as well as from Poe's criticism at the time (roughly, 1841–46). The paragraph in question must first be examined in Hugo's French, especially since one of the influences upon Poe resides in *sangsue*, the French word for "leech" that Poe used under pretence of its being a legitimate English term. Other words to be noted are *tonneau* and *fortunate senex*, taken from Vergil. The situation must be indicated: Archdeacon Claude Frollo, who has vainly pursued the gypsy dancer La Esmeralda with lustful passion and has finally denounced her to the ecclesiastical court as a witch, has offered her a chance to escape from the dungeon in which she has been languishing. Rejected by her again, he has watched her being taken to the gibbet in front of the cathedral, has assumed her execution as inevitable, and has wildly coursed through Paris, finally ending his day of frenzy at the house of assignation on the Pont Saint-Michel, the scene of his earlier encounter with Esmeralda. Now he spies on his young brother Jehan just before the latter comes out, and he throws himself to the ground in hope of escaping detection in the dusk:

> Il remua du pied dom Claude, qui retenait son souffle.
> —Ivre-mort, reprit Jehan. Allons, il est plein. Une vraie

sangsue détachée d'un tonneau. Il est chauve, ajouta-t-il en
se baissant: c'est un vieillard! *Fortunate senex!*[1]

In one standard translation this is rendered thus:

> He pushed Dom Claude with his foot, the archdeacon
> holding his breath the while.
> "Dead drunk!" resumed Jehan. "Bravo! he's full!—a very
> leech, dropped off a wine-cask. He's bald," added he, stoop-
> ing over him; "it's an old man—*Fortunate senex!*"[2]

The italics are given in all of the many editions of the work
that I have examined; they were, therefore, an aspect of the
passage that could easily have caught Poe's eye, while he was
reading and using *Notre-Dame* intensively during this period.

Several features of the passage which went into the two
tales can be briefly indicated: the use of the word *sangsue* for
"leech" in "A Tale of the Ragged Mountains," and, in "The
Cask of Amontillado," the name Fortunato, the basic idea of
self-destructive drunkenness, and the word *cask* in both title
and plot. The dungeon in this section of the novel is also
important in Poe's developing the catacomb setting of the
latter tale.

There is no doubt about Poe's knowledge of Hugo's novel
at this time. I have presented in the preceding chapter in full
both the evidence and the significance of his many allusions to
the story during the 1840's. It may be concluded that Poe
knew well the portion of Hugo's novel that contained the passage quoted above. The *sangsue* or leech played a critical role
in "A Tale of the Ragged Mountains."[3] It was the means by
which Poe arranged for the demise of the Virginia protagonist,
Mr. Bedloe, the counterpart of Mr. Oldeb, the British officer
who had died in the insurrection at Benares of Cheyte Sing,
as Poe tells it, through a poisoned arrow lodged in his temple.
It was actually a passage of anecdotal description borrowed
largely and almost verbatim from several passages in Thomas
B. Macaulay's review of G. R. Gleig's three-volume compilation of the *Memoirs of the Life of Warren Hastings, First*

Governor-General of Bengal. Poe had read this in the October, 1841 *Edinburgh Review.* The plagiarism—for it is necessary to call it that bluntly—has been traced by Maurice Le Breton, who overlooks one piece of borrowing from this source which tells much about Poe's methods and his frank disdain for the literary culture or perceptiveness of his reading public.[4] I refer to Macaulay's reference to the very name which Poe gives to Mr. Bedloe, his main character. Since the mystic correspondence of events and of deaths—from 1780 to the date of the story, 1844, depends upon the palindrome in Bedlo-Oldeb, I must cite Macaulay's passage. He is discussing the shift in Hastings' fortunes in India, when company officials were trying to wrest power from the Governor-General and almost everyone was turning against him:

> Immediately charges against the Governor General began to pour in. They were eagerly welcomed by the majority, who, to do them justice, were men of too much honour knowingly to countenance false accusations, but who were not sufficiently acquainted with the East to be aware that, in that part of the world, a very little encouragement from power will call forth, in a week, more Oatses, and Bedloes, and Dangerfields, than Westminster Hall sees in a century.[5]

William Bedloe had confirmed the false testimony of Titus Oates in the false charges against the Catholics in 1678, in consequence of which thirty-five men were judicially murdered.[6] It seems to me that Poe, reading this passage in Macaulay, was struck by the almost palindromic effect of the phrase, "Oatses and Bedloes," both names being of two syllables with prominent *o*'s in reversed positions, equivalent *e*'s, and *t* and *d* (the same sound, voiced and unvoiced). There is no need to underline Poe's musicality of ear or his love for word play. Since the entire story rests on the parallel of the visionary participation of Mr. Bedlo(e)[7] in the Benares revolt in which Oldeb is killed, this double borrowing from Macaulay is noteworthy.[8]

The weird correspondence is completed when we find Dr. Templeton, in attendance upon the ill Mr. Bedloe, seeking to

cask"—although not very scientific. Hugo wishes, of course, to remind the reader of the bloated body of the creatures after they have gorged on blood, even though as parasites they always choose animals for their source of food. In the text of "The Cask of Amontillado" the word *pipe* is used repeatedly as a synonym for *wine cask*. Poe also uses *cask* and *puncheon* (Harrison, 6.167–175): "I have received a pipe of . . . Amontillado" and "A pipe? Impossible" (6.168). As they proceed, the drunken Fortunato again asks about "the pipe." They pass through walls of piled bones, "with casks and puncheons intermingling" (6.171). One might add that it is absurd of Poe to write about an ossuary as being gruesomely combined, at random, with the appurtenances of a wine cellar, but it is probably proof of his wizardry that readers do not question this irregularity any more than they do the description of a burial vault that goes far beyond the limits of one family.

The theme of the drunken Fortunato, however, is one of Poe's major debts to Hugo's passage. Hugo italicized the phrase *"Fortunate senex,"* as coming from Vergil's "First Eclogue," specifically the passage in which Meliboeus is congratulating Tityrus, the old man, on his tranquil, pastoral life. Twice he addresses him thus: "Fortunate senex, ergo tua rura manebunt, / et tibi magna satis" (lines 46–47) and "Fortunate senex, hic inter flumina nota / et fontes sacros frigus captabis opacum" (lines 50–51). The passage of course has nought to do with being full of wine and is unlikely to have occurred independently to Poe's mind as a name-source for this short story. We know his willingness to borrow three other Latin expressions from Hugo's novel, as indicated above. The name itself was peculiarly apt for Poe's purposes. It is doubly ironic, as Professor Mabbott points out, meaning both "fated" and "fortunate."[18] It is true that Poe might have been aware of *Old Fortunatus* by Dekker or at least of the excerpts published by Lamb in *Specimens of English Dramatic Poets Who Lived about the Time of Shakespeare*.[19] The plot of the play certainly has nothing in common with the tale of Poe. I do not hold it impossible for the two sources, if Dekker's work was one, to result in a single use by Poe; in view of the coincidence of so many useful and, I believe, used elements in the Hugo passage, this onomastic aspect as a contribution to the tale should not be ignored. It is noteworthy too that the "senex" part of Hugo's quotation from Vergil is indirectly carried into the story, for Montresor, who tells the tale, speaks of "the thousand injuries of Fortunato" and of his waiting *"at length"* (Poe's italics) to be "avenged." A long time is implied in "You are rich, respected, admired, beloved; you are happy, as once I was. You are a man to be missed" (6.170).[20]

The intoxication of Fortunato is a key element borrowed from Hugo's passage with its "ivre-mort." Poe's victim literally becomes "mort" because initially "ivre," hence not on his guard. The fact is established at the beginning: "He accosted me with excessive warmth, for he had been drinking much." His eyes were "filmy orbs that distilled the rheum of intoxication." Montresor cleverly intensifies his dupe's drunken state by encouraging him to imbibe as a defense against "the damps" and leads him to the niche prepared for his immurement. His weeping when he realizes himself to be trapped shows that "the intoxication of Fortunato had in a great measure worn off" (6.174). I do not claim that a complex work of art is without many sources. Poe certainly derived something also from the details of Headley's account, in *Letters from Italy*, of a man immured in the wall of an Italian church.[21] Headley, however, speaks of the antecedent physical tortures of the victim of a plot for revenge; he has been walled up above the ground. Part of the power of "The Cask of Amontillado" lies in the extraordinary unpleasantness of the crypts through which Montresor leads Fortunato to his doom, and this, I feel certain, comes largely from *Notre-Dame*.

In Hugo's novel after Esmeralda is tortured into a confession, she is condemned and is then led to the "subterraneous vaults" under the Palais de Justice. The heading of the chapter, "Lasciate Ogni Speranza," epitomizes her incarceration and suffering, and the grim horror of the delicate girl's being buried alive makes this one of the most effective portions of the work. From the first paragraph, chapter iv of Book VIII becomes a sort of *étude* for "The Cask of Amontillado," as a few details will show:

> The subterraneous vaults . . . formed another edifice, in which you descended instead of ascending. . . . The stories of these prisons, as they went deeper into the ground, grew narrower and darker. These dungeon funnels usually terminated in a low hollow, shaped like the bottom of a tub . . . in which society placed the criminal condemned to death. When once a miserable human existence was there interred —then farewell light, air, life, *ogni speranza*—it never went out again but to the gibbet or the stake. Sometimes it rotted there—and human justice called that forgetting. Between mankind and himself the condemned felt weighing upon his head an accumulation of stones and jailers, and the whole prison together . . . was now but one enormous complicated lock that barred him out of the living world. (pp. 297–298)

This matches Poe's stress upon the long, continual descent into the extensive vaults of the mansion, into the "inmost recesses," and still "we passed through a range of low arches, descended, passed on, and descending again, arrived at a deep crypt" of foul air. It is a crypt, four feet, by three feet, by seven, just such a "dungeon funnel" as Hugo describes; in fact, all the details correspond closely including the padlock by which Fortunato is "barred" out of the living world "to rot" forgotten, behind an "accumulation of stones." There is further correspondence between the "mouldy stones" of Esmeralda's prison and the wet "flag-stones" and the "insufferably damp" vaults "encrusted with nitre" of Montresor's domain (Harrison, 6.169). Another detail in Hugo's gallery of horrors may have contributed to Poe's grimly ironic ending: "For the half of a century no mortal has disturbed them [the bones]. *In pace requiescat!*" Twice Hugo uses a term which, in its italics, might have directed Poe's mind to this ending. Hugo says: "It

was one of those low damp holes, in the oubliettes excavated
by St. Louis in the *in pace* of the Tournelle, that . . . they had
deposited La Esmeralda . . . a poor fly that would not have
stirred the smallest of its stones" (p. 298) and "the vault of
the *in pace*" (p. 299).

Perhaps not even all his French readers knew the origin
and exact meaning of Hugo's term "*in pace*" to designate the
cell of Esmeralda. The *Dictionnaire de la Langue Française*,
of 1863, defines it as a "very secure prison, in which the monks
formerly put those of their brethren who had committed some
grand fault." Its origin lies in the Latin, of course, "by a cruel
play of words on the peace of a prison."[22] Hugo's application
of a conventual term to the vaults under the Palace of Justice
is a little surprising but can be shown to derive, I think, from
a front-page article in *Le Figaro* on August 22, 1829, issued
just while Hugo was in the process of writing *Notre-Dame*.
The liberal political journal published "L'In-Pace" to emphasize the black repression of the government of Charles X, the
year before the July Revolution. As justification, it uses the
occasion of the publication of an anonymous old manuscript
entitled *Le Couvent de Baiano*, with an eighty-page preface
by P. L. Lacroix (in reality, the highly respected antiquarian
P. L. Jacob). It cites Jacob's account of the *in pace* cells, which
were found to contain the skeletons of the victims of monastic cruelty when the religious foundations were opened and
sacked by the revolutionaries in 1789. *Le Figaro* drives home
the point that the *in pace* resembled the "oubliette" of feudal-
ism (the latter term was also used by Hugo in this passage).
No reader could miss the implication of this article concerning
the modern French police state, and Hugo was unquestionably
a reader of *Le Figaro*.[23]

Thus, by a curious stream of association, the sardonic use
of the monastic phrase through Hugo may have suggested to
Poe the very real sarcasm of the double pun, at the end of
"The Cask of Amontillado," whereby Montresor asks that the
bones be left "in peace" and in the place of perpetual imprisonment that he had so cunningly prepared for Fortunato. Poe,

a lover of rare and new expressions, would have consulted a dictionary of French. As for the ingenious explanation—that by metathesis of personality Montresor has sacrificed his own peace forever, as symbolized by the ending, I find little justification for equating the two men with William Wilson and his double or for denying that this is indeed a tale of mad or obsessive vengefulness.[24] After the loss of the *Broadway Journal*, Poe's mood during 1846, when the tale was published, might have urged him to treat this very theme.[25]

Another phase of Poe's tale that leads me back to Hugo's total atmosphere in *Notre-Dame* concerns the many touches of France, and specifically of Paris, in the story. It would be convenient to think of the carnival as being Venetian, as does Mary Phillips in her book on Poe.[26] But Venice is obviously eliminated by the sentence, "We are below the river's bed" (6.171). Headley's *Letters from Italy* stresses the dry quality of the wall and the fact that it is on the main floor of the church. Poe himself tells us that the crypts are much like "the great catacombs of Paris" (6.172), a detail which I have not seen discussed by any commentator. Poe had apparently been reading an account of the rather new necropolis for the city of Paris, deliberately constructed out of the granite quarries which spread out under the Faubourg St. Jacques, finally imperiling the buildings of the district. In 1770 the king's ministers had decided to shore up the galleries and put them to some good use. The officials of both church and state eagerly embraced the plan of clearing out the overcrowded cemeteries and churches, piling the skeletal remains of three million former denizens of Paris along the walls of the renovated "catacombs." These eventually became one of the tourist sights of Paris, and even today the guidebooks advise tourists to see them but to dress warmly against the infernal cold or, as Poe would have it, the "damps."[27] Poe had read descriptions of the macabre aesthetic effects sought by the planners:

> The bones are stacked up between the pillars and against the walls so as to show as ornaments or visible surfaces, raised and flat, on which stand out horizontal bands of

juxtaposed heads, long bones placed crisscross, and other decorative forms compatible with the nature of the place.[28]

It was not long before the galleries of the catacombs became a morbid attraction, so that under the Second Empire, Nadar took photographs of them, by artificial light, of course. One of these, used as a frontispiece illustration for Paul Fassy's account of *Les Catacombes de Paris,* might well serve as an illustration for "The Cask of Amontillado."[29] Poe correctly speaks of the "fashion of the great catacombs of Paris" and then states that "three sides of this interior crypt were still ornamented in this manner" (6.172). As I have personally observed in Paris, there is an overwhelming effect of deliberate ornamentation through the geometric patterning of the figures and varied shapes produced by cementing skulls and the knobby ends of long bones all together to comprise the catacomb walls. Obviously the Montresor family alone could not produce the wealth of bones described throughout the tale, but the many churchyards of Paris could do so. Poe also speaks of the "circumscribing walls of solid granite"—the stone of the quarries of Paris.

I believe that I have found one of the specific sources for Poe's initial interest in the catacombs and for his ghastly idea of merging the burial vaults with the wine cellar of the Montresor family. In *The Knickerbocker Magazine* for March, 1838, the "Editor's Table" features a letter from a Paris correspondent on the catacombs of Paris. This feature of New York's leading periodical was read regularly by Poe, the "magazinist," as he called himself.[30] He must have read the account, which I shall excerpt:

> After having reached the spot, I followed my guide, who was provided with flaring tapers, down a long flight of steps. At length, more than a hundred feet from the surface of the ground, we paused, and entered one of the low passages leading to the catacombs. . . . As the door was closed behind me, a cold shudder crept over me, at the thought that I was shut up with three millions of skulls! . . . tier after tier, and

one above another, like bottles in an extensive wine-cellar.
. . . how many victims of ambition—how many votaries of
pleasure—how many slaves to passion—how many wretched
and oppressed.[31]

Here are many motifs of importance in the story: the guide,
the taper, the descent, the chill, the skulls, the wine cellar,
and the victims—strong evidence of a link between the "Table"
and the tale.

There can be no doubt that Poe had a French setting in
mind, although he is very casual about mixing Italian and
French names. While this approach produces no real confusion
and no ill effect upon the uncritical, spellbound reader, it
serves to show us how strong was the pull toward a French
mise-en-scène, a pull stimulated in part by Hugo's role in the
inspiration. Montresor is the name of an eminent French family which included Claude de Bourdeille, comte de Montrésor,
a noted intriguer and memoir-writer.[32] By contrast Fortunato,
in form, and Luchesi, in fact, are names with the aura of Italy.
For the actual record, there was a celebrated General Lucchesi who endangered the impending victory of Frederick the
Great at Niemen, December 5, 1757, by charging Driesen's
cavalry unexpectedly.[33] Poe's mistaken spelling of the family
"from Lucca" is interesting chiefly for its being a tacit admission of weakness in his Italian. In the earliest form of the tale,
published in *Godey's Lady's Book*, November, 1846, the name
appears as "Luchresi." This is a strange spelling, since the *h*
is phonically unnecessary and non-Italian, unlike the *esi* ending of the name. It matches Poe's strange notions of Italian
pronunciation as evidenced in his "Sonnet to Zante" (see chap.
vi). Someone must have told Poe of his error, for he altered
the name throughout the copy that Griswold used for his
printing—from "Luchresi" to "Luchesi," a spelling which is
equally incorrect in its lack of two *c*'s. The relatively few
changes for this tale, as well as their generally sound nature,
would argue that Poe himself inserted them all into the copy
that Griswold used, about which Harrison says: "The Gris-

wold reading may be preferred to the Godey's; but as we
have no positive evidence that Poe made these changes, the
latter form has been followed in the text" (6.294). Professor
Mabbott apparently credited Poe with the shift to "Luchesi"
on two scores. First, he traced Poe's acquaintance in West
Point with a Frederick Lucchesi, a piccolo-player. Second, he
noted the similarity of the altered name to that of the French-
man in "Why the Little Frenchman Wears His Hand in a
Sling," of 1840 (republished in the *Broadway Journal* of
September 6, 1845 [2.128]). Therein the hero, Sir Pathrick
O'Grandison spells out the Frenchman's calling-card name as
"the Count, A Goose, Look-Aisy, Maiter-di-dauns." Professor
Mabbott believes that since "Look-Aisy" is a homonym for
"Lucchesi," Poe must have thought the name to be French.[34]

I am less confident about the provenance and nationality of
Poe's names in this tale than of those attached to the wines in
this story of drinking. The French atmosphere enters strongly
into those with which Montresor plies Fortunato: "Medoc"
(*sic* for Médoc) and "De Grâve" (*sic* for Graves).[35] There
are other French touches, such as the "flambeaux" which
Montresor uses to light their passage and the "roquelaire" in
which he wrapped himself.[36] Poe seems to have thought that
amontillado was an Italian wine, as is clear in Montresor's
saying, "I was skilful in the Italian vintages myself, and bought
largely whenever I could," at the beginning before he speaks
of buying a pipe of amontillado; Fortunato thinks this trans-
action unlikely, especially in the "middle of the carnival," which
would deplete the stocks of wine. This is unquestionably his
buying of Italian vintages "largely." Even if Poe had not made
the error about the Spanish origin of amontillado, I fear that he
would have found it difficult to differentiate between sherry
and amontillado, everywhere defined as "pale dry sherry."[37]

To return to our original passage from *Notre-Dame*—there
is another small touch which makes me suspect that this is a
mardi gras in Paris: Jehan leans over his brother, whom he
believes to be "ivre-mort," on the Pont Saint-Michel over the

River Seine. We are told that the catacombs of Poe's tale lie under a river; since they owe their origin in Poe's imagination to Paris, the ambience of that great city thereby pervades "The Cask of Amontillado." For both tales the passage has aroused a host of associations, most of them macabre, and all in keeping with Poe's intentions and with his demonstrated power. It is not in derogation of that power to claim a role for Hugo's great novel in directing its application to these two of Poe's stories: "The Tale of the Ragged Mountains" and "The Cask of Amontillado."

3

THE MOTTO OF POE'S "ELEONORA": ITS SOURCE AND SIGNIFICANCE

LATE IN 1841, in *The Gift: A Christmas and New Year's Present for 1842,* Edgar Allan Poe published the story "Eleonora," one of his most admired prose pieces.[1] Scarcely an adverse criticism of this arabesque allegory can be found. The terms of the eulogies serve to point out the essential nature of the tale and also suggest the problem of explicating Poe's interpretation of the motto which he added to the story when it was reprinted with revisions in his *Broadway Journal* of 1845.[2] The epigraph, "Sub conservatione formae specificae salva anima," was borrowed from Victor Hugo, who had drawn upon Henri Sauval; Sauval had acknowledged his use of Raimon Lull, thirteenth-century philosopher. Arthur Hobson Quinn, Poe's foremost biographer, terms "Eleonora" "one of his finest stories . . . an arabesque masterpiece," and "the idealized, the spiritualized version of the theme of spiritual integrity, made concrete by its association with the death of a beautiful woman."[3] It is generally agreed that Virginia Poe's latent tuberculosis, become overt in January, 1842, in an attack which threw Poe into a frenzy of desperation, was the chief stimulus for the writing of the tale, which has the simplest of plots. Pyrros, as the narrator is called in the first version of the story, tells about the growth of love between himself and Eleonora, both living with her mother in the remote Valley of the Many-Colored Grass by the River of Silence. After they recognize their love for each other, the river gushes with sounds of delight, multicolored birds come to the valley, the flowers become ruddier, and the sky grows brilliant through a mystically descending cloud of crimson and gold. But when Eleonora sickens and dies, after receiving a vow of his eternal fidelity, the valley returns to silence and drabness. Pyrros leaves for a city and weds Ermengarde.[4] Thereupon, Eleonora as a spirit visits him once to indicate her forgiveness.

George E. Woodberry stresses the "myth" quality of the piece, "pictorial like a medieval legend," and declares that "symbolism has seldom been more simple and pure, more imaginative, childlike, and direct . . . than in this unreal scene."[5] Marie Bonaparte finds it a "perfect symbolic description of the sentimental retirement in which Poe lived with Virginia and her mother in their little world of three" despite what she alone calls a "repellent" landscape.[6] A perceptive editor of a recent collection of Poe's work, Eric W. Carlson, aptly says: "As Poe's most poetic, arabesque fantasy, this tale weaves a complex and rich pattern of symbolic images within its larger allegorical frame." With even more praise Hardin Craig declares: "In the perfect plot of 'Eleonora' Poe worked for a balance between elements of ideal beauty for the achievement of what might be called poetic satisfaction."[7] It would appear that such widespread admiration warrants an attempt to cast light upon whatever is problematical or obscure in its symbology or its epigraph.

The first problem is the source and meaning of the quotation used as the motto: "Sub conservatione formae specificae salva anima, Raymond Lully."[8] There is no question about the person referred to in Poe's ascription, "Raymond Lully." The "Doctor Illuminatus" (1235–1315), born Ramón Lull or Llull in Palma, Majorca, saw the spiritual light after a career as soldier and noble roister, then devoted himself to converting the Moslems, engaged in controversy chiefly in Paris and Montpellier with the Averroës-followers, and was finally stoned to death at Bugia (or Bougie) in Algeria. His works numbered almost three hundred in Latin, Catalán, and Arabic, and presented a once celebrated system for the "acquisition of knowledge with the solution of all possible problems by a systematic manipulation of certain fundamental notions derived from the Aristotelian categories."[9] Scholars do not now accept the works on alchemy once attributed to him; yet it is in a context of alchemy in Victor Hugo's novel and in his source, Henri Sauval, that we find the passage which Poe borrowed.[10] Lull is discussed under "Ramon Lully" in two English-language encyclopedias which Poe knew well.[11] Very apt for Poe's tale was the motto concerning *form* and *soul*. My examination of authentic texts of Lull for insight into the contemporary usage of certain crucial words in the motto may throw some light upon the meaning of the sentence and hence of Poe's tale.[12]

The words of the quotation were not read by Poe in any medieval writing but unquestionably in Hugo's *Notre-Dame de Paris*. Poe evidently began reading *Notre-Dame* early in 1842, for it was in the February, 1842 issue of *Graham's Magazine*, in his review of the poem *Wakondah* and his review of *Barnaby Rudge*, that he first praised Hugo's novel, directly and by implication. Therefore, Poe had no opportunity to include the motto in any of the six 1841 printings of "Eleonora," indeed not until his own 1845 republication.[13] It is a coincidence that in the same month that Poe added the motto to his reprint of "Eleonora," he made his only other allusion to the name "Raymond Lully." This was in the first of the "Fifty Suggestions" that he published in two installments in *Graham's Magazine* of May and June, 1845. In this paragraph, packed with scraps of erudition about the physical properties of color, "blue-stocking" women, and Gargantua, Poe's climactic sentence is "Your 'blue,' when we come to talk of stockings, is black in *issimo—'nigrum nigrius nigro*—like the matter from which Raymond Lully first manufactured his alcohol" (Harrison, 14.170). Now this was, in fact, manufactured by Poe out of the obiter dicta of *Stanley*, a novel published in 1838 by

Horace Binney Wallace under the pseudonym William Landor. Two widely separated passages from *Stanley* are drawn upon here, the first a reference to Bulwer Lytton, who, "to use a happy phrase of Walpole, always writes in *issimo*," and the second, a reference to a man who "is like the substance from which Raymond Lully first made alcohol, 'nigrum nigrius nigro,' . . ." In actual fact, Lully's name is generally connected not with alcohol but with nitric acid, which he prepared by a new process and called *eau forte*.[14] Poe's inclusion of the entry perhaps indicates his assumption of Lully's background in alchemy, and it may explain his readiness to add the Lully quotation to "Eleonora," which has an aura of the supernatural.

To return to *Notre-Dame*—the new motto confirms the impression that Poe was again dipping into the book, for in the March 15, 1845 issue of the *Broadway Journal* his reference to the "Romain qui sauve sa patrie" also comes from Hugo.[15] Later, in his *Broadway Journal* reprint, October 4, 1845, of "The Island of the Fay," he substitutes for the original poem, "To Science," a motto in Latin derived from Hugo's novel, although said merely to be from Servius. The Lull passage in fact occurs in the chapter immediately following the one containing the Servius motto and is in the same chapter as the reference to the patriotic Roman. The Archdeacon of the cathedral, Claude Frollo, has descended to the street with one of the officials of the ecclesiastical court, Maître Jacques Charmolue. In order to draw him away from his tower room in which Jehan, Frollo's younger brother, has been hiding, he has suggested that they examine the sculpture over one of the portals of the cathedral. Jehan follows and overhears them:

> He approached them on tiptoe, and heard the archdeacon say in a whisper to Charmolue, "It was Guillaume de Paris that had a Job engraven on that stone of lapis lazuli, gilt at the edges. By Job is meant the philosopher's stone, which must be tried and tortured to become perfect, as Raymond Lully says, Sub conservatione formae specificae salva anima."[16]

Poe was, in fact, paying close attention to this section of the novel, perhaps because of his deep interest in the subject matter of necromancy and alchemy, as shown in "Ligeia" and also in his late story "Von Kempelen and His Discovery" (April, 1849).[17] There are resemblances between "Ligeia" and "Eleonora," chiefly on the score of metempsychosis.

Hugo had probably not read the passage in Lull, for his erudition was almost as largely borrowed and splendidly displayed as was Poe's.[18] It is doubtful that he intended to deceive his readers since in his text he names as sources Du Breul, Pierre Mathieu, Jean de Troyes, Commynes and, twice, Sauval.[19] The Lull passage, as it first appeared in Sauval, is interesting because it enables us to observe Hugo's deft revision of material transplanted into his own work:

> But to return to our alchemists and their visions, it is, they say, the same Bishop William who had them engrave at the portal on a stone of deep blue, gilded at the edges, the Job seen in the midst of his friends, mocking him with their words, *Patientia Job.* And by Job he represented the philosopher's stone, whose material must suffer every sort of change and torture, in the report of Raymond Lulle, before it arrives at its perfection, *sub conservatione formae specificae salva anima.*[20]

Unfortunately Sauval does not identify the source of the Lull sentence, so that we cannot examine the whole context. Could we do so, we might be helped a bit in ascertaining what meaning Poe ascribed to the quotation, especially since the terms *forma* and *anima* have highly specialized meanings in scholastic philosophy. The word *specifica* is not classical Latin at all and is susceptible to such varied interpretations as "characteristic," "definite," or "specific" in the sense of "constituting or falling into a named category." Another possible meaning is "exerting a distinctive influence," as in the medical use of *a specific*. These are, of course, modern uses as well. In medieval Latin the word had these implications and, in addition, a highly individual meaning of "pulchra" or "beautiful."[21] In conjunction with *forma* this is possibly quite significant.

Forma had a host of meanings, of which I should allude only to a few, in the order given by Du Cange (3.563): the first, "figura or imago," namely, "copy or likeness"; the fifth, "phantasma or imago apparens," namely, "apparition"; the sixth, "habitus, ornatus," that is, "dress, costume, equipage." Even *conservatione* offers its difficulties, being translated by Guyard by the equivalent French term "conservation" or, in English, "preservation" (p. 326), whereas Du Cange's closest word, "conservator," is drawn from juridical terminology to yield a meaning more consonant with "protection" than "preservation."[22] *Anima* might appear to keep its classical meaning of "the vital principle or life," being sometimes equivalent to "animus," or the "rational soul of man, the mind."[23] However, we might also consider the medieval shift in meaning to "that which possesses the life," or simply "homo" as Du Cange and others indicate (for example, D'Arnis, p. 158). The word *forma* meant not simply its modern equivalent of "shape," but it also meant "visage, physiognomy" about 1312, close to Lull's date of writing (Du Cange, 3.565); this is also a classical meaning, and it might have its implications for the interpretation both in "Lull" and in Poe.

With respect to these possibilities, passages in the works of the philosopher Ramón Lull which are of the general period of the motto throw a small amount of light on our object of inquiry. In his *Liber de Praedicatione,* in the section "De Anima Rationalis" he declares: "Anima rationalis est substantiva spiritualis, creata, coniuncta. Et habet tres potentias, scilicet: Intellectum, memoriam, et voluntatem." Equally pertinent is another passage: "Anima naturaliter est maior quam corpus, eo quia ex nobilioribus et altioribus principiis est constituta quam corpus." Here it would seem that *anima* represents "life" or "living principle" within the man or his soul in the sense of "rational soul," almost like "judgment." Two other words, mooted above, occur in a passage from the same work.

Lull asks: "De Elementiva, per regulas deducta. De Quo? 1.
Per primam speciem regulae de Deo quaeritur: Elementativa
de quo est. Et respondendum est, quod est de se ipsa, eo quia
forma specifica est et species generalis tamquam essentia; et
suum concretum sive esse est elementatum."[24] I am inclined
to think that *forma specifica* may be used by Lull in the sense
of characteristic shape or individuality. In slight confirmation,
I cite a passage from another of Lull's works, his *Liber Prov-
erbiorum:* "De Forma," no. 13: "In prima et generali Forma
sunt seminatae individuae Formae, quae expectant naturalia
agentia."[25] The matter remains vague, however, and it is with
the utmost uncertainty that I suggest that the sentence in Lull
might be translated as "In the preservation of its characteristic
form, each soul is inviolable or intact." I believe that there is
no doubt about its referring to the same entity in both parts
of the sentence, but I am not sure that Poe understood it thus.

Let us now examine a few of the translations of the sentence
offered before deciding upon Poe's probable interpretation.
In the Hugo text, Guyard gives us: "Sous la conservation de
la forme spécifique, l'âme est intacte," that is, "Through the
preservation of its specific form, the soul is (kept) whole or
untouched." This is not very helpful, in itself. Alterton and
Craig offer: "The safety of the soul lies in the preservation of
the specific form."[26] This evades, for one thing, determining
the ownership of the "soul" and the "form" through the use
of personal pronouns. Following closely upon this definition is
Eric W. Carlson's: "In the preservation of its specific form lies
the safety of the spirit of life."[27] Finally, with a somewhat
changed emphasis is Professor Mabbott's "Under the protection of a specific form, the soul is safe."[28]

There is a slight verification of Professor Mabbott's inter-
pretation of "protection" in my discovery of a marginal note
translating the motto in the 1845 *Broadway Journal* reprint of
"Eleonora" (1.322).[29] The writing is that of Poe's fiancée, Mrs.
Whitman ("H. W."), probably inscribed in October, 1848.
"Eleonora" starts five lines from the bottom of the second col-

umn, and the following sentence of translation is written in the space directly under the text: "Under the conservation / protection of specific forms the soul is safe." The index page at the front of the first volume of the two-volume set bears the notation, "Given to S. H. W. by E. A. P. October 1848," in Mrs. Whitman's writing. I assume that this item, like several others, reflects Poe's conversations with the attractive Providence widow, whom he was courting. Hence the translation, however faulty, may show a little of Poe's interpretation of the motto of a story which was particularly interesting to Mrs. Whitman. Obviously Poe would not make a mistake about the singular number of *formae specificae,* which she renders in the plural, but the presence of "protection" directly after the closely related "conservation" for *conservatione* makes me believe that Poe preferred this and, therefore, the idea of "under" for *sub.*

Another marginal notation relating to "Eleonora," also in the hand of Sarah Helen Whitman,[30] makes especially relevant her desire to fathom the meaning of the motto and of the whole fable. A month after Poe included "Eleonora" in the issue of May 24, 1845, he reprinted, on June 24, his tale "Morella," which had first appeared in the April, 1835 *Messenger.* Probably after receiving the celebrated love letter of October 1, 1848, from Poe, Mrs. Whitman, reflecting ideas in his letter and in conversations with him, inserted a series of names in one continuous string on the left-hand margin (1.388):

Robert Stannard Helen Stannard Helen Whitman—Helen —Ellen Elenore Lenore!

Poe had implied to Mrs. Whitman that his early and enduring partiality for various forms of the name Helen, including "Eleonora," revealed their basic "soul-love" for each other. The notes at the side of the tale show that Helen Whitman was probably trying to place an early tale into this onomastic penumbra through the "ella" portion of the name "Morella." The insertion of "Ellen" in the annotation suggests just this.[31] Helen

Whitman, we know, was inordinately proud of Poe's use of
forms of her name, as in the first "To Helen," supposedly addressed to "Helen" (that is, Jane Stith) Stanard in 1831, a Poe
assertion which others have disputed;[32] "Lenore," the name
given the earlier "A Paean" when it was revised for Lowell's
Pioneer of February, 1843; the Lenore of the 1845 poem "The
Raven"; and finally the second "To Helen" of 1848. Indeed,
after Poe's death, Mrs. Whitman commented: "I believe that
the spirit of her who bore this beloved name, has always hov-
ered around him, and that it was in some way through *her*
influence that he was drawn to *me*."[33] Notice here Mrs. Whitman's concept of "Helen-Eleonora" as hovering over the pro-
tected poet, just as in the tale itself.

Poe himself, in his celebrated October, 1848 letter, provided
Mrs. Whitman with this idea as well as with other themes
that bear on my interpretation of "Eleonora." A few of the
background circumstances are needed.[34] Mrs. Whitman had
sent Poe a valentine poem to be read February 14, 1848, at
a New York party. The verses, entitled "The Raven," were
published in Willis's *Home Journal*, March 18, 1848, through
the good offices of Miss Lynch and Mrs. Osgood. After mailing
his first "To Helen" verses to Mrs. Whitman, Poe sent her his
new "To Helen" in June, 1848 (publishing it in November).
Allusions to these events are made in Poe's long, passionate
letter of October, which I here excerpt:

> Immediately after reading the Valentine, I wished to
> contrive some mode of acknowledging . . . the honor you
> had conferred on me. . . . my eyes fell upon a volume of my
> own poems; and then the lines I had written in my passion-
> ate boyhood, to the first, purely ideal love of my soul—to the
> Helen Stannard [*sic* for Stanard] . . . flashed upon my recol-
> lection. . . . Think, too, of the rare agreement of name—Helen
> and not the far more usual Ellen—think of all these coinci-
> dences . . . [which] wore an air of positive miracle. . . .
> I said to myself—The sentiment—the holy passion which
> glows within my spirit *for her*, is of Heaven, heavenly, and

has no taint of the Earth. . . . As you entered the room, pale, timid, hesitating, and evidently oppressed at heart; as your eyes rested appealingly, for one brief moment, upon mine, I felt, for the first time in my life . . . the existence of spiritual influences altogether out of the reach of the reason. I saw that you were *Helen—my* Helen . . . she whom the great Giver of all Good had preördained to be mine—mine only —if not now, alas! then at least hereafter and *forever,* in the Heavens. . . . I grew faint with the luxury of your voice and blind with the voluptuous lustre of your eyes. . . . Do you not feel in your inmost heart of hearts that the "soul-love" . . . is . . . the most absolute of realities? . . . that it is my diviner nature—my spiritual being—which burns and pants to commingle with your own? Has the soul *age*, Helen? Can that which began *never* and shall never end, consider a few wretched years of its incarnate life?[35]

Here are many details that link Poe's courtship of Helen with his ideas in "Eleonora" and also with her interest in the story itself at the time of Poe's gift of the two volumes. It is noteworthy that Poe addresses Mrs. Whitman in phrases seemingly derived from the pages of "Eleonora" itself. The tale could have been identified only with Virginia, but Poe is here proclaiming the statuesque Helen Whitman as his "preordained soul-love."[36] Certainly the "spiritual influences" and the ageless soul contrasted with "carnate life" might be drawn directly from "Eleonora." In the exaggerated tone Poe reveals the contrived and histrionic nature of his courtship, as in his reference to growing "blind" before the "voluptuous lustre" of her eyes —in reality, her best feature. Poe eulogized them in the second "To Helen":

> All—all expired . . .
> Save only the divine light in thine eyes—
> Save but the soul in thine uplifted eyes.
>
> . . . .
>
> I see them still—two sweetly scintillant
> Venuses, unextinguished by the sun!
> [Harrison, 7.108–109]

Poe has, of course, done much better than this in his "Eros-inspired" poetry, but Mrs. Whitman was delighted,[37] especially since Poe included a reference to her eyes in the margin of his *Broadway Journal* reprint of "Ligeia," September 27, 1845, just before this ardent letter: "The poem which I sent you contained all the events of a *dream* which occurred to me soon after I knew you. Ligeia was also suggested by a *dream—* observe the *eyes* in both tale and poem."[38]

Since "Ligeia," one of his most cherished stories,[39] dates from 1838, it is clear that Mrs. Whitman's "orbs" may have had a deep-seated power of attraction for Poe; "early and late" he lavished his powers on heroines with these "twin" charms, usually with more success than the "Cheshire Cat grin" effect in the second poem entitled "To Helen."[40] Certainly, "Eleonora" originally made its palingenetic point through the description of the eyes, "gateway to the soul," before Poe abridged these passages in order to turn the theme from the path taken by "Morella" and "Ligeia." Poe expressed his essential dissatisfaction with this aspect of "Eleonora" in a published, although uncollected, source. In *Graham's Magazine* for November, 1841 (19.249–250) Poe reviews *The Gift: A Christmas and New-Year's Present for 1842* as "superior to any yet published" and, after listing several of its items, says, "We ourselves have one which is not ended so well as it might be —a good subject spoiled by hurry in the handling." Accordingly, for the 1845 *Broadway Journal*, he revised the final section.

The motto to "Eleonora" that he then provided helps to focus this point. Professor Mabbott saw no discrepancy between the theme and the motto, interpreted as "Under the protection of a specific form, the soul is safe." For Poe's tale I am inclined to favor this construction, wherein *anima* seems to refer to the narrator and *forma* seems to refer to Eleonora, with her gentle kiss after death and her last words of forgiveness and of heavenly promise at the end. In that case, *anima* would mean either *homo* (man) or "the spirit or life of another" and it would not be impossible for *forma* to be not

merely "form" but also "beauty" as in classical Latin. The original version of the story would then be a more fully "realized"
expansion of the motto, which, in effect, he added so late. I
refer to two passages which describe Eleonora and Ermengarde in terms which seem to make them equivalent. After
the sentence which begins paragraph seven in the *Broadway
Journal* version, following "The loveliness of Eleonora was that
of the Seraphim," Poe originally described her tall, fragile stat-
ure and "the hues of her cheek," obviously the disease tokens or
hectic flush of phthisis. The deleted passage continues thus:

> With the nose, lips, and chin of the Greek Venus, she had
> the majestic forehead, the naturally-waving auburn hair,
> and the large luminous eyes of her kindred. Her beauty,
> nevertheless, was of that nature which leads the heart to
> wonder not less than to love. The grace of her motion was
> surely etherial [*sic*]. Her fantastic step left no impress upon
> the asphodel—and I could not but dream as I gazed, enrapt,
> upon her alternate moods of melancholy and of mirth, that
> two separate souls were enshrined within her. So radical
> were the changes of countenance, that at one instant I
> fancied her possessed by some spirit of smiles, at another by
> some demon of tears. [Harrison, 4.314]

The passage dropped from the description of the second
beloved, Ermengarde, in the thirteenth paragraph, follows
after the corresponding "seraph Ermengarde" and includes
many attributes parallel to those of Eleonora, such as "the
blue depths of her meaning eyes," and "the wavy flow of her
auburn tresses" and the "fantastic grace of her step"; there is
also "the identical transition from tears to smiles that I had
wondered at in the long-lost Eleonora." The only trace of the
duality of spirit in both girls who, in their duality, also originally represented a "soul's identity," is Poe's final sentence in
the paragraph: "Oh divine was the angel Ermengarde! and as
I looked down into the depths of her memorial eyes I thought
only of them—and *of her*" (Harrison, 4.314 and 243).[41] In both
versions two more paragraphs tell us that Eleonora's spirit

comes through the night once to comfort him with the knowledge that in "taking to thy passionate heart her who is Ermengarde, thou art absolved, for reasons which shall be made
known to thee in Heaven, of thy vows unto Eleonora"
(4.244).[42]

Let us assume then that *formae specificae* refers to the spirit
of Eleonora, whose "familiar and sweet voice" speaks to him
at the end, thereby mystically demonstrating the "form" of
the soul even after death and its waiting for his soul, in its
"post-life" form, to join hers in heaven. In that case, is it his
continued condition of love, his "passionate heart," which,
even though directed toward another, makes him eligible to
join her as a spiritual being in heaven? This "redemption by
love" is a possible interpretation of the allegory.[43] In that event,
the hovering of the spirit over him twice is no act of protection but merely of communication, and *conservatione* may
be judged to be "preservation," whether in her own spiritual
form or, less likely, through that of Ermengarde, the new-old
love object.

I rather think that Poe wisely decided to suppress the dual
nature of both girls, which helped to complete their identity
but which detracted from the major theme. He also subordi-
nated the idea of the transmigration of the soul, which he
had treated frequently before. One of the earliest and best
known of Poe's tales was "Morella" (1835) with its pointed
reference to the "modified Palingenesía of the Pythagoreans,"
serving as a motif of this tale of the mother who assumes the
identity of her daughter at the latter's birth and her own
death.[44] "Ligeia" (1838) uses more of the supernatural in the
usurpation of the identity of the second wife by the spirit of
the first—an enchantress. Other tales of Poe toyed with the
idea or mentioned it. For example, in "Metzengerstein" (1936)
Poe spoke of the belief in metempsychosis prevailing in Hungary, as a prelude to his story of the reincarnated, avenging
horse (Harrison, 2.185). *Burton's Magazine* of December,
1839, presented his "Conversation of Eiros and Charmion,"

two souls who have been liberated from earth by an all-consuming comet. This theme, of souls conversing in heaven, is continued in the 1841 "Colloquy of Monos and Una." In 1884 Poe includes a significant statement in "The Premature Burial": "The boundaries which divide Life from Death, are at best shadowy and vague. . . . The silver cord was not for ever loosed, nor the golden bowl irreparably broken. But where, meantime, was the soul" (Harrison, 5.256)? This strongly suggests the beginning of his poem "Lenore" of 1843: "Ah, broken is the golden bowl! the spirit flown forever! / Let the bell toll!—a saintly soul floats on the Stygian river" (7.53). In June, 1845, in the *Democratic Review*, Poe published another in his series of "conversations of spirits," this being "The Power of Words," in which Oinos and Agathos, spirits "new-fledged with immortality"—although it seems to be three centuries since their death—discuss divine creativity; it seems to emanate from divine thought but with a hint of passion (6.139–144). In a sense, this tale is a continuation of the 1844 "Mesmeric Revelation" dialogue between Vankirk, the mesmerized and moribund consumptive, and the author "P" concerning the power of God's thought to create "new individualities" and the "painful metamorphosis" of death, which enables the "inner form" of the body to be perceptible to the spirit world (5.241–254).

Certainly Poe had always shown considerable interest in the ways and forms of spirits. Since his most definite treatments of the theme of palingenesis tended to be extremely sinister, we can understand his effort to reduce this element in "Eleonora," which preserves a rather idyllic tone even after the first girl's death. In his revision he may have moved his theme further away from the probable meaning of the motto from "Lull." Yet, Eleonora's spirit still preserves its essential form, that of an angelic being, who causes Pyrros to hear the swinging "of the censers of the angels" and smell "streams of a holy perfume." Since she had the "loveliness" of the "seraphim" when alive, the "anima" must indeed be hers. If, however, we

think of "love" as revealing or expressing a universally "seraphic form," then there is less difficulty in seeing in the "seraph Ermengarde" the "preservation" or "conservation" of the
soul of Eleonora. Years before, in one of the "Pinakidia" items
of the *Messenger*, August, 1836, Poe had written: "Josephus,
with Saint Paul and others, supposed man to be compounded
of body, soul, and spirit. The distinction between soul and
spirit is an essential point in ancient philosophy" (Harrison,
14.55–56). Poe may now be simply implying that Eleonora's
spirit becomes a liberated soul, after death, ready for commu-
nion with another soul.

In this respect there is one small item of change in the tale
which is tucked into the notes of Harrison. I refer to Poe's giving the narrator the name Pyrros, which is totally omitted in
1845. In the second paragraph there are still retained phrases
which relate to the skepticism or pyrrhonism suggested by the
name, Pyrros:

> . . . a condition of shadow and doubt, appertaining to the
> present, and to the recollection of what constitutes the sec-
> ond great era of my being. Therefore, what I shall tell of the
> earlier period, believe; and to what I may relate of the later
> time, give only such credit as may seem due; or doubt it
> altogether. [Harrison, 4.237]

This has a correspondence also to the "glimpses of eternity"
and the learning of "the wisdom which is of good" and "the
mere knowledge which is of evil" in paragraph one. Despite
the difference of spelling, Pyrrho of Elis may have been intended by Poe in the fact also that the narrator learned his
ultimate wisdom in an Eastern city, the adjective "Eastern"
being dropped from the final version along with the narrator's
name.[45] Pyrrho (c. 360–270 B.C.) went to the East in the
train of Alexander and studied in India under the Gym-
nosophists and in Persia under the Magi.[46] According to one
brief account, his basic principles were those of "acatalepsia"
or the impossibility of knowing things in their own nature,

intellectual suspense or "epoché," equilibrium or "arrepsia," and noncommittal silence or "aphasia"—all of which would desirably lead to the attitude of imperturbability or "ataraxia."[47] By chance there is something of this in Hardin Craig's stress upon the tale as a presentation of the "balance of the elements of ideal beauty" and "a balanced equality as the root of all beauty," although he ignores the initial name given to the hero and believes that the passages on the duality of spirit —melancholy and mirth and smiles and tears—were dropped in order to produce a superior "indefiniteness."[48]

It must be admitted that the word "indefiniteness" must be applied to any theories eventuating from a discussion of Poe's conception of Lull's motto. We know that his Latin was adequate to handle any variation of which we might conceive.[49] We can be quite definite about the aptness of the borrowing, which leads us directly to the central issues of the idyll—the return and forgiveness of the loving and love-lorn man by the spirit of the beautiful mate (no marriage to Eleonora is recorded in the tale). As with the splendidly apposite lines from Béranger's "Le Rufus," added to the reprinted "Fall of the House of Usher" (see chap. iv) the epigraph of "Eleonora" shows Poe's genius for associating with finished tales mottoes that seem to be *leit motifs*. This gift for summation and for insight into essentials sometimes served him brilliantly as critic and as observer of trends in the arts. To Victor Hugo, to Henri Sauval, to Ramón Lull, and above all to Edgar Allan Poe the reader owes the pleasure of a fruitful and provocative motto for a poignant tale.

BÉRANGER IN THE WORKS OF POE

IN 1909 KILLIS Campbell advanced the theory that two lines from "Le Refus" by Pierre-Jean de Béranger were the basic inspiration for Poe's "Israfel," first published in April, 1831. He repeated this view in his authoritative edition of Poe's *Poems* in 1917.[1] Since that time many commentators appear to accept the hypothesis.[2] Yet it seems difficult to maintain that by April, 1831, Poe could have read the lines in "Le Refus":

> Mon coeur est un luth suspendu;
> Sitôt qu'on le touche, il résonne.[3]

In fact, I believe Poe never read a volume of Béranger's verses although he used these two lines later as a motto for "The Fall of the House of Usher," reviewed a translation of a few of Béranger's poems with authoritative allusions to the French originals, and referred to the name and style of Béranger in six more pieces of criticism and one extended comment in the "Marginalia." In all, there are nine separate published references to the poet or his poems in Poe's writings and one in a manuscript note. Two of his major critical works—the review of Hawthorne's *Twice-Told Tales* and "The Poetic Principle"— have important passages discussing Béranger as a poet. Obviously it is necessary to consider Poe's methods of citation as well as his knowledge of the French contemporary figure.

It was quite normal for Poe to be aware of the songs of Béranger, who was then feted throughout the western world for the lyrical quality of his verse and his very apt commentaries on personalities and events in France. Perhaps few reputations have more sharply fallen than that of Béranger, whose *chansons* were being published in one, two, or three volumes almost every year throughout Poe's maturity.[4] It was not only the French who were infatuated with these lyrics, composed by Béranger for popular melodies of his own and earlier days; we find also an 1837 London volume of translations; another published in Philadelphia in 1844 by Poe's successor as editor, the indefatigable anthologist Rufus W. Griswold; and an 1850 New York translation of two hundred of the lyrics.[5] Continuing evidence of his popularity is shown in another translation of *Béranger's Songs,* dedicated to Dante Gabriel Rossetti (London, 1856), and still another (New York, 1888).[6] In short, Poe had to be aware of a body of poetry of which Griswold said: "This is the first collection that has been made in this country of the writings of the greatest of the living poets of Europe. . . . The edition has selected such songs as in their English dress give the most true impression of the author's genius"; similarly the preface of Young's 1850 English edition declares: "Béranger, the darling poet of his countrymen and the admiration of the lettered world, is a master of song, not the founder of a creed."[7]

Since the many collections of *Chansons inédites* and *Oeuvres* began coming out in 1828, there was sufficient opportunity for Poe to become acquainted with Béranger's work. On this assumption, Killis Campbell postulated that "Le Refus" was somehow known to Poe in time for the publication of "Israfel" in *Poems* "by Edgar A. Poe, Second Edition." The date of this book, as noted by Quinn,[8] was probably April, 1831. Campbell requires us to be fastidious about the month because he specifies that "Le Refus" came out in January or February, 1831, early enough to enable Poe to gain inspiration for "Israfel." Poe, I believe, actually first saw the two lines in the article on Béranger in Robert M. Walsh's translation of *Sketches of Conspicuous Living Characters of France,* which Poe reviewed in the April, 1841 issue of *Graham's Magazine.* Not long afterwards, in October, 1841, in the same magazine, Poe reprinted "Israfel," with a subtle but significant change in the poem and in the motto, ascribed to the Koran. In 1831 the motto read: "And the angel Israfel, who has the sweetest voice of all God's creatures." In 1841 it read: "And the angel Israfel, or Israfeli, whose heart-strings are a lute, and who is the most musical of all God's creatures" (19.183). In the poem itself the second line of the 1831 version is now furnished with quotation marks: "Whose heart-strings are a lute"; these imply that it is a quotation from Sale's version of the Koran. (In actual fact, the 1831 version leaves out the Koran as source, while that of 1841 leaves out Sale, inserted only in the 1845 printing.) I suspect that Poe would not be displeased with Harrison's suggestion, elaborated by Campbell, that Béranger's "lute" lines were connected with the genesis of "Israfel."[9] Both of these critics may be following the curious 1841 "lead," which I believe derived from Poe's reading in Walsh.

Briefly this is Campbell's argument for an early inspiration. Béranger had refused the offer of a pension from General François Sébastiani, minister of the successful new monarch, Louis Phillipe, whom Béranger had supported despite his protestations of republicanism. "Le Refus" speaks bravely of his desire to be independent and maintain a heart responsive to his own thoughts and desires and those of the people:

> Gardez vos dons: je suis peureux
> Mais si d'un zèle généreux
> Pour moi le monde vous soupçonne,
> Sachez bien qui vous a vendu:
> Mon coeur est un luth suspendu;
> Sitôt qu'on le touche, il résonne.

This is rendered thus by William Young:

> Keep, keep your gifts, then; fears I'm apt to feel:
> Yet, if too great for me your generous zeal
>   Should by the world be found,
> Know well who your betrayer was—my heart,
> Like lute suspended, ever plays its part:
>   When touched it *will* resound.[10]

In reality, he declared in 1840, his refusal sprang chiefly from sheer laziness; in his posthumous autobiography, he ascribed it to his having an income from his books of verse without need for aid from the public treasury.[11] Whatever the motives of Béranger, the main idea of the poem is very different from "Israfel," with its aesthetic and mystical creed, and also from the hypochondriac dilettantism of Roderick Usher. Campbell ingeniously supposes that a Paris newspaper, probably *Le Figaro*, in January, 1831, published the first instance of "Le Refus," chiefly because another Béranger poem, "A mes amis devenus Ministres," appeared in the paper in that month. Campbell admits that Poe would have had to see the Paris newspaper in West Point—which he left on February 19, 1831 —or in New York City, in order to include his "resultant" poem in the volume published in April; surely this was unlikely in the days when passengers took more than a month to cross the Atlantic.

Le Figaro, as a leading anti-royalist organ, took great interest in the work and popularity of Béranger. In its January 14, 1831 issue (Vol. 6, no. 14) it announced its first-page publication of his poem, "A mes amis devenus Ministres": "A new song by Béranger . . . it is the awakening [*réveil*] of that voice . . . too long mute with joy. . . . If this spirit of the muse who had anticipated, counseled, celebrated in advance our political regeneration is revived, the opposition in France is neither dead nor splintered" (author's translation). This poem was reprinted on January 15 in *Le Voleur*, of similar political persuasion, under the title "Le Réveil de Béranger." Obviously, if "Le Refus" had come out soon afterwards, *Le Figaro* and *Le Voleur* would have printed or at least spoken about it as a major literary event. Only in September is there another Béranger poem (see below) and a short, disappointed article on Béranger on December 14, 1831. Moreover, Béranger published his recent political poems late in 1831, in a twenty-four page pamphlet "au profit du Comité polonais," of which he was a member; the only poems included were "Poniatowski,"

"Hâtons-Nous," "Chansons dédiées au Général Lafayette," "Le 14 Juillet, 1829," and "A mes amis devenus Ministres." This last item contained the significant notation: "This poem was printed in the *Figaro* a few months ago" (p. 23). Clearly during the intervening months "Le Refus" had not been published anywhere.

In the absence of any positive proof from Béranger or his editors, it is difficult to establish the exact date of "Le Refus." It first appeared—according to our knowledge, not Campbell's inferences—in *Chansons Nouvelles et Dernières de Béranger* in 1833. I have looked for it in a Brussels edition of *Oeuvres Complètes* which is dated 1830 but which includes poems from 1831, among them "A mes amis devenus Ministres" (pp. 559–561) as well as "A M. de Chateaubriand," which is dated, "Paris, 14 septembre 1831" (pp. 570–571); *Le Figaro*, I found, printed the latter in its September 6, 1831 issue, with this proleptic date. The absence of "Le Refus" from this volume argues clearly that "Le Refus" belongs to a later date than September, 1831, and therefore could not have been seen by Poe before he published "Israfel" in April, 1831. On the other hand, it does appear in a Brussels edition of 1833 (pp. 117–118). The only edition that attempts to date "Le Refus" at all, among the many that I have examined, is the *Oeuvres de Pierre-Jean de Béranger* (Paris, 1872), which lists it without a definite date in the text (2.308), but which ascribes it to 1831 in the "Table" (2.389). The subject matter certainly places it in 1831, as Campbell says, but it is fantastic to think that Poe could have seen it then.[12]

Far more plausible is Quinn's claim that a major source of "Israfel" is Thomas Moore's "The Light of the Haram," with its lute and "Angel Israfil."[13] Incidentally, Poe shows a confusion about the nature of the lyre and lute throughout the poem, in which Israfel seems to be singing to a lute in stanza 1, to a lyre in 3, to a lute in 6, and, by implication, to a lyre in 8. He makes the same error in the first paragraph of "The Island of the Fay" in speaking of "those who love the lyre for its own sake, and for its spiritual uses," since players on the

lute in 1841 were conceivable but not players on the ancient
instrument called the "lyre." The lute would have been appropriate for a Moslem angel, since it had come to Europe via
the Arabs.[14] The lyre is more reminiscent here of Shelley's
"lyre" of the "forest" in the "West Wind Ode" and has overtones of "The Skylark."[15] To Béranger the lute in "Le Refus"
and in several other poems was a symbol of the carefree song-
ster, the troubadour strolling about and delighting a succession of auditors, as in the paintings of Watteau.[16]

There is no need to belabor the point, since in 1831 Poe had
probably no more than heard Béranger's name. In 1836, he
presented a bona fide discussion of one of Béranger's poems,
however ignorant of the text itself he may have continued to
be. As editor and major reviewer of the *Southern Literary
Messenger,* in January, 1836, Poe published a long review of
three volumes of poetry by three women: *Zinzendorff, and
Other Poems* by Mrs. L. H. Sigourney; *Poems* by Miss H. F.
Gould (3rd ed., 1835); and *Poems; Translated and Original*
by Mrs. E. F. Ellet (Philadelphia, 1835). It is the third volume
which is of interest because of Poe's dicta on Mrs. Ellet's translations of Béranger and Lamartine.[17] Poe first gives the facts
of her book—that in two years most of its fifty-seven poems
had appeared in periodicals and that eighteen were "credit-
able" translations from French, German, Spanish, and Italian.
Yet he ironically observes: "A too scrupulous adherence to the
text is certainly not one of her faults—nor can we yet justly
call her, in regard to the spirit of her authors, a latitudinarian."
She neglects the "*poetical characters*" of the original. In proof
of this, he says, "Let us refer to the lady's translation of the
Swallows. We have no hesitation in saying that not the slightest conception of Pierre Jean de Béranger, can be obtained by
the perusal of the lines at page 112, of the volume now before
me." Given below are the lines in question (stanza 2) from
"Les Hirondelles," followed by William Young's translation of
1850 and then Mrs. Ellet's version. Hers appears to me to be
as faithful in content as Young's, for example, and perhaps

more felicitous in style, despite Poe's carping and despite her
being ignored by anthologists of Béranger translations.

> Depuis trois ans je vous conjure
> De m'apporter un souvenir
> Du vallon où ma vie obscure
> Se berçait d'un doux avenir.
> Au détour d'une eau qui chemine
> A flots purs, sous de frais lilas,
> Vous avez vu notre chaumine:
> De ce vallon ne me parlez-vous pas?
> [ed. 1840, p. 358]

> Thrice the year hath rolled, since from you first
>   I besought some token, to be brought
> From the valley where, obscure, I nursed
>   Dreams of life with future blessings fraught.
> Where the limpid streamlet winds between
>   Banks bedecked with lilacs fresh and gay,
> Ye our little cottage must have seen:
>   Have ye nothing of that vale to say?

> Bring me, I pray—an exile sad—
>   Some token of that valley bright,
> Where in my sheltered childhood glad,
>   The future was a dream of light.
> Beside the gentle stream, where swell
>   Its waves beneath the lilac tree,
> Ye saw the cot I love so well—
>   And speak ye of that home to me?[18]

There is little reason for Poe's conclusion: "We have no fault
to find with these verses in themselves—as specimens of the
manner of the French chansonnier, we have no patience with
them." This stricture, which he levels also at her translation
of the "Sepulchres" of Foscolo, he applies to Lamartine's "Loss
of the Anio," "in the original of which, by the way, we cannot
perceive the lines answering to Mrs. E.'s verses:

> All that obscures thy sovereign majesty
> Degrades our glory in degrading thee."

Mrs. Ellet devoted five pages of her book (pp. 42–46) to her translation of this entire poem. Since she does not identify the exact source, aside from the subtitle, I doubt that Poe either knew enough or cared to consult the original in Lamartine when he made this contumelious statement, which matches the irrelevancy or cruelty of his stricture on her Béranger translation. In fact, her entire poem is a fine, faithful translation of "La Perte de l'Anio" in the *Harmonies Poétiques et Religieuses*.[19] For the original of the above chapter, Lamartine wrote:

> En tout ce qui flétrit ta majesté suprême
> Semble en te dégradant nous dégrader nous-mêmes!

Clearly Poe had not looked at the text before making this harsh charge against Mrs. Ellet.

The rest of his discussion of her volume is less apposite to our investigation, but it illustrates further Poe's critical approach. He praises her translation of a Quevedo sonnet, "Rome in Ruins," which gives him a chance to decry Quevedo's "plagiarism" from Girolamo Preti. He is equivocal about the merits of her original poems, and attacks an epigram on Echo as a "silly joke upon a threadbare theme." He hints at plagiarism in her *Teresa Contarini*, a tragedy included in this volume which was lauded upon its performance in March, 1835, but is really "better suited to the closet." Finally, he prints the six stanzas of a poem "rich in vigorous expression and full of solemn thought," containing "condensation and energy." It begins:

> Hark—to the midnight bell!
> The solemn peal rolls on
> That tells us, with an iron tongue,
> Another year is gone!

Could not these lines have lingered in the retentive memory of Poe for many years as a suggestion for

> Hear the tolling of the bells—
> Iron bells!

What a world of solemn thought their monody compels!
　　In the silence of the night,
　　How we shiver with affright
At the melancholy menace of their tone!

[Harrison, 7.121]

Poe himself thought that his criticism, including this kind of "cutting and slashing," was "just." Indeed, he scarcely saw it as unkind, and affirmed that in regard to the poems of Mrs. Ellet "praise slightly prevails."[20]

In 1839 Poe had another occasion to mention the French poet's works. He was reviewing George P. Morris's works, for *Burton's Gentleman's Magazine* (December, 1839). Morris was author of the extremely popular "Woodman, Spare That Tree" and a frequent contributor to the magazines of the day. His many song lyrics were often published in books. Now he forms the subject of a Poe article, "George P. Morris," featured simply as "our best writer of songs" (Harrison, 10.41–45). This inevitably suggested comparison with the best French "song-writer," here termed by Poe "De Béranger." Poe first claims that the popularity of a song is a test of its merit. He then associates the "indefiniteness" of the composer's creation with that of the "lyricist." Poe here seems to identify "definiteness" or "determinateness" with imitative or program music, such as Kotzwara's "Battle of Prague." He manages to equate indefiniteness with *"abandonnement,"* which, he says, is exemplified in old English ballads and carols. This is the "essence of all antique song," and he enumerates Homer, Anacreon, and Aeschylus. "It is the vital principle in De Béranger." Without "this quality no song-writer was ever truly popular." Next, Poe defends the use of "hyperbole" and the poetic "conceit" —as used by Morris. Béranger is brought in again, rather strangely: "To all reasonable persons it will be sufficient to say that the fervid, hearty, free-spoken songs of Cowley and of Donne—more especially of Cunningham, of Harrington, and of Carew—abound in precisely similar things; and that they are to be met with, plentifully, in the polished pages of

Moore and of Béranger, who introduce them with thought and retain them after mature deliberation" (10.44). His last commendation of Morris speaks of his "Woodman, Spare That Tree" and "By the Lake Where Droops the Willow" as "immortal." Now one may ask whether this rigmarole of names and ill-matched qualities, intended to set off Poe's erudition and refinement, gives the slightest hint of the real merits of Béranger. Can one find any evidence here that Poe had read the French poet, who is neither indefinite nor metaphysical nor above imitative effects in his poems?[21] It is clear, I think, that to this date, 1839, Poe had read no Béranger in French.

His ignorance was alleviated early in 1841 when he received, for review in *Graham's Magazine*, *Sketches of Conspicuous Living Characters of France*, translated by R. M. Walsh (*Graham's*, 18.202–203). The original author, although unknown to Poe and Walsh, was Louis Léonard de Loménie. Poe accepts the "impartiality" of these sketches of contemporary figures and asserts: "We are most pleased with those of Thiers, Hugo, Sand, Arago and Bèranger [*sic*]" (p. 202); although he devotes his entire review to the accounts of Hugo, Arago, Berryer, Chateaubriand, and George Sand, his awareness of details in Loménie's eulogy of Béranger can easily be proved. Elsewhere I have analyzed the pastiche of unjust remarks about Hugo that Poe concocted from Loménie's chapter.[22] Conversely, Poe would have received the impression of a man of extraordinary genius from the account of Béranger. Since the substance and the cited examples of his chapter entered largely into future references made by Poe, I shall briefly summarize it (*Sketches*, pp. 231–247). The famous eulogy by Chateaubriand, prefacing his *"Historical Studies"* as the epigraph terms the work, is cited: "Under the simple title of *song writer*, a man has become one of the greatest poets that France has produced"; also cited is Béranger's statement in the preface to his works: "The people is my muse" (p. 231). A long account of his life is first given, with three brief poetic excerpts, in French, that help to underscore important dates. He is said to be "careful to conceal his profound knowledge" (p. 241) and to have the "stuff of an historian, a philosopher, or a states- man" (p. 242).

A discussion of "the general character of his poems" is intro- duced with "Mon coeur est un luth suspendu; / Sitôt qu'on le touche il résonne" from "Le Refus." "The genius of Béran- ger is like his heart; it echoes every sound, from whatever quarter it may come" (p. 242). Loménie deplores his "loose songs" and praises his satirical poetry which has been "a pow- erful influence upon the great events of recent years." Eight lines are here cited. His "elegiac poetry" is next praised for its pervading tone of "sadness" and "The Swallows" is one of those mentioned. Eight lines from the sentimental "Jacques" are quoted to illustrate his sympathy with the wretched of the earth; Loménie notes "that *refrain* which is heard at intervals, like the tolling of a funeral bell; 'Lève-toi, Jacques, Lève-toi; / Voici venir l'huissier du roi.'" The harmonious combination of his lyric poems is highly praised, and an example is given in "this admirable strophe of the piece entitled *Fools* ('Les Fous')." The last four lines of the eight which conclude this poem we shall find Poe citing *in toto* in 1849. The author ends with mock reproof of Béranger for deprecating his "glory" and his "genius" which have been lavished on the song, "that im- perishable species of manifestation. When you have chosen, you have inspired the people with the instinct of noble things, you have impressed upon their soul . . . the grand ideas of glory, honour, patriotism, and humanity. . . . The remotest gen- erations will repeat your strains and your name will never perish from the earth" (p. 247).

Before indicating the more far-reaching effect upon Poe's view of Béranger given by this translated chapter, I should like to offer an amusing sign of his careful reading of its pages. Eight years later, Poe prepared for the *Southern Literary Messenger* of June, 1849, a set of "Marginalia." One paragraph, which has not been traced to my knowledge, comes directly from Loménie-Walsh's chapter on the poet, with minor changes:

A clever French writer of "Memoirs" is quite right in saying that "if the *Universities* had been willing to permit it, the disgusting old *débauché* of Teos, with his eternal Batyllis, would long ago have been buried in the darkness of oblivion." [Harrison, 16.164]

This can be found printed verbatim in Walsh (p. 243), with the erroneous spelling "debauchee," (referring to Anacreon), but Poe, in correcting this error, should also have corrected "Batyllis" into "Bathyllus." Poe also adds the emphasis of italics. It would appear that he retained his notes on this chapter from 1841 or the book itself—a fact which becomes more significant in his 1849 quotation of Béranger, from the same chapter, as well as his 1842 addition of the motto for "The Fall of the House of Usher."

It is not a mere paragraph, however, nor even a set of quotations that Poe chiefly derived from this source, but a wholehearted respect for the French poet. This was much more intense than any feeling that firsthand acquaintance with Béranger's middle-level strains could have given to Poe. Yet Loménie was not unusual at this time in his adulation. For example, William Young, in his translation, asserts: "Béranger's songs are the wonder of the critic, no less than the delight of the artisan, who cannot read them, but yet knows them by heart."[23] Béranger himself knew the truth about his mediocrity; in his preface to the *Chansons Nouvelles et Dernières* of 1833 he wrote: "In short, a great number of my songs are no more than the inspiration of intimate sentiments or of the whims of a vagabond spirit. . . . Despite all that friendship has been able to do, despite the noteworthy tolerance and indulgence of the interpreters of public opinion, I have always thought that my name would not survive me, and that my reputation would decline faster for having, of necessity, been greatly exaggerated by the interest of the party which has adopted it."[24] This sentiment accords with his reply to a letter of glowing tribute to Béranger, "chansonnier," sent by Chateaubriand on September 24, 1831 (alluding also to his high praise in the *Etudes*).

It appears to follow Béranger's poem of tribute to Chateaubriand of September 14. Béranger's reply, of October 4, 1831, concerns his inflated reputation: "I am a good little poet, a clever artisan, a conscientious worker to whom the old airs and the corner where I am confined have brought happiness, and that is that. . . . I shall have a line in history."[25] Béranger correctly assayed his merits, although his reputation lingered a little longer than he had anticipated.

In 1879 Walter Bagehot, in a long chapter on Béranger in his *Literary Studies*, thought him influential in political affairs, quick, gay, precise, and epicurean—therefore, "superficial."[26] In 1896 Alcée Fortier regarded him as "vulgar, bombastic, and grandiloquent" but not without genius.[27] Gustave Lanson left him out of his *Histoire de la Littérature Française* but elsewhere granted him a skill in ear-catching, dramatic rhythms; he compared him to Scribe in his song structure.[28] Even more contemptuous is Pierre Moreau, who says: "He waved a panache of popular patriotism which made him for a time a great man." A brief but penetrating evaluation is offered by L. Cazamian, who thinks his "unrivalled popularity" to be owed to "neatness, light and deft phrasing, easy, short, well-marked rhythm . . . humour and a touch of sentiment"—qualities appealing to "the taste of the middle classes" rather than "artists and intellectuals."[29]

Mindful of these few critical dicta about Béranger, we return to his contemporary, Edgar Allan Poe, who has just read the sketch by Walsh-Loménie. In September, 1841, Poe was reviewing for *Graham's* the novel *Joseph Rushbrook, or the Poacher* by Captain Marryat (19.142–143; Harrison, 10.197–202). Poe had little respect for Marryat: "He has always been a very *popular* writer in the most rigorous sense of the word. His books are essentially 'mediocre.' His ideas are the common property of the mob, and have been their common property time out of mind. We look . . . in vain for the slightest indication of originality . . . sentiments rather than ideas; and properly to estimate them, even in this view, we must bring ourselves into a sort of identification with the sentiment of the mass. Works composed in this spirit are sometimes purposely so composed by men of superior intelligence, and here we call to mind the *Chansons* of Béranger." This spirit is called by critics *"nationalty"* (in this sense, a Poe nonceword) and Poe doubts that it is "a fit object for high-minded ambition" (10. 197–198).[30] One wonders whether "nationalty" is indeed what critics do call the mixture of popularity and simplicity about which Poe *may* be writing (for there is certainly little straightforward meaning in any of it). It would appear, however, that Béranger's writing for the people, whom he calls "ma muse," has been driven home by Loménie, but the comparison with Marryat is utterly discordant and shows no real understanding or knowledge of Béranger.

It was during 1841 that Poe recorded a few lines from Béranger which are not in Loménie's article, the only such instance, but he did not make any published use of the citation. The matter is, perhaps, too petty to concern us for long, and may be followed in the illuminating account of "What Poe Knew about Cryptography" by W. K. Wimsatt, Jr.[31] Sometime during 1841, while he was continuing his articles on "Secret-Writing" or cryptography, begun in *Alexander's Weekly Messenger* over a year earlier,[32] Poe jotted down three lines from Béranger's "Petit Homme Gris" on an envelope which he was using for notes on cryptography: "Et dit, moi je m'en / Et dit, moi je m'en / Ma foi; moi je men [*sic*] ris." This is the refrain of the poem, save for the last line: "Oh! qu'il est gai [*bis*] / le petit homme gris!" (1840 ed., pp. 27–29). The envelope can be identified as one sent by F. W. Thomas to Poe, July 19, 1841. Various aspects of Poe's magazine exhibition of decoding cryptograms made it appropriate for him to record this mocking kind of refrain. He could easily have picked it up from hearing the song, "Le Petit Homme Gris."[33] It was not necessary for him to derive a refrain from reading a collection of Béranger's works, and in the light of his further uninformed references, I believe that the sketch in Walsh's book remained his sole contact with Béranger's work in the original French. The connection between "A Few Words on Secret Writing" in the July, 1841 issue of *Graham's* and the April review of Walsh's book is noted by Poe (19.35); Poe refers to the phrase "le gouvernement provisoire" which had been discovered by Berryer, subject of one of the Walsh chapters, to be the key to a cipher involving the Duchesse de Berri (18.203). In a further notice on "Secret Writing" Poe alluded to the Berryer discovery of the cipher solution (August, 1841, 19.96). A brief note on "Secret Writing" was again included in *Graham's* for October, 1841 (19.192). Clearly, elements from the *Sketches* were lingering with Poe during the rest of the year and afterwards, to provide him with ideas and allusions adequate for his purposes.

Accordingly, in May, 1842, in his second review of Hawthorne's *Twice-Told Tales* in *Graham's* he invokes Béranger's name, in the often-cited passage on the superiority over long compositions of the "tale proper" and of the "rhymed poem" which can be read in an hour. In discussing the epic as "offspring of an imperfect sense of Art," he evaluates a "poem *too* brief" to produce "an intense or enduring impression" (Harrison, 11.107). I shall give the conclusion with its misinterpretation of Béranger:

> Without a certain continuity of effort—without a certain duration or repetition of purpose—the soul is never deeply moved. There must be the dropping of the water upon the rock. De Béranger has wrought brilliant things—pungent and soul-stirring—but, like all immassive bodies, they lack *momentum*, and thus fail to satisfy the Poetic Sentiment. They sparkle and excite, but from want of continuity, fail deeply to impress. Extreme brevity will degenerate into epigrammatism; but the sin of extreme length is even more unpardonable. *In medio tutissimus ibis.*

This is replete with errors, the most objectively demonstrable of which is the length of Béranger's poems. In the 1840 edition, which is virtually complete, there are 320 "chansons," of which only three percent or exactly eleven are as brief as eight lines in length. Since these "couplets" as Béranger terms them are usually written in tribute to real persons the danger of mere "epigrammatism" is slight.[34] Almost all of the remaining 309 are forty lines long, much greater, one might add, than the average length of Poe's poems. How could Poe have made such a surprising mistake? one asks. The answer is simple and inescapable—by looking solely at the excerpts published in the Béranger chapter of Walsh's book. From the same source derives the notion that he wrought "brilliant things—pungent and soul-stirring." Merely read the ending of that chapter given above, to observe this. Even the wording derives from it. Apparently, with regard to French literature, Poe felt secure from any accusation of error.

Poe next drew upon the chapter in Walsh's *Sketches* for the important motto to "The Fall of the House of Usher." In his *Tales* "by Edgar A. Poe" (New York, 1845), he reprints the tale of 1839, this time with the motto. It had appeared twice in 1840 without the motto.[35] I emphasize that 1840 was the year before his review of Walsh's *Sketches;* hence, Poe had no previous knowledge of the lines from "Le Refus." Without suspecting this situation Quinn controverts by implication Campbell's suggestion about "Israfel" by stating that if both works were based on the excerpt, "It would be a remarkable example of Poe's retention of an idea for fourteen years!" (Quinn, pp. 466–467). In fact, Poe would have been capable of such a retention, *if* he had actually read Béranger's poem in 1831, but this was impossible. There is no question that, taken out of context, the lines are very well suited to Roderick Usher, who responds to so many suprasensual phenomena with fear, evasion, and eventually disintegration. To point up the application Poe did not hesitate to change Béranger's "mon coeur" to "son coeur" in the motto. This is one of the many instances in which Poe shows a kind of genius in borrowing and adapting short-story mottoes well after the original genesis and printing of the work.[36] In his article in *The Dial* Campbell

carelessly overlooks the lack of motto in the first three printings
of "The Fall of the House of Usher," and confidently declares
that the tale uses it ten years *after* it enters into "Israfel."

After 1845 there is a lapse in Poe's references to Béranger
until the last two years of his life, when we find three. The
first to be printed (see below for his lecture of 1848) is the
comparison of George P. Morris with Béranger, because of
their both being "song-writers." This is identical with Poe's
article in *Burton's Gentleman's Magazine* of December, 1839,
and it is now included as one of the long items in the "Marginalia" of the *Southern Literary Messenger* of April, 1849
(Harrison, 16.136–140). Harrison is in error in his headnote
and footnote which maintain that it was given the title "National Melodies of America" and reprinted "revised" and "with
slight alterations" (10.41). Its appearance indicates Poe's continuing misconceptions about Béranger's works—for example,
their being written for music of "indefiniteness."[37] In the
stresses of the year of Virginia's final decline and afterwards
while courting the literary ladies of New York, Lowell, Providence, and Richmond, Poe probably had little time or inclina-
tion to look into Béranger's poems.

At least once he glanced into his notebook jottings from
Walsh's *Sketches* or into the book itself, for in the June, 1849
"Marginalia" of the *Messenger* we find him using four of the
eight lines from "Les Fous," which Loménie had quoted. The
brief item illustrates Poe's method of embellishing his "Marginalia" quotations and also provides insight into Poe's prevailing attitude on important issues:

> I have great faith in fools:—self-confidence my friends will
> call it:—
> > Si demain, oubliant d'éclore,
> >   Le jour manquait, eh bien! demain
> > Quelque fou trouverait encore
> >   Un flambeau pour le genre humain.

By the way, what with the new electric light and other matters, De Béranger's idea is not so *very* extravagant. [Harrison, 16.165]

For lack of a faithful translation by Mrs. Ellet of these lines from Béranger's satire on followers of St. Simon, Fourier, and Enfantin, I shall give that of William Young. He translates the poem as "Madmen" and concludes it with:

> If day should fail to-morrow duly
> To break—why then, to-morrow, truly,
> Some madman would in such a case
> Light with his torch the human race.
>
> [p. 318]

Béranger's full satire on social reformers would certainly be pleasing to Edgar Allan Poe. Many are the instances of Poe's strictures against Fourier and Condorcet and those that he sweepingly called the "human-perfectibility men." More ambivalent was his attitude toward the progress of the sciences, quite apart from their application to the betterment of the life of the average man. He shows this equivocal appreciation of the new science in the heavily footnoted "Thousand-and-Second Tale of Scheherazade" with its references to rapid trains, Babbage's early computer, electrotype, the "Voltaic pile," the "Electro Telegraph," the daguerreotype, etc. (February, 1845); less directly, in the "anti-democratic" and "anti-progressivist" story "Some Words with a Mummy" (April, 1845); and, especially, in his "looking-backward" fantasy, "Mellonta Tauta" (February, 1849). These are only a few of the *loci* for references by Poe to scientific development.[38]

It may appear strange to the reader of today that Poe should reach out to Béranger in order to make such an observation. One might note, in passing, that Poe knew about Sir Humphry Davy's experiments of 1801 with the electric arc (exhibited by him in 1808) as well as about the many developments of the 1840's intended to improve electric arc lamps.[39] Poe's interest here may also have coincided with his work on "The Light-House" during his last year of life.[40] Lighthouses were often

discussed as a primary goal of efficient electric illumination.[41]
Whatever the source of his interest, Poe certainly forces Béranger into an odd application, since the French poet is not
talking about science at all, and says nothing so *very* extravagant at the end; the image is as old as the idea of Prometheus's
enlightening mankind with fire. But it certainly leads to an
insight into Poe, for he implies his feelings about the majority
of mankind—"les fous"—despite the wry humor of his placing
himself on the same level. There is also the implication of
pleasure in a universal holocaust—easily substantiated from
Poe's self-destructiveness, especially after the death of Virginia.

The last instance of Poe's use of Béranger's poetry was in
"The Poetic Principle," prepared as a lecture late in 1848 and
published posthumously in 1850.[42] The Béranger section of this
celebrated statement of Poe's aesthetic credo, with its definition of the function of poetry as "the rhythmical creation of
beauty," was adapted from his earlier passage in the May,
1842 *Graham's Magazine* review of *Twice-Told Tales*. We can
date with accuracy its entrance into his lecture and consequent
essay through a letter to Sarah Whitman of November 26, 1848:

> I . . . ask you to mail me, *as soon as possible,* three articles
> of mine which you will find among the *critical papers* I gave
> you, viz: "The Philosophy of Composition—Tale-Writing—
> Nath Hawthorne"—and a review of "Longfellow's Poems." I
> wish to refer to them in writing my Lecture & can find no
> other copies. Do not fail to send them . . . as soon as you
> get this. Enclose them *in a letter*—so that I may be sure to
> get them in season. [Ostrom, 2.411; Poe's underlining]

Poe lectured in Providence on "The Poetic Principle" on December 20, 1848, with great success according to his letter of
the 28th (Ostrom, 2.413). Henceforth the lecture-article, with
its prominent reference to Béranger, became a major source
of income for Poe during the last year of his life.[43] In view of
the importance that Poe and literary critics have attached to
this work, Poe's use of Béranger's "chansons" to illustrate a
leading point deserves attention.

The passage in the Hawthorne review, with its capitalized "Poetic Sentiment," may have suggested the lecture and essay title, "Poetic Principle," as well as various themes. It is interesting to observe the way in which he has altered the original —by no means for the better. I do not wish to suggest causes for the loss of his customary skill or judgment in this matter. Some changes, of course, derive from the need, in 1848, to consider poetry alone, whereas "tale-writing" was his primary theme in 1842. The Béranger portion of the original, long paragraph now is given paragraph emphasis by itself:

> On the other hand, it is clear that a poem may be improperly brief. Undue brevity degenerates into mere epigrammatism. A *very* short poem, while now and then producing a brilliant or vivid, never produces a profound or enduring effect. There must be the steady pressing down of the stamp upon the wax. De Béranger has wrought innumerable things, pungent and spirit-stirring; but in general, they have been too imponderous to stamp themselves deeply into the public attention; and thus, as so many feathers of fancy, have been blown aloft only to be whistled down the wind. [Harrison, 14.268–269]

The former image of "the dropping of the water upon the rock" has been supplanted by two references to "the stamp upon the wax," probably suggested by his original use of "impression" and "impress." The phrase, "extreme brevity degenerates," of the first essay has become "undue brevity" and has been shifted to the beginning from its penultimate position, while the pretentious last sentence, in Latin, has been dropped. The paragraph is another proof that up to the very end of his career Poe persisted in believing that Béranger's poems were chiefly short, a misconception that a mere glance into a collection would have banished. In this new passage he has committed another blunder, for in the original, Béranger's poems were too "immassive" to "satisfy the Poetic Sentiment," whereas now, being still "imponderous," they fail to receive significant "public attention." This is, as we have seen from the large number of editions and the extravagant praise and popularity of his works, a wrong estimate by Poe, willing to derive one error from another in justification of his original thesis about the short poem. In the new version he adds to the notion by a comparison with feathers 'blown aloft," despite the marked staying power, at least up to 1849, of Béranger's poems. Moreover, rhetorically the development is peculiarly inept for poems which start out as "brilliant or vivid," turn into "stamps upon the wax," then become "pungent," and finally dance lightly in the breeze. Poe's conspicuous use of synesthesia can scarcely justify this mixture. Quinn judges his style in the essay to be "almost beyond criticism"—apparently in other passages than this one.

In conclusion, then, Béranger appears not to have contributed very much to Poe's concepts or practices in creative work. He probably played a very minor role in the revision of "Israfel" and furnished only a reminder of the theme—a mere addendum—in "The Fall of the House of Usher." In his criticism we find Poe willing to adapt views about Béranger gleaned from secondary sources, such as Loménie, and to neglect elementary precautions in making generalizations about a presumably well-known author. His two definite citations of verses appear intended primarily to display his knowledge, although in touching upon important strands in Poe's total fabric of thought the citations provide us with insight into his mental processes. Several of Poe's references to Béranger also show a lack of appreciation of contemporary movements in French literature, entirely understandable in the harried American, who was desperately eager to establish a reputation for sophistication and omniscience. In surveying the ten instances we learn something about Poe and about his contemporary reading public and audience.

THE ROLE OF BYRON
AND MARY SHELLEY
IN POE'S "MASQUE"

ALMOST EVERY MASTERPIECE of literature reflects a variety of sources, recent and remote, major and minor, all absorbed and held by the creative spirit in a state of dynamic but subliminal flux, until the moment of conception. It may be argued that the pinpointing of this moment and of the particular stimulus involved, can never be definitively verified either through analyzing the finished work or tracing the sequence of the author's major and trivial personal affairs. I emphasize the multiplicity of the origins because I consider Poe's acknowledged source in Hugo's play, treated in chapter i, to be only one of the many which flowered into "The Masque of the Red Death." Two more writers remain to be discussed in the present chapter. These two were friends who shared a common background and who, together, had a singular influence in establishing and linguistically sharpening Poe's underlying theme. Through my discussion of Lord Byron and Mary Shelley, I mean to place Poe's tale in the stream of one of mankind's major preoccupations—the question of man's ultimate fate on earth, both as individual and as a species. I put aside, for the moment, the fairly easily settled matter of Poe's knowledge of the writings of the two authors.

Byron's poem "Darkness" can be properly presented as a widely known statement of the romantic theme "The Last Man," which engaged the interest of many leading writers.[1] *The Knickerbocker Magazine* of New York, in October, 1833,

shows awareness of this in its observation that Mary Shelley's
The Last Man is a detailed, prose copy of the "terrible painting" of Byron's "Darkness."[2] The poem was only one of several
of Byron's contributions to the subject that Poe admired. It was
a product of Byron's sojourn at Geneva during the summer of
1816, when he constantly associated with Shelley, Mary, and
Claire. Its weird and nightmarish concept of the death of all
living creatures on earth, when the sun goes out, reminds us
of the grim stories that were told nightly at Villa Diodati.[3]
Mary's *Frankenstein* was another product of those sessions.
Byron's eighty-two lines of blank verse in "Darkness" present
a succession of horrors: howling men who build their own
pyres, vipers consumed for food, sailorless ships rotting on the
motionless seas, and famine-stricken multitudes. It concludes:

> The winds were wither'd in the stagnant air
> And the clouds perish'd! Darkness had no need
> Of aid from them — She was the Universe.

The poem shocked Jeffrey and Scott and probably most of
those who read it upon publication in 1816 as part of *The
Prisoner of Chillon and Other Poems*.[4]

Although Byron's manuscript notes defensively assert: "The
thoughts I claim as my own," they have been traced by Eugen
Köbling to a work of some popularity at a period when many
in Europe under the heel of Napoleon thought that the day of
Armageddon had indeed come; this was the two-volume novel
of 1805 by Jean-Baptiste François Cousin de Grainville, *Le
Dernier Homme; ou, Omégare et Sydérie*.[5] Obviously the subtitle owes its origin to Revelation 22:13: "I am Alpha and
Omega, the beginning and the end, the first and the last."
Revelation is rich in scenes of final destruction. The rather
full account of the novel in Michaud's *Biographie Universelle*
points out that it was published after the suicide of the author
early in 1805 and was then issued in 1806 in English, with no
indication of the original authorship.[6] The book subsequently
received so much attention through a long reference to it by
Sir Henry Croft in his 1810 edition of the odes of Horace

(Book II, Ode 1) that it was republished by Charles Nodier in Paris in 1811. Its continuing popularity may be indicated by a poetic adaptation as late as 1831.[7] Byron may have read any of these editions of the novel or even the detailed analysis given in *L'Esprit des journaux* of May, 1811. At any rate, de Grainville tells about the universal sterility of all mankind and the extinguishing of the heavenly bodies through a vast conflagration. The absence of warmth and of growth becomes Byron's major theme. It is not impossible that Poe derived in part the concept of the dotage and death of the earth from Byron. He used that idea in "The Conversation of Eiros and Charmion" in December, 1839, and was to mention it at the end of "The Power of Words" in June, 1845. An intervening work, undoubtedly familiar to Poe, was a *Blackwood's* story of March, 1826, "The Last Man," which was followed by a published controversy in the January, 1827 issue over the claim of Thomas Campbell as opposed to Byron to be the "originator" of the idea. Poe, of course, had studied *Blackwood's Edinburgh Magazine* closely for his tale "How to Write a Blackwood Article."[8]

Quite apart from the concept of the extinction of all life, which prevails in "The Masque of the Red Death" (since the plague is presented as universally inescapable), there is a similarity of phrasing in the two works of Poe and Byron. The Red Death, after being accosted by Prospero at the masquerade, afflicts and fells every one of the thousand courtiers. I shall have so many reasons to allude to this famous last paragraph that it should be cited in its entirety:

> And now was acknowledged the presence of the Red Death. He had come like a thief in the night. And one by one dropped the revellers in the blood-bedewed halls of their revel, and died each in the despairing posture of his fall. And the life of the ebony clock went out with that of the last of the gay. And the flames of the tripods expired. And Darkness and Decay and the Red Death held illimitable dominion over all.[9]

The last sentence, it seems to me, has links with Byron's "Darkness had no need / Of aid from them—She was the universe." Byron, in turn, may have borrowed it from a familiar source which has been assumed to be Poe's original—Pope's conclusion to the *Dunciad:*

> Light dies before thy uncreating word;
> Thy hand, great Anarch! lets the curtain fall,
> And universal Darkness buries All.[10]

Certainly Poe shows an awareness of Pope's celebrated poem, but of his eight allusions to the *Dunciad* only one is to specific lines, and these are drawn from Book I, "at random," Poe tells us; the others refer merely to the title as a standard of satirical style.[11] It is Byron with whom Poe shows a thorough familiarity, both in his varied references and in the many echoes from diverse works.[12] Moreover, the context of the conclusion of the *Dunciad* is scarcely relevant to the theme of Poe's "Masque of the Red Death," while Byron's "Darkness" has much in common with the tale.

A definite influence from Byron appears in Poe's final paragraph in the words, "and died each in the despairing posture of his fall." The end of Byron's *Lara* gives us:

> And she would sit beneath the very tree
> Where lay his drooping head upon her knee;
> And in that posture where she saw him fall,
> His words, his looks, his dying grasp recall;
>
> .   .   .   .
>
> Then rising, start, and beckon him to fly,
> From some imagined spectre in pursuit.[13]

Poe would find significance himself in the coincidental use of *posture* and *fall* in Byron's poem for the "dying" man, both of which he applies to the stricken stage figures of Prospero's court.[14] Patrick Quinn rightly points out the theatrical effect of the story: "The reader . . . understands that the drama is not being played out on any realistic stage."[15] Byron again is not totally lacking in responsibility for this, since he starts "Darkness," originally entitled "A Dream," with "I had a dream, which was not all a dream." Poe, midway in his tale, while discussing the "phantasms" which the courtiers have become through their grotesque costumes, says: "There were delirious fancies such as the madman fashions. . . . To and fro in the seven chambers there stalked, in fact, a multitude of dreams. And these—the dreams—writhed in and about. . . . The dreams are stiff-frozen as they stand. . . . And now again the music swells, and the dreams live" (4.254). It is the "factual dream" quality of both pieces, determined throughout by the strange settings and the specific details, which produces the horrified tension of our response.

In other well-known works Byron had also given the effect of utter desolation with the extinction of virtually all human life, and these too may have provided Poe with a general orientation toward the theme of "The Last Man," if not with specific ideas. For example, *Heaven and Earth: A Mystery*, founded on Genesis, deals with the flood and the elimination of almost all life. One passage in the soliloquy of Japhet, when he contemplates the death of all mankind except for Noah's family, gives us the feeling of universal annihilation, especially with its rhetorical repetition of "no more": "Oh, men—my fellow-beings! Who / Shall weep above your universal grave, / Save I. . . . No more to have the morning sun break forth. . . . No more to have / Day's broad orb drop behind its head at even. . . . / No more to be the beacon of the world, / . . . And can those words 'no more' / Be meant for thee, for all things, save for us . . ." (I, iii). This was possibly also a suggestion for Poe of several of his uses of "no more" or variations thereof in his poetry, as in the "Sonnet to Zante."[16] *Heaven and Earth* derives from a later period in Byron's career, having been written at Ravenna in October, 1821. Mary Shelley saw it in the second number of Hunt's *The Liberal*, as she notes in her letters.[17] Since she and Shelley shared most of their reading, its presence on Shelley's list for December 14, 1821, also indicates her familiarity with it.[18]

After the death of Shelley on July 8, 1822, followed by that of Byron on April 19, 1824, Mary Shelley felt peculiarly alone, since she had been tied emotionally to both poets. Soon after hearing of the second loss she wrote in her journal: "The last man! yes, I may well describe that solitary being's feeling, feeling myself as the last relic of a beloved race, my companions extinct before me."[19] In 1826, her third novel, *The Last Man*, conceived after Shelley's death and given much impetus by Byron's death, rather closely represents her husband as Adrian and Byron as Raymond and incorporates Byron's adventures in Greece into the narrative. Her journal exclamation suggests that she derived elements from de Grainville's book and also from "Darkness," which she knew well, having been present during its gestation.[20] With these she combined the idea of widespread death by plague, which came to her from a variety of sources, as she admits in her novel—chiefly the works of Boccaccio, Charles Brockden Brown, and Defoe.[21] She does not mention de Grainville's *The Last Man, or Omegarius and Syderia* either by main title or subtitle, but two facts make me think that it influenced her as well as Byron. Chapter viii of the second volume of her novel ends with this sentence: "There was much of degradation in this: for even vice and virtue had lost their attributes—life—life—the continuation of our animal mechanism—was the Alpha and Omega of the desires, the prayers, the prostrate ambition of human race" (p. 212). Omegarius, the name of de Grainville's hero, is undoubtedly from the "Alpha and Omega" passage in Revelation, as I have indicated. Secondly, Mary Shelley was living with Godwin during much of the time that she was working on *The Last Man* and continued to see him frequently when she moved to another address in London. Godwin records in his journal for January, 1826, that he is reading the two volumes of *Omegarius.* it is likely that this was connected with the imminent publication of his daughter's novel.[22] Perhaps Godwin wished to check on the new novel's closeness to this source, in expectation of the reviews that would soon be published. He was correct, for one article at least wondered why one *Last Man* was not suffi-cient.[23] Part of her motivation, of course, was the growing interest in the spread of plague from the Orient. Year by year Asiatic cholera had been moving westward from Bengal, hav-ing recently ravaged Asia Minor; hence, the inclusion of epi-sodes at Istanbul and then at Athens. In point of fact, the plague reached England only in 1831 and the next year one of its victims was Mary's half-brother, William Godwin, Jr., a promising novelist and journalist. Poe saw its incursion into Baltimore in 1831.

I suggest that the whole theme of her novel, the death by plague of all in the world save the narrator, could easily have directed Poe's mind to the subject. In addition, the work fur-nished Poe with specific details and even phrases, I think. In "The Masque of the Red Death" Prospero removes one thou-sand of his courtiers to a "castellated abbey" where they are shut inside to revel and forget the fearful epidemic. Finally after their half year of seclusion, the masquerade ball is given in the suite of seven differently colored rooms. The Red Death enters in a spectral or corpselike costume, his mask sprinkled with blood, like the face of a plague victim; Poe here is chang-ing the characterizing buboes or sores of the bubonic plague (first called Black Death in English only in 1823) to a horri-fying new symptom, bleeding at the pores.[24] The Red Death strikes the accosting Prince with the plague, and the rest of the company succumb almost at once. The details of the plot of *The Last Man* need not be given. The first part is a tangle of relationships involving the throne of England in the twenty-first century; it is being abdicated by Adrian, or Shelley, in his democratic fervor. The major episodes involving Lionel Ver-ney, married to Idris, Adrian's sister, are set chiefly in the castle at Windsor and nearby Marlow, prominent in Shelley bi-ography. The fifteen hundred English survivors of the plague, in 2096, decide to seek refuge in Switzerland, which, they dis-cover, has also been losing its population, and finally the small remaining group travels to Italy. Both locales give Mary a chance to describe in vivid detail memorable scenes from her life with Shelley. At last, Adrian and his niece die by drowning (p. 321), just as Shelley had died, leaving Lionel Verney alone to tell his story.[25]

Certain resemblances are evident, even from this short summary: the annihilation of all within the purview of the story by plague, except for the narrator; the locale of Italy at the end of the story, and the use of a castle as an ineffective refuge. Other resemblances are the importance of a masquerade at one point in the story; the intrusion of a black-cloaked figure representing Death, and at least two striking verbal similarities, which I shall give later. The masquerade enters into chapter vi of the first volume, when the plague has attacked England. Near Windsor a "mock fair" is being held. "The park was speckled by tents, whose flaunting colours and gaudy flags, waving in the sunshine, added to the gaiety of the scene" (p. 173). As Verney continues reflecting, "The gay dance vanished, the green sward was strewn with corpses, the blue air above became fetid with deathly exhalations" (p. 174). It was this sort of charnel atmosphere interspersed throughout the book that disgusted the reviewers—if not the public, since *The Last Man* reached a second printing in 1826. The same masquerade episode yields several other details for comparison. Verney says: "The lightness of heart which had dressed them in masquerade habits, had decorated their tents and assembled them in fantastic groups, appeared a sin against, and a provocative to, the awful destiny that had laid its palsying hand upon hope and life" (p. 176). Change the "tents" to "rooms" and this might be a motto for Poe's tale. The sudden death brought by the plague in both Poe's and Mary Shelley's work is unique, for other authors, such as Defoe, give at least a few hours for the career of the disease from its symptoms to its termination.[26] This is made clear in the same episode in her book: the Lord Protector Ryland becomes terror stricken, for "One of his servants, while waiting on him, had suddenly fallen down dead. The physician declared that he died of the plague" (p. 176).

Similarly, Mary emphasizes that throughout the world only Verney recovers from it, while Poe has Prospero and his thousand courtiers succumb almost instantaneously.[27]

Shortly after the "masque" scene just mentioned, Mary repeats this contrast, obviously derived from Boccaccio,[28] in describing the shallow merrymakers in London; they tried "to banish thought and opiate despair . . . assemblies of mourners in the guise of revellers" (pp. 200–201).[29] Reminding us of the courtiers in their costume and the Red Death in his, she has a maniac warn them: "Apparel yourself in the court-dress of death. Pestilence will usher you to his presence" (p. 190). The inevitability of its coming to all, indicated ironically in Poe's choice of name for Prospero, the absolute monarch, is reflected also in Mary's more obvious homily: "The pomp of rank, the assumption of power, the possessions of wealth vanished like morning mist" (p. 212). Likewise, "To chambers of painted state farewell—To midnight revelry, and the panting emulation of beauty, to costly dress and birth-day shew, to titles and the gilded coronet, farewell" (p. 233)! (This last is very much, in phrasing and sentiment like Calderon, whom Mrs. Shelley cites twice, pp. 136 and 195.) "Death sat at the tables of the great . . . seized the dastard who fled, quelled the brave man who resisted" (p. 198) and "Nature . . . invited us to join the gay masque" (p. 198). The idea of investing death with spectral garb is also used, derived, I assume, from standard representations of the dance of death, dating from the Middle Ages.[30] On the road toward Geneva, the company is "haunted for several days by an apparition, to which our people gave the appellation of the Black Spectre." They see it only at evening when all believe it to be a "token of inevitable death." Eventually the spectre turns out to be a lonely French nobleman, somewhat shyly following them until he dies of the plague at the moment of his unmasking (p. 299).

Two similarities of phrasing establish more circumstantially the probability of Poe's having read Mary Shelley's work. One phrase occurs in Mary Shelley's description of the dance: "The band played the wild eastern air of Weber introduced in Abon Hassan" (p. 173). Poe speaks repeatedly of the dance in the "Masque of the Red Death" as being the waltz. This same importation from the Continent produced Byron's "The Waltz, an Apostrophic Hymn" (1812), which condemns the "voluptuous" dance.[31] One must remember that in the costumes of Poe's courtiers there was "much of the wanton." The orchestra plays "wild music" (4.254), and as "the music swells," the "dreams live, and writhe to and fro more merrily than ever." Spurred on by this music "the masquerade licence of the night was nearly unlimited." Only the "spectral image" moves among the waltzers "with a slow and solemn movement" as if to remind them of his restraining purpose.

The "wild music" of the waltz also forms a curious and rather intricately wrought link with both Mary Shelley's *Last Man* and Poe's "last man" story of "The Fall of the House of Usher" of 1839. In this earlier tale the narrator is remembering his last days with the demented Roderick Usher. "I hold painfully in mind a certain singular perversion and amplification of the wild air of the last waltz of Von Weber" (3.282–283). A little later we are told that he "confined himself upon the guitar," for which he wrote both the words and the notes of "wild fantasias" or "rhapsodies," as illustrated by "The Haunted Palace" (actually, added to the story after the first printing).[32] However strange the waltz would sound on a guitar, the adjective "wild" is interesting in comparison with Mary Shelley's "wild eastern air of Weber introduced in Abon Hassan" (p. 173), in a scene of revelry in the Windsor Castle park, just when news of the advent of the plague in London is to be announced. She does not specify that the dance was a waltz. Mary Shelley must have attended a performance of *Abon Hassan* in 1825; this was the name given in England to Weber's *Abu Hassan,* a two-act play with music, derived by his librettist, Franz Carl Hiemer, from a story in *The Arabian Nights' Entertainments.* The growing popularity of Weber's music and his widely heralded arrival in London for the first performance of *Oberon* may have led to two separate productions of *Abon Hassan:* a farce by William Dimond and a Drury Lane version by Thomas S. Cooke, both using Weber's score.[33] Since Weber tries to provide an exotic atmosphere in a few arias and in an overture marked *presto,* Mary's reference to a "wild eastern air" is not inappropriate at the time.

This reference in *The Last Man* or Poe's possibly direct knowledge of *Abu* (or *Abon*) *Hassan* may have been merged in Poe's retentive memory with the title of another work attributed to Weber. It was a popular piece, originally for the pianoforte, called "Weber's Last Waltz." In Poe scholarship, Professor Mabbott appears to be the first to observe that it was not really Weber's at all; Kenneth Graham and others mention its being a composition by Karl Reissiger.[34] Reissiger, who had succeeded Von Weber as conductor of the Dresden opera, wrote many popular chamber music compositions. His *Danses Brillantes pour le pianoforte,* op. 26 (1824), includes the so-called "Last Waltz."[35] As with so many of Poe's references, no simple explanation will suffice. The piece in reality was Reissiger's "Weber's Last Thought" (*Gedanke*), either mistranslated or misapplied. Percy Scholes supplies the interesting information that Weber had heard Reissiger play it in February, 1826, just before Weber left for London, bearing a donated copy of the piece. A few months later, after Weber's death, it was found among his effects and published or republished in England with the erroneous title of "Weber's Last Waltz" and was attributed to Weber himself. Years later, when Johann Peter Pixis sent Reissiger his own "Fantasia" on the theme ascribed to Weber, the composer discovered the error, now too widespread in English-speaking lands to be corrected.[36] Not only was the piece frequently played but many adaptations and variations on the theme were composed. I have found three in two major music libraries of New York City: a "Fantaisie" for piano and clarinet by Friedrich Berr, piano "Variations Brillantes" by Henri Herz, and a four-hand duet by Henry Karr; all are ascribed to "Weber's Last Waltz." Roderick Usher's "perversion and amplification of the wild air of the last waltz of Von Weber," the "fervid *facility*" of his "impromptus" (3.283), and his "wild fantasias" induct him into the large company of musical enthusiasts who were varying Reissiger's air.

For the twentieth-century listener, however, there is one drawback to the designation of "wild"—the nature of the music itself, which is happily available in a well-known collection called *Masterpieces of Piano Music*.[37] It is difficult to imagine anything more utterly pedestrian, more tame, more standard in its sequence of notes than this salon theme, devised by a composer of the early nineteenth century who completely reflected his period. It may be that Poe, impressed by the fame of the piece in its original form or in one of the sets of variations, used the title for a prestigious effect without listening to it for validation of his adjective "wild." Perhaps Mary Shelley's reference to the "wild eastern air of Weber" contributed a theme to Roderick Usher's wild playing on the guitar.

Whatever the case, I feel that Mary Shelley's *The Last Man* may have entered into the earlier tale and into "The Masque of the Red Death." It is noteworthy that immediately after the dance sequence in *The Last Man*, Ryland, formerly an ambassador to the United States, declares that "all the world has the plague!" Adrian responds, "Then to avoid it, we must quit the world" (p. 175). A bit further in the chapter Ryland reproves him: "It is well, shut up in your castle, out of danger, to boast yourself out of fear." Their conversation is "weighed with intolerable heaviness from the knowledge that the earth's desolator had at last, even as an arch-fiend, lightly over-leaped the boundaries our precautions raised, and at once enthroned himself in the full and beating heart of our country" (p. 177). These details connected with the music at the opening of the chapter are good indications of a link between the novel and the tale.

There is another phrase used by Poe which is strongly reminiscent of a passage in Mary Shelley's book. In describing the reaction of different types of men to the pestilence, she says:

"Death, which had in our younger days walked the earth like 'a thief that comes in the night,' now, rising from his subterranean vault, girt with power, with dark banner floating, came a conquerer. . . . They endeavoured to exchange terror for heedlessness, and plunged into licentiousness, to avoid the agonizing throes of worst apprehension" (pp. 196–197). The unidentified phrase, placed in quotation marks by her, is derived from Sir Thomas Browne's *Religio Medici:* "How comes He then like a Theefe in the night, when He gives an item of His coming?" (Pt. I, sec. 46). This is found soon after Browne's discussion of the ending of the world. "I believe the World grows near its end, yet is neither old nor decayed, nor shall ever perish upon the ruines of its own Principles. As the work of Creation was above nature, so is its adversary, annihilation; without which the World hath not its end, but its mutation. But no one knows the secret of the date."[38] Sir Thomas is taking his phrase from 1 Thessalonians 5:2: "The day of the Lord so cometh as a thief in the night" and possibly also from Revelation 16:15: "Behold, I come as a thief." Mary had cited Sir Thomas Browne by name only a few pages earlier: "It is too late to be ambitious. We cannot hope to live so long in our names as some others have done in their persons: one face of Janus holds no proportion to the other" (p. 189). This is from his *Hydriotaphia* (chap. v, para. 4), another storehouse of Browne's macabre ideas. We know that Shelley had read the *Religio Medici* aloud to her on March 14, 1815, according to an entry in her journal.[39] Shelley's admiration for Sir Thomas Browne, expressed in his letters, must have affected her deeply.[40]

It is true but unlikely that Poe may have picked up the phrase from his own reading of the Bible or of Sir Thomas and may have made the same adaptation by supplying "death" as the subject. He refers to Sir Thomas at least twice, but neither context is from the *Religio Medici*. In August, 1841, he cited the familiar reference to the Sirens from *Hydriotaphia*.[41] Even more generalized is his "Marginalia" note of November, 1844 (Harrison, 16.2) describing how he will "talk" in the "Marginalia"—"freshly—boldly—originally—with *abandonne-ment*—without conceit—much after the fashion of Jeremy Taylor, and Sir Thomas Browne." As for his biblical references, Killis Campbell disbelieves the figure of sixty passages from that source attributed to him by William M. Forrest and doubts any intimate knowledge on the part of Poe. Most of the passages, Campbell reasonably asserts, are stereotyped expressions; therefore, the transformation of one Bible passage in the same way as Mary Shelley's seems unlikely.[42] Except for "dark banner floating" every detail in her context corresponds to those in Poe's.

At this point one may ask whether it is probable that Poe had read and to some degree remembered Mary Shelley's novel. I believe that several factors favor this premise. The book had been issued twice during 1826 by the well-known London publisher, Henry Colburn and also in Paris by Galignani. After the cholera epidemic in America, beginning in Baltimore in 1831 and attacking New York in 1832,[43] a great demand for a novel about plague must have stirred the important Philadelphia publisher, Carey, Lea, and Blanchard to pirate it in a two-volume edition in 1833. Poe was well acquainted with the works and the prestige of this company, to whom he had offered *Al Aaraaf* in May, 1829, when it was called Carey, Lea and Carey.[44] In 1834, the year after the Philadelphia publication of *The Last Man*, he offered his "Tales of the Folio Club" to the firm, which declined it. Carey, at least, did accept "Ms. Found in a Bottle" for the first issue of the annual *The Gift* for 1836 (published in 1835), and "William Wilson" was in *The Gift* for 1840 (1839).[45] Clearly Poe was fully aware of the books which bore the imprint of this firm in its transformations during the 1830's.

Secondly, one might ask whether the name of Mrs. Shelley would mean anything to him, aside from his known and often professed admiration for the works of Shelley. During his Philadelphia period, particularly, Poe had reason to become aware of Mrs. Shelley as a writer. In 1838–39 Mary Shelley and a group of collaborators published in London a book entitled *Eminent Literary and Scientific Men of France*. This was reprinted or, rather, pirated by Lea and Blanchard in Philadelphia in 1840 as *Lives of the Most Eminent French Writers* and was reviewed by Poe in *Graham's Magazine* in January, 1841. The item has not been collected by Harrison but is so typical of Poe's method of brief reviewing and of his authoritative style as to warrant fairly certain attribution. The last sentence speaks of Mrs. Shelley's reputation with the implication, I believe, that readers as well as the reviewer are familiar with her writings. I shall furnish the whole of this short item, not easy of access:

"French Writers of Eminence," By Mrs. Shelley, and others. 2 vols. Lea & Blanchard.

This compilation, for it is nothing more—has the merit of presenting well-known Encyclopaedia biographies of French authors, to the general public, in a cheap and portable form, —thus bringing down much valuable information within the means of those who could not afford to purchase the larger and more comprehensive work. The design is praiseworthy.

The sketches of Rabelais, Racine, Corneille, Moliere, Voltaire, Rochefoucald, and others, will prove highly interesting to those who have not perused them before. A more valuable work, when considered solely as an introduction to French literature, has not, for some time, been issued from the American press. We would guard our readers, however, from fancying that Mrs. Shelley was the principal author of these sketches, as it would neither be truth, nor, in fact, add to her reputation.[46]

In addition to the writers mentioned, the book contained articles on Condorcet, Mirabeau, Mme. Roland, and Mme. de Stael; in the last account, undeniably by Mary, the reader finds information about Byron's visit in 1816 when they were all together on the shores of Lac Leman, where "Darkness" was written.[47]

Another compilation was prepared by Mrs. Shelley during

this period, in collaboration with Sir David Brewster, James Montgomery, and others; it was called *Lives of Eminent Literary and Scientific Men of Italy* and was similarly pirated by Lea and Blanchard in 1841. This too was reviewed by Poe in *Graham's Magazine,* not long before he began planning and writing "The Masque of the Red Death." Perhaps the Boccaccio article suggested the Italian *mise-en-scène* to the tale. This brief review, also uncollected by Harrison, will be given *in toto* and *literatim:*

> The lives embraced in these volumes are those of Dante, Petrarch, Boccacio, Lorenzo de Medici, Bojardo, Berni, Ariosto, Machiavelli, Galileo, Guicciardini, Vittoria Colonna, Guarini, Tasso, Chiabrera, Tassoni, Marini, Filicaja, Metastasio, Goldoni, Alfieri, Monti, and Ugo Foscolo. We have no clue to the names of the respective writers—but the biographies are, without exception, well written—although at times their brevity is annoying. As a whole, the work is not only interesting, but of value.[48]

And finally—Poe's deep awareness at that time of Mary Shelley's *Frankenstein* is attested through the published memories of one of the Smith family. Poe was accustomed to visit the matriarchal Mrs. William Moore Smith, whose fine house was at the falls of the Schuylkill River. "His favorite seat was in the doorway of the family mausoleum . . . where he read such books as Lewis's 'Tales of Terror,' Mary Wolstonecraft's [sic] 'Frankenstein,' and 'Five Nights at Saint Albans.' "[49] The account is entirely credible. One might justifiably conjecture that Poe sought out and read another of her macabre novels, if he had not indeed seen it earlier, not long before he wrote "The Masque of the Red Death." Certainly, there were many other influences working to produce this small, colorful tapestry of a story, but Byron and his admirer Mary Shelley contributed their threads to its total fabric.

6

POE'S "SONNET TO ZANTE": SOURCES AND ASSOCIATIONS

AMONG THE CURIOUS medley of references in Poe's *Al Aaraaf* of 1829 is one to the name of the island of Zante:

> And thy most lovely purple perfume, Zante!
> Isola d'oro!—Fior di Levante!—[1]

More mystifying is Poe's use of the name as the germ of his entire "Sonnet to Zante" in the *Southern Literary Messenger* of January, 1837. In this the last couplet is almost identical with that in *Al Aaraaf*, save for the first phrase, which emphasizes the flowery nature of the island and the alleged source of its name:

> Fair isle, that from the fairest of all flowers
>   Thy gentlest of all gentle names dost take!
> How many memories of what radiant hours
>   At sight of thee and thine at once awake!
> How many scenes of what departed bliss!
>   How many thoughts of what entombéd hopes!
> How many visions of a maiden that is
>   No more—no more upon thy verdant slopes!
> *No more*! alas, that magical sad sound
>   Transforming all! Thy charms shall please
>   *no more*—
> Thy memory *no more*! Acccurséd ground
>   Henceforth I hold thy flower-enamelled shore,
> O hyacinthine isle! O purple Zante!
>   "Isola d'oro! Fior di Levante!"[2]

The use of quotation marks is also noteworthy. We may infer Poe's partiality to the poem from his causing it to be printed

four more times[3] and his copying it out twice, once for Richard
H. Stoddard[4] and once in an incomplete article, called "A
Reviewer Reviewed" and left in manuscript.[5] Not only does
the prominence of the Italian name of the island in Poe's poem
seem strange; there is also a teasing quality in the pattern of
his phrases, such as "entombéd hopes" and "*no more*," and in
the images, such as "a maiden" upon "verdant slopes."[6] Rarely,
however, has the poem been singled out for special mention
and never for special study.[7] I suggest that an inquiry into its
three major literary sources and into two minor influences
(Isaac Disraeli and John Hewitt) may help to place the Zante
sonnet in the total development of Poe's poetry and thought
and may explain a little the strange effect of the poem upon
its readers. Of the three sources—Byron, Chateaubriand, and
Keats—only the second has been considered at all by critics.

First, consider the associations that the Ionian island of
Zante would have for an educated young man in the 1820's.
Lemprière lists several allusions by classical writers to the
island of Zacynthos, to give it the name by which it was
known to Homer, Vergil, Ovid, and Pliny.[8] The first two call
it "woody," and Ovid calls it "high"; both of these adjectives
may explain Poe's "verdant slopes." His familiarity with these
three authors would have given him only a subliminal awareness of the island, the Italian name of which dates from its
domination by medieval Italian overlords and, from 1482, by
Venice. It formed part of the Heptanesus or "Seven Islands,"
with Corfu, Cephalonia, Santa Maura, Ithaca, Cythera (Cer-
igo), and Paxos. Most of these names arouse echoes of Greek
mythology and history. The current history, for Poe, included
their being taken from France, 1809–1815, to be held by
England through the Treaty of Paris. In 1829 Poe's interest
in the Heptanesus appears in his lines in *Al Aaraaf* on "lilies
such as rear the head / On the fair Capo Deucato" (p. 15).
Poe's footnote calls this island "Santa Maura—olim Deucadia."
As Leucadia, a name derived from the white appearance of
its rocks, it is well known for Sappho's famous leap, indicated in

another of Poe's footnotes. His reference to "Deucadia" is a pardonable misconception, derived from Capo Ducato, the modern Italian name for the 2,000-foot cliff at the southern tip.[9]

The transformation of another name in *Al Aaraaf* illustrates Poe's awareness of classical literature and its Greek background at the time. "Zanthe" occurs in Part II as one of the angelic figures inhabiting the mystical, starry region of the poem:

> She paus'd and panted, Zanthe! all beneath!—
> The fairy light that kiss'd her golden hair
> And long'd to rest, yet could but sparkle there![10]

It seems evident from the context that Poe is using a name suggested by the Homeric word for "yellow," *xanthos*,[11] with a change of *x* to *z*, a phonic influence carried over from the earlier Zante.[12] Another reason for inferring Poe's preoccupation with the Greek background here is his inclusion of a trio of associated names, all Nereids, as George H. Green has pointed out,[13] and probably derived from Vergil's fourth *Georgic*, which mentions several including Ligea (*Al Aaraaf*, p. 30), Nesaea (*Al Aaraaf*, pp. 14, 18, and 27—"Nesace"), and Xantho.[14]

Whatever the connection in Poe's mind between Zante and other names, it cannot be doubted that in both *Al Aaraaf* and the "Sonnet to Zante" Greece played an important role and was "Holy Land" as he calls it in "To Helen" of 1831.[15] In *Al Aaraaf* are references to "hills Achaian,"[16] "Capo Deucato," "Parian marble," "Lemnos," and the "Parthenon" (pp. 14, 15, 25, 35, 36). In the sonnet the Greek island itself forms the theme. For a most significant clue to Poe's concern we must remember Lord Byron's death in 1824 at Missolonghi, located directly opposite the island of Zante—a death which seemed to be a sacrifice to the cause of Greek freedom. This had been so appealing to Poe that he tried to create the legend of his enlisting in the Greek revolutionary effort, via the autobiographical fragment that he left to Griswold: "Mr. A refused to pay some of the debts of *honor*, and I ran away from home without a dollar on a quixotic expedition to join the Greeks, then struggling for liberty. Failed in reaching Greece, but made my way to St. Petersburgh, in Russia."[17] The fantastic tale clearly shows the direction of Poe's mind in 1827 when he left the University of Virginia.[18] As Stoddard aptly wrote concerning Poe's fantasy: "Byron had done so, and had died at Missolonghi two or three years before and public honours had been decreed to his memory. Campbell was shouting, 'Again to the battle, Achaians,' and Halleck was raising a monument to Marco Bozzaris in his martial verse."[19] Zante was a name inextricably linked with Byron's in the minds of his fervid admirers, including Poe, at the University.[20] On the walls and ceilings of his room, number 13, West Range, Poe had copied out, in charcoal, many engravings from an illustrated volume of Byron's works.[21] It is reasonable to assume, as does Hervey Allen, that many of the notes and lines of *Al Aaraaf* were conceived at this time when Poe had available both a library and leisure time.[22]

It is relevant to indicate briefly the extent to which Zante entered into the Byronic legend. Zante, one of the earliest of the Ionian Islands to be brought under British control, was the seat of a British Resident. Byron discussed this control in a long note, entitled "Thoughts on the Present State of Greece," which was appended to Part I of *Childe Harold's Pilgrimage*. Rather prophetically he wrote: "The islanders look to the English for succour, as they have very lately possessed themselves of the Ionian republic, Corfu excepted. But whoever appears with arms in their hands will be welcome."[23] More specifically, he was to know the island of Zacynthos or Zante with its good harbor, fertile soil, and strategic position. Most of the 277 square miles were highly cultivated, and the crops included a dwarf vine whose "currants" (from Corinth) are excellent for wine or when preserved; hence Poe's adjective "purple," unless he means to apply it only to the hyacinth flower, which is indeed profuse on the island. Poe's reference to "verdant slopes" is also borne out by the ridge of low hills on the eastern part of the island which are covered by a rich growth of subtropical plants and trees and justify the "nemorosa" or "wooded" of Homer and Vergil.

Poe's awareness of the nature and appearance of the island may have arisen also from allusions in the accounts of Byron's life and death. In 1823 Byron had left for Greece, intending to establish his first headquarters on Zante before direct participation in the obscure, confused situation on the mainland of the Morea. He sought information of Marco Bozzaris, fighting north of Missolonghi, with his Suliotes. In August, Byron located himself on Cephalonia because the Resident there was reputed to be friendlier to the Greek cause than was Sir Frederick Stoven, Resident at Zante. On December 29, 1823, he finally sailed directly to the south, arriving the next day at the main city of Zante to transact financial matters before proceeding to his last home, at Missolonghi.[24] His little villa there was close to a rock commanding a view of Zante and the surrounding Ionian Sea.[25] In a slight rally during his mortal illness, April 11–13, 1824, Byron planned to leave Missolonghi with his household for Zante, but was prevented by a sudden sirocco.[26] After his death on April 19, most of Greece mourned for its great benefactor. On April 25 his body, in a sealed coffin, was transported to Zante, where it arrived to a mournful salute of guns and remained for almost the whole of May. On the 25th Byron's body was put aboard the *Florida* for the trip to England. Perhaps even in Poe's Italian phrase *fior di Levante*, derived of course from other sources, lies a trace of this carrier's name. Details of Byron's life and death were available to Poe in the current accounts of the 1820's and also in Moore's editions (1832, 1835) of Byron's works.[27] The students at the University of Virginia most probably circulated copies of these memoirs.

Poe did not merely revere Byron as a guide in literature and in reckless behavior; he sometimes felt himself to be almost an avatar of Byron. His comparison of his swimming prowess with Byron's is an indication of this.[28] More to the point, with regard to the Zante sonnet, is his general comparison of his youthful frustrated passion for Sarah Elmira Royster, in Richmond before he left for college, with Byron's unrequited love for Mary Chaworth, immortalized in "The Dream."[29] Killis Campbell is firm about the application of the Zante sonnet to Poe's broken romance, especially since it was first published in 1837, perhaps in token of his leaving the city of Richmond.[30] In addition, Campbell claims a like relevance for "To One in Paradise" and "I saw thee on thy bridal day . . ." to the marriage of the seventeen-year-old Sarah Elmira to the wealthy Mr. Shelton, Poe's letters to her having been intercepted by her father.[31] Poe's full knowledge of Byron's youthful passion is shown in his piece on "Byron and Miss Chaworth," in which he says that in her very name there seemed to exist an "enchantment."[32] She was "the incarnation of the ideal that haunted the fancy of the poet" and "the Egeria of his dreams— the Venus Aphrodite that sprang, in full and supernal loveliness, from the bright foam upon the storm-tormented ocean of his thoughts." We are here reminded of the lines in *Childe Harold's Pilgrimage:* "Egeria! sweet creation of some heart / Which found no mortal resting place so fair / As thine ideal breast." Most telling, perhaps, is a fact that I have not seen mentioned—that in "Ligeia" Poe names the second bride, Lady Rowena Trevanion of Tremaine, after Byron's charming and intelligent grandmother, Sophia Trevanion.[33]

I have alluded to Poe's fantasy of having gone off like Byron to fight for Greek independence. A link here is provided directly with Halleck, since we know that Poe had asked the eminent author of "Marco Bozzaris" to contribute to the *Southern Literary Messenger* in June, 1836. In March, 1837, he had attended a booksellers' dinner with Halleck in New York.[34] The continuing relationship with Halleck needs no underscoring; I shall mention only Poe's review of Halleck's "Alnwick Castle, with Other Poems," in the *Messenger* of April, 1836, a year before the Zante sonnet.[35] While his praise there of "Marco Bozzaris" is tempered, he commends its "lyrical" beauty and its "force" and gives extensive quotations. Byron had paid tribute to the Suliotes exiled from Albania in *Childe Harold* and lamented the death of Bozzaris battling against the Turks in the mountains of Acarnania above Missolonghi, on August 21, 1823.[36] Pietro Gamba gives the affecting account of the burial of part of Byron's remains, vouchsafed to the Greeks, in the church of St. Nicholas at Missolonghi, next to the remains of Marco Bozzaris.[37] Not only through his poem on Bozzaris did Halleck arouse Byronic associations, as Poe's review indicates.[38] In 1832 Halleck had published a 700-page edition of the *Works of Lord Byron, in Verse and Prose, including His Letters and Journals, with a Sketch of His Life.*

Early and thoroughly Poe absorbed the style, themes, moods, and attitudes of Byron's poetry into his own work. In the 1827 version of *Tamerlane*, Tamerlane speaks of himself as "Alexis" and of his love as "Ada,"[39] a name in Byron's family which came to supersede Augusta as the first name of Byron's daughter.[40] In Woodberry's opinion, *Tamerlane* is "as clever and uninteresting an imitation of Byron as was ever printed."[41] Byron's influence upon the early poetry as well as attitudes of Poe has received frequent comment; Quinn links *Tamerlane* with *The Giaour, Childe Harold,* and *Manfred,* the last of which he finds conspicuous in *Al Aaraaf* as well.[42] Byron's poem "To Ianthe" (Lady Charlotte Harley), which prefaces *Childe Harold,* is an obvious source of "Ianthe" in *Al Aaraaf.*[43] Still the best summary of the ever-prevalent traces of Byron in Poe's poems is Campbell's 1909 article in *The Nation.*[44] Poe's disavowal of "Byron as a model" in the letter of May 29, 1829, to John Allan is better proof of his awareness of that influence than of its obliteration.[45] Since the "Sonnet to Zante" was written in the 1830's, Poe's comment to Isaac Lea, in a letter of May, 1829, seems quite significant: *Al Aaraaf,* Poe says, "commences with a sonnet (illegitimate) as la mode de Byron in his prisoner of Chillon."[46] In reality Byron's sonnet is in the strict Italian form,[47] while both Poe's sonnet to "Science," prefacing *Al Aaraaf,* and his Zante sonnet are in the English

form. Incidentally, the Greek ambience of the earlier sonnet
is also strong in the sestet, with its allusions to Diana,
Hamadryad, and Naiad.

With reference to the Zante sonnet, I suggest that the role
of Zante in the funeral rites of Byron first brought the island
to Poe's attention as "accursed ground" although beautiful in
itself, being "hyacinthine," "purple," "flower-enamelled," and
golden. Perhaps continued reflection on the fancied parallel
between Byron's Mary Chaworth and Poe's Sarah Elmira
Royster, now Shelton, suggested the merger in one sonnet
of the two themes: disappointment in love and death. This
double subject, I believe, accounts for the somewhat divergent
streams of emotion that flow through the sonnet: the beauty
of the island, with its "entombéd hopes," and the beauty or
charm of the maiden that is "no more"—at least as an unwed
maiden. One might almost say, in T. S. Eliot's phrase, that
Poe's deep passion has no satisfactory objective correlative in
the stereotyped situation of the departed girl. It is clear that
Poe wishes to avoid saying that she is "entombéd." Indeed,
this is very like the poem of 1834, "To One in Paradise," with
its "green isle in the sea" allusion at the beginning, "wreathed
with fairy fruits and flowers," and with its repetition of "no
more" in the second stanza. The canceled stanza which Campbell prints in his edition of the poems makes more obvious the
departure of the loved one for "an unholy pillow" rather than
a tomb.[48] The link with Byron is made quite definite by the
fact that Poe first printed "To One in Paradise" as part of "The
Visionary," later called "The Assignation," which is thought
to be much in the Byronic manner.[49] Most conclusive is Poe's
printing the poem in 1839 under the Byronic title, "To Ianthe
in Heaven."[50]

A very specific source of the last line of "Zante," reprinted
from Al Aaraaf but with quotation marks, is Chateaubriand's
Itinéraire de Paris à Jérusalem, et de Jérusalem à Paris
(1811). This connection has been pointed out by Woodberry
in his biography of Poe.[51] The French writer, one should note,
is not named by Poe in any of the notes to Al Aaraaf, although

he is taxed for several other allusions, such as the 1687 date at which the unimpaired Parthenon could still be seen.[52] I have not found any reference in Poe studies to the fact that the final line—"Isola d'oro! Fior di Levante!"—was not original with Chateaubriand either, as seen in his italics for both phrases: "Je souscris à ses noms *d'Isola d'oro*, de *Fior di Levante*."[53] Emile Malakis suggests that Chateaubriand derived the first phrase from *Voyage d'Italie, de Dalmatie, de Grèce, et du Levant* by Jacob Spon and George Wheler.[54] In the first edition of 1679, published at Amsterdam, I find, "Zante a été autrefois appellée par Boterus l'Isle d'or."[55] The two authors then explain the sobriquet in terms of the wealth that the cultivation of the Corinth grapes brings to the island. They do not, however, give the second phrase, used by Chateaubriand and Poe. Its common application to Zante may be seen in an 1850 work by Aubrey De Vere, *Picturesque Sketches of Greece and Turkey*, which says that Zante "deserves its Italian title, 'Fior di Levante.'" I might add that upon leaving Zante and gliding past Missolonghi, De Vere "thought—who would not? —of Byron."[56]

John W. Robertson is mistaken, I believe, in thinking that the sonnet was written to embody a particular couplet that Poe was proud of having composed years before.[57] Although the Italian phrases of the last line fit well into the thought pattern of the poem and may indeed have evoked it, the line is metrically unsuitable for both *Al Aaraaf* and the Zante sonnet; it is only by distorting *fior* into two syllables that five beats can be "read into" the pentameter line.[58] I strongly suspect that Poe regularized the whole by shifting the accent of *isola* as well, so that it must have been intended to sound thus: *Isóla d'óro! Fíor dí Levánte!* The great rarity of trochaic openings in the iambic pentameter lines of *Al Aaraaf* and the insertion of "O" for the first syllable of the concluding couplet of the sonnet confirm Poe's mispronunciation of the Italian. Without the "O" the thirteenth line is improved and chimes more musically with the last, when correctly pronounced.

Poe's more scrupulous punctuation of the last line, in quotation marks, does not indicate that he is citing his own earlier use of these words; it may be that the source in Chateaubriand's *Itinéraire* had been pointed out or that he feared that it might be. Had he not excised from the first version of *Tamerlane* Byron's line "A sound of revelry by night" for a more original conclusion?[59] For Poe, with his obsessive interest in plagiarism, this was no trivial factor.

Unfortunately, Poe also borrowed from Chateaubriand the false derivation of the name of the island—from the hyacinth plant (ὑάκινθος) rather than from Zacynthos (Ζάκινθος), an error easier in the French form, *jacinte,* than *hyacinthe.*[60] I should note that Chateaubriand's mention of "nemorosa Zacynthos" may have helped to foster Poe's "verdant slopes." He also speaks of the tradition that Zante was a refuge for political exiles, being reputedly the resting place for the "cendres de Cicéron." This may be relevant to Poe's "entombéd hopes," and yet does not deny the impact of the more recent illustrious exile, whose bier was shown for a month on Zante.

The splendid penultimate line of Poe's sonnet bears within itself a curious origin, from Horace via Isaac Disraeli, which illustrates not only the variety of Poe's creative inspiration but also the remarkable ability of genius to profit from criticism, although sometimes most grudgingly. At the beginning of the chapter, I pointed out that the line from *Al Aaraaf*—"And thy most lovely purple perfume, Zante!"—had become "O hyacinthine isle! O purple Zante!" The revision greatly improves the meaning and avoids the oppressive alliteration of "purple perfume" and the monotonous gallop of iambs. The sense of the line, of course, confirms the ideas of the preceding "Accurséd ground / Henceforth I hold thy flower'enamelled shore." In reading *Al Aaraaf* one has to infer that Zante is an island full of purple flowers with a lovely perfume. Since hyacinth as color is purple and as flower is odoriferous, Poe's footnote in the 1829 volume (p. 17), which reads: "The Hyacinth," seems to be adequate. Moreover, Part I of *Al Aaraaf* contains many references to the scent of flowers. Yet there is something a little odd about "purple perfume" as well as the phrase directed to Nesace, "to whose care is given / To bear the Goddess' song, in odours, up to Heaven" (p. 17).

The explanation for the oddity might lie simply in synesthesia, used extensively by Poe even in this early poem. I believe, however, that it lies in a source which Poe later acknowledged using in the "Pinakidia" or "tablets" of the *Messenger* of August, 1836—a title and section which Poe explains as the siftings from "a confused mass of marginal notes, and entries in a commonplace-book" (Harrison, 14.40). Earl L. Griggs traced many of the 171 paragraphs to five sources; over two dozen are attributable to Isaac Disraeli's *Curiosities of Literature*.[61] Obviously Poe had begun early to collect notebook or "tablet" items for his many footnotes in *Al Aaraaf* and for the many recondite references in his early tales.[62] Disraeli's work also provided Poe with prefatory mottoes.[63] I believe that "purple perfume" was picked up by Poe when he was leafing through the *Curiosities*.[64] Poe paid particular attention to the long article "Poetical Imitations and Similarities," which includes the relevant text:

> It is extremely difficult to conceive what the ancients precisely meant by the word *purpureus*. They seem to have designed by it any thing *bright* and *beautiful*. A classical friend has furnished me with numerous significations of this word which are very contradictory. Albinovanus, in his elegy on Livia, mentions *Nivem purpureum*. Catullus, *Quercus ramos purpuroes*. Horace, *Purpureo bibet ore nectar*, and somewhere mentions *Olores purpureos*. Virgil has *Purpuream vomit ille animam;* and Homer calls the sea *purple*, and gives it in some other book the same epithet, when in a storm.[65]

I submit that Horace's phrase "Olores purpuroes," standing thus alone, would be taken by most reasonably well-educated persons to mean "purple perfumes" or, according to the paragraph, "beautiful perfumes or fragrances." Indeed, I have given the two-word phrase to three university teachers of

Latin and elicited this sort of response in each case. Memories
of *olfactory* or of *oloroso,* the Spanish word for "fragrant,"
inevitably direct one's mind to this association. From this Latin
phrase in Disraeli's paragraph, I think, came Poe's phrase, for
even the word "lovely" is subsumed in his context.

The fact is, however, that *olores* is the plural form of the
Latin poetic word for "swan," the word *cygnus* being reserved
for the commonplace, everyday, prosaic species, one might say.
Olor as the Latin for "odor" is found only in ante- and post-
classical periods, with the Latin word *odor* derived from it
for regular classical use.[66] Disraeli's phrase, with modifications,
is from Horace's first ode in the fourth book, in which he is
addressing Venus; it is an ode which has become much more
famous today than it was in Poe's time, because of Ernest
Dowson's use of the opening: "Non sum qualis eram bonae /
sub regno Cinarae." The third stanza in Horace reads:

> Tempestivius in domum
>   Paulli, purpureis ales oloribus,
> Commisabere Maximi.[67]

This is rendered by Horace Gregory as

> More timely hie thee to the house
>   (With thy bright swans) of Paulus Maximus.[68]

More literally "purpureis ales oloribus" means "winged" or
"furnished with wings by means of gleaming swans."[69] In another instance, Horace cites *olores* or swans as being the
motive power of Venus, who visits Paphos "iunctis oloribus,"
that is, "with her yoked swans."[70] I seriously doubt that Poe
could have remembered this poetic term for swan, despite his
many references to the names and works of Horace, with occasional conventional citations.[71] But his absorptive mind would
pluck the phrase from the pages of Disraeli and store it, perhaps with the aid of a "tablet" notation, for just such a use as
the one in *Al Aaraaf.*

Poe's misconception was to have an amusing consequence,

which perhaps even motivated him to revamp the line in his 1837 sonnet. One of the two known reviews of *Al Aaraaf* in 1829 was thoroughly adverse. John Hill Hewitt, poetaster and editor of the Baltimore *Minerva and Emerald,* was the reviewer;[72] although it was anonymous, Poe quickly found out who had damned his book with such comments as this: "On page seventeen, we learn the color of a *smell* in the following line: 'And thy most lovely purple perfume, Zante!' "[73] This was the beginning of his strong dislike of Hewitt, increased when Hewitt became the editor of the *Saturday Visiter* of Baltimore late in 1832[74] and took from him the prize for best poem in the *Visiter's* contest of June, 1833. Hewitt's entry was submitted under the pseudonym of "Henry Wilton," but the inferiority of "Song of the Winds" to "The Coliseum" and Hewitt's editorial post inflamed Poe into provoking a fist fight on the sidewalk by accusing Hewitt of influencing the judges.[75] As a result of the review, Poe had previously thrust Hewitt into his satirical "Loss of Breath," first printed as "A Decided Loss," the theme of which facilitates an allusion to perfume. The narrator is searching for his lost breath: "At one time, indeed, I thought myself sure of my prize; having, in rummaging a dressing-case, accidentally demolished a bottle of (I had a remarkable sweet breath) Hewitt's 'Seraphic, and highly-scented double extract of Heaven, or Oil of Archangels,' which, as an agreeable perfume, I here take the liberty of recommending."[76] Poe merely dropped the parenthesis and the word "double" in the printings of the September, 1835 *Messenger* and the *Tales* of 1840.[77] Perhaps he changed the name of "Hewitt" to "Grandjean," a wigmaker,[78] in the *Broadway Journal* reprint of 1845 because of a small favor which Hewitt accorded Poe in Washington, March, 1843.[79] Previously, however, Poe revealed the depth and nature of his grudge against Hewitt in a letter of June 4, 1842, to Joseph Evans Snodgrass, new proprietor of the *Saturday Visiter* from which Hewitt had long departed.[80] Poe sent his good wishes and an offer of "The Mystery of Marie Rogêt" for publication. It was refused, per-

haps because of his tactless remark about Snodgrass's new
enterprise—"a journal which has never yet been able to recover
from the mauvais odeur imparted to it by Hewitt."[81] Certainly
one must admire or at least wonder at the persistence of
resentment in Poe against a third-rate personality.

Ironically, in Hewitt's poem "The Song of the Wind," that
took the poetry prize of the *Visiter*, there are echoes of *Al
Aaraaf* which perhaps imperceptibly tipped the scales in
its favor with the judges. Compare the opening and closing
of Hewitt's poem with the passages from *Al Aaraaf* which
were initially cited as illustrative of Poe's emphasis upon
odors; Hewitt wrote: "Whence come ye with your odor-laden
wings, / Oh, unseen wanderer of the summer night?" and "But
shrink not; I've gathered the sweets of the flowers, / And,
laden with perfume, I come to thee now."[82] Hewitt must also
have been reading "Israfel" in Poe's *Poems* of 1831, with its
lyre and line, "None sing so wildly well," to judge from the
succeeding lines of the first stanza:

> Why, sportive, kiss my lyre's trembling strings,
>   Fashioning wild music, which the light
> Of listening orbs doth seem in joy to drink?

Surely this is as fantastically synesthesiac as "purple perfumes"
and as another line by Poe, "Flap shadowy sounds from visionary wings," about which Hewitt had observed: "We learn that
sound has form and body."[83] Hewitt seems to be aping a technique that he once decried, although his new role makes him
no better a poet. But Poe appears to have profited from
Hewitt's criticism, for the revised line, inserted into the "Sonnet
to Zante," is incomparably better than the first form of it
in *Al Aaraaf*.

A third major source for the Zante sonnet, I suggest, can be
found in the works of Keats. There is, first, the fact that Zante
lies in the classical Greek "realms of gold," being part of the
kingdom of Ulysses himself; it was one of the "western islands
. . . / Which bards in fealty to Apollo hold." On nearby Saint

Maura or Leucas—or "Capo Deucato," as Poe calls it in *Al Aaraaf*—was a shrine to Apollo; thus he was often called "Leucadius." The Eldorado theme, the quest for an unattainable land of beauty and of gold, was to haunt Poe throughout his life of penury, incessant work, sordid evasions, and unrewarded self-development. Well did he know the "Ode to a Nightingale" and feel the point of "No hungry generations tread thee down." In his 1836 article on Drake and Halleck he referred to this poem as "of the purest ideality" (Harrison, 8.299*n.*). There is a reminder of Keats in Poe's stress upon "no more," which is vocalically and rhythmically like the "forlorn" of the "Ode." There is also a correspondence both in situation and in language closer than mere coincidence would grant: In Keats we find "charm'd magic casements" and a "plaintive anthem" that "fades . . . up the hill-side"; in Poe we find "visions of a maiden that is / No more . . . upon thy verdant slopes," the phrase itself being a "magical sad sound / Transforming all! Thy charms shall please *no more*." A little less significant is the second stanza of the "Ode" with its vinous elements: the "beaker full of the warm South, the blushful Hippocrene," and "the purple-stained mouth." To Poe, Zante was characterized by purple because of its hyacinth blossoms, but its well-known grape produce could implicitly lend it this color. In another of Keats's most famous poems, "Ode on a Grecian Urn," I find a strong suggestion of the rhetoric of Poe's sonnet, which moves by a series of questions from lines 3 through 8. In similar fashion, Keats first apostrophizes the "bride of quietness," and then asks rhetorically about the pictured deities and mortals, with an abrupt close on "wild ecstasy." More moderately, but with a definite sense of climax, Poe speaks of memories of "radiant hours / At sight of thee and thine" and of "scenes" of "departed bliss," ending with "thy charms shall please no more."

It is not difficult to validate Poe's reverence for Keats in other ways than through the review of Halleck cited above.[84] Hervey Allen and Francis Winwar believe that Keats could be

found on the shelves of his college study, a plausible inference.[85] Later Poe expressed himself unequivocally on the merits of Keats, alluding to the "bolder, more natural and more
ideal compositions of . . . Keats, . . . the sole British poet who
has never erred in his themes. Beauty is always his aim."[86] In
his letter to Lowell of July 2, 1844, he speaks of Keats as one
of "the *sole* poets."[87] Obviously, the effect of Keats upon Poe's
practice and theory of poetry was profound. In Poe's use of the
sonnet form itself and in the atmosphere, ideas, images, and
language, I propose Keats as one of the strands in the complex fabric of the "Sonnet to Zante." By weaving this in with
the threads from the Italian and classical past of the island,
from Chateaubriand's treatment, and from the colorful life of
Lord Byron, Poe created an original masterpiece, evocative,
nostalgic, and melancholy.

7

GODWIN AND POE

IT HAS LONG seemed clear to me that the themes and atmosphere of Poe's tales often resemble those of William Godwin's "nightmare" novels. In many of the tales, the protagonist experiences inordinate curiosity, as in *Caleb Williams* or *St. Leon;* manifests jealousy or suspicion, as in *Mandeville* and *Deloraine;* indulges in debauchery, as in *Fleetwood;* or yields to irrational, murderous rage, as in *Cloudesley.* Often he is isolated from society or finds an unstable adjustment in a doomed marriage, and sometimes, as in the novels of Godwin, he combines the language of rationality with the caprices of madness. It was not a modern study of Poe's works that led me to trace the more exact interrelationship but rather two articles more than a century old. One was by Edouard Forgues in the Paris *Revue des Deux Mondes* of October, 1846, and the other was in the *Edinburgh Review* of April, 1858. Since their brief suggestions, however, no attempt has been made to indicate the considerable evidence of Godwin's work and influence in Poe's writings of every type. In contemporary studies of Poe I have found only one brief comment on Forgues's aperçu, despite ample acknowledgment of early French contributions to Poe criticism.[1]

Poe himself, it is reported, was much encouraged by the essay of Edouard Forgues in the *Revue,* published during a particularly despondent period in Poe's career. In 1849 Poe publicized "that justice which had been already rendered me by the 'Revue Française' and the 'Revue des Deux Mondes.' "[2] Forgues, the French translator of the "Descent into the Maelstrom," speaks of Poe's characters as "wearing the fantastic livery of Hoffmann or the grave and magisterial costume of

Godwin, renewed by Washington Irving and Dickens." Significantly he rounds off his long article by returning at the end to the connection between Godwin and Poe:

> We have already likened the talent of Mr. Poe to that of . . .
> William Godwin, whose dark and unwholesome popularity
> has been so severely censured by Hazlitt, *Spirit of the Age.*
> . . . However, it is necessary to recognize in the author of
> *Saint Leon* and *Caleb Williams* more true, philosophic
> knowledge and less tendency toward purely literary paradox.

He concludes by referring to common qualities in Poe and Charles Brockden Brown, Godwin's disciple in the novel.[3]

Twelve years later, in 1858, the *Edinburgh Review*, gullibly accepting the denigrations of Griswold's memoir in the edition of Poe being reviewed, regards the influence of Godwin and Brown as a very dubious benefit to Poe:

> We are disposed to think that we can trace his inspiration
> in a great measure to the writings of Godwin and Charles B.
> Browne [*sic*]. There is in each the same love of the morbid
> and improbable; the same frequent straining of the interest;
> the same tracing, step by step, logically, as it were, and
> elaborately, through all its complicated relations, a terrible
> mystery to its source. . . . Their personages are little more,
> after all, than stately abstractions or impersonations of cer-
> tain moods or guesses of their own minds, the results of
> solitary thinking.[4]

It is true that Poe was deeply conscious of the peculiar genius of Charles Brockden Brown, whose inspiration in turn was self-ascribed to Godwin.[5] It is my intention to show that Poe was sufficiently aware of Godwin's many novels and other writings to require no intermediary contact at all, whether it be Brown, Bulwer-Lytton, or others. We shall be concerned chiefly with the long overdue checking of the exact references to Godwin in Poe's writing and the significance of each. We observe, first, that in separate and distinct writings, including tales, criticisms, and letters, Poe alluded to Godwin or his

books seventeen times.[6] Many of these are not casual references, but rather the keystones of his criticism, or they are
thematic germs out of which develops an entire narrative
rationale. They run throughout Poe's mature productions, from
1835 to 1849, and occur in such a variety of works as to demonstrate that Godwin represented for Poe the apex of narrative and stylistic achievement. This was chiefly after Godwin's
death in 1836, when he had lost much of his literary credit
in England and America, although less in France.[7]

Chronologically—and that will be my approach to this topic
—the earliest reference is in the tale "Loss of Breath," published in the *Southern Literary Messenger*, September, 1835,
although composed much earlier. Poe remarks, "William Godwin, however, says in his 'Mandeville,' that 'invisible things
are the only realities,' and this, all will allow, is a case in
point."[8] It may be assumed that the observation, plucked from
the end of Godwin's novel, represents a reading of the entire
work by Poe. Echoes of the quotation can be found in "Berenice," also published in 1835. "Realities of the world affected
me as visions . . ." (Harrison, 2.17). The mixture of the real
and the unreal, of the world of the imagination and that of
detailed, mundane reality, runs through the whole body of
Poe's work. It is not surprising to find a strong echo of this
very phrase in the preface to "Eureka," the work that Poe considered his greatest contribution to thought: "To the dreamers
and those who put faith in dreams as in the only realities"
(16.183). Godwin, too, was a visionary, although he believed
in the eventual realization of a different type of dream from
those which haunted Poe.

The next item is the review by Poe of the New York (1835)
edition of Godwin's *Lives of the Necromancers*. It was a book
of great interest to the British and American public of the day,
to judge from extensive reviewing and excerpting and frequent
reprints.[9] Poe, with his profound interest in the abnormal and
the occult, would naturally have enjoyed reviewing the book
and demonstrating some familiarity with works of the same

nature. Indeed, his comparison of Godwin's work with Sir
David Brewster's *Letters on Natural Magic,* of 1832, reminds
one of his famous examination of "Maelzel's Chess Player,"
of April, 1836. Therein Poe was to lean heavily on Brewster's
very able presentation of Von Kempelen's device which Maelzel had more recently been displaying.[10]

To my knowledge, no one has given more than passing
attention to Poe's review of *Necromancers,* the last work by
Godwin published in his own lifetime. He first remarks:

> The name of the author of Caleb Williams, and of St. Leon,
> is . . . a word of weight, and . . . a guarantee for . . . excel-
> lence. . . . There is about all the writings of Godwin one
> peculiarity which we are not sure that we have ever seen
> pointed out for observation . . . an air of mature thought—
> of deliberate premeditation. . . . [Harrison, 8.92]

Here clearly is the implication of wide familiarity with other
works of Godwin as well as with critical writing about him.
He continues by commenting on his style as having

> artificiality, which in less able hands would be wearisome,
> in his a grace inestimable. We are never tired of his terse,
> nervous, and sonorous periods. . . . No English writer . . .
> with the single exception of Coleridge, has a fuller apprecia-
> tion of the value of *words*; and none is more nicely dis-
> criminative between closely-approximating meanings.

Poe's interest in style became a trademark of his criticism.[11] It
is interesting to speculate whether he knew the essay on style
in Godwin's *Enquirer* (1797), the only portion of the book
which Godwin revised in the second edition of 1823.[12] There is
no indication that Poe knew about Godwin's Juvenile Library
publication of a school text devoted to usage and grammar.

He mentions the "avowed purpose" of *Necromancers* as
being "to exhibit a wide view of human credulity," quoting
Godwin's rationalistic preface, and declares that "we differ
with him," in that "there are many things more curious than
even the records of human credulity." Then he adds that God-

win's fine accounts of the necromancers convince him that human experience has surpassed human credulity in being "curious." This brief statement suggests one of the fundamental cleavages of purpose in fiction between the two writers and is a reminder that the tracing of hints and inspirational sources does not presuppose an identity of temperament or basic philosophy. He also asserts Godwin's purpose—in which "he has fully succeeded"—to be the display of "the great range and wild extravagance of the imagination of man." He laments Godwin's prefatory statement that this concludes his literary labor (*Necromancers*, pp. xii–xiii); "The pen which wrote Caleb Williams should never for a moment be idle." In conclusion, he refers to Godwin's article or chapter on Faustus (*Necromancers*, pp. 330–358) with an impressive remark that Godwin "very properly contradicted . . . the idea that Fust the printer and Faustus the magician are identical." This pronouncement about an ancient confusion is the sole comment specifically on Godwin's text. It demonstrates Poe's amazing facility in convincingly pretending to more knowledge than was possibly his.

In the same December, 1835, issue of the *Southern Literary Messenger*, Poe discussed one of the novels of a not inconsiderable dramatist and novelist of the period, Dr. Robert Montgomery Bird, the author of *Calvar* and *The Infidel*. In reviewing *The Hawks of Hawk-hollow* (Harrison, 8.63–73), Poe reveals his awareness of significant traces of Godwin in later works of fiction:

> At the opening of the tale, however, a Captain Loring resides upon the estate, and in the mansion of the Gilberts holding them as the agent or tenant of a certain Col. Falconer, who is a second edition of Falkland in Caleb Williams,— and who has managed to possess himself of the property at Hawk-Hollow. . . . [pp. 65–66]

> The crime with which the young man is charged, is the murder of Henry Falconer, who fell by a pistol shot in an affray during the pursuit. The criminal is lodged in jail

at Hillborough—is tried—and, chiefly through the instru-
mentality of Col. Falconer, is in danger of being found
guilty. [p. 69]

The persecution theme, indicated here, certainly provides
enough parallel between the two books to enable Poe legiti-
mately to make the point. It is one which no one, to my
knowledge, has made about Bird since this review.[13]

The fourth and fifth references to Godwin concern one book,
although widely separated in the dates of publication. In January, 1837, for the *Southern Literary Messenger,* Poe reviewed
Beverly Tucker's *George Balcombe* (Harrison, 9.243–265),
"upon the whole . . . the best American novel. Without being
chargeable in the least degree with imitation, the novel bears
a strong family resemblance to the 'Caleb Williams' of Godwin." This high opinion is borne out in Poe's articles on autography in *Graham's Magazine* of November, 1841 (Harrison,
15.195), in which he again asserts it to be "one of the best
novels ever published in America." Similarly, he had praised
Tucker's "literary character" in a latter to Thomas White, of
May 30, 1835 (Harrison, 17.6). Poe's article found the novel
to be replete with "ingenuity" and finish of plot (9.265), qualities which he also imputed to Godwin's work. Hence he repeats his basic sentiment about the book, this time summarized
as a paragraph for the "Marginalia" in the *Southern Literary
Messenger* of April, 1849 (Harrison, 16.142). This note combines his partiality for Godwin with his antipathy to the North-
ern critics: "Had the 'George Balcombe' . . . been the work
of any one born North of Mason and Dixon's line, it would
have been long ago recognized as one of the very noblest fictions ever written by an American. It is almost as good as
'Caleb Williams.' "

In *Graham's Magazine* of November, 1841, we find a review
of *Guy Fawkes; or the Gunpowder Treason: an Historical
Romance,* by William Harrison Ainsworth (Harrison, 10.214–
222). Here Poe lauds "autorial comment" in a novel, a some-

what surprising view from a writer whose best works embody a clean directness of narration:

> The writer never pauses to speak, in his own person, of what is going on. It is possible to have too much of this comment; but it is far easier to have too little. The most tedious books, *ceteris paribus*, are those which have none at all. . . . The *juste milieu* [*sic*] was never more admirably attained than in De Foe's "Robinson Crusoe" and in the "Caleb Williams" of Godwin. This latter work, from the character of its incidents, affords a fine opportunity of contrast with "Jack Sheppard" [of Ainsworth]. In both novels the hero escapes repeatedly from prison. In the work of Ainsworth the escapes are merely narrated. In that of Godwin they are *discussed*. With the latter we become at once absorbed in those details which so manifestly absorb his own soul. We read with the most breathless attention. We close the book with a real regret. [pp. 218–219]

Unquestionably, Poe has stressed the quality which has caused *Caleb Williams* to go into over fifty separate reprints and translations since 1794. This "absorption" of which he speaks is, of course, the element that Poe demanded as the response appropriate to any effective work of fiction and that caused him, eventually, to evolve his theory of the one-sitting work of literature. He is not clear, however, about one phase of the "autorial comment," in failing to differentiate between novels told in the third person, like those of Ainsworth, and those told in the first person, like all of Godwin's novels and many of Poe's own tales. Since the author and the suffering protagonist are the same, Godwin's comments serve to reveal the underlying motives and heighten the emotional tension of the plot. Ainsworth's remarkable objectivity and clarity of detail, as in the Chat Moss episode of *Guy Fawkes*, require a technique different from Godwin's.[14]

Yet Poe is right to compare the works of the two authors, even though perhaps for the wrong reason, since Ainsworth's plots involving criminals and pursuits, in a measure, spring from Godwin's novels.[15] Ainsworth might have derived this influence from direct contact with Godwin and Mary Shelley as members of a group often found in Lamb's home, which Ainsworth began visiting in 1825.[16] It is true, however, that Ainsworth's sense of plot construction was markedly inferior to that which Poe attributed to Godwin, even in the opinion of Ainsworth's most adulatory biographers.[17] Poe also deplores Ainsworth's inability to vivify characters who owe their pallid existence, remotely at least, to Godwin's models.

Godwin as a standard of excellence was now firmly implanted in Poe's mind, and one of the last pieces of his writing as editor of *Graham's*, in the December, 1841 issue, includes a reference to the British author. Poe is reviewing Simms's *Confession: or The Blind Heart, a Domestic Story* (*Graham's*, 19.306) and incidentally brings in a more important work by Simms: " 'Martin Faber' did him honor; and so do the present volumes, although liable to objection in some important respects. We welcome him home to his own proper field of exertion—the field of Godwin and Brown—the field of his own rich intellect and glowing *heart*." In this item, uncollected by Harrison, Poe shows his association of Godwin not only with the well-constructed novel but also with the novel of strong, even melodramatic emotional tone. Consider the tortured, even grotesque nature of *Martin Faber*, the novel which evokes this comparison. Poe is quite right, of course, in linking Godwin with his disciples, Charles Brockden Brown and Simms.

Of all the references by Poe to Godwin's works, perhaps the only one which has occasioned any critical notice is that involving the visit of Dickens to Philadelphia in 1842. The story is told in biographies of Poe and Dickens and, in detail, by Gerald G. Grubb.[18] Poe's later use of Dickens's statement about *Caleb Williams* for the germ of his "Philosophy of Composition" undoubtedly makes it the most significant link between our two authors. Yet even the basic facts of the initial episode have been misinterpreted. The letter from Dickens to Poe, of March 6, 1842, in response to Poe's sending him books and papers together with a letter requesting an interview, now lost, has become widely known. The last of Dickens's five sentences reads: "Apropos of the 'construction' of 'Caleb Williams,' do you know that Godwin wrote it *backwards*,—the last volume first,—and that when he had produced the hunting down of Caleb, and the catastrophe, he waited for months, casting about for a means of accounting for what he had done?" (Harrison, 17.107). Professor Grubb, correctly I believe, surmises that the papers sent by Poe and mentioned by Dickens included the first review of *Barnaby Rudge*, which Poe had written for the *Philadelphia Saturday Evening Post*, of May 1, 1841, before the final part of the novel had been printed, and that the books sent were the two volumes of Poe's tales. He fails to state, although he implies, that Poe also sent Dickens the long review of *Barnaby* that had just been printed in the February, 1842, issue of *Graham's Magazine*, timed for Dickens's arrival. In effect, Dickens's letter includes a specific comment even on the wording itself of Poe's second review. The postulate of Hervey Allen, concerning a fancied similarity between the riots near the end of *Barnaby* and a scene in Godwin's novel, cited with approval by Gerald Grubb, is not confirmed by an examination of the two works; there is no such similarity.[19] Moreover, it is unthinkable that Poe could have expressed cursory remarks on Godwin in his first note to the literary lion whose aid in publishing his works in England he was planning to seek.

The fact is that even in punctuation and wording, Dickens's letter shows the source of his own reference to Godwin; it lies in Poe's second review which pointedly criticizes Dickens for his lack of power in the "construction" of a novel—a power which Poe preeminently attributed to Godwin. Poe first asserted that "the thesis of the novel [*Barnaby*] may thus be regarded as based upon curiosity" (Harrison, 11.49). He then pointed out the inconsistency in the maintenance of the mystery and the adventitious use of the riots, which detracted from the horror of the murder story; the reason lay in the lack

of a predetermined "particular plot when he began the story."
Its being an example of that misbegotten species, a "periodical novel," explains this looseness of structure without excusing
it, Poe asserts. "Our author discovered, when too late, that *he
had anticipated, and thus rendered valueless, his chief effect*"
(11.57). He concludes his long critique by awarding the palm
for "construction" to Godwin:

> That this fiction, or indeed that any fiction written by Mr.
> Dickens, should be based in the excitement and maintenance
> of curiosity we look upon as a misconception, on the part
> of the writer, of his own very great yet very peculiar powers.
> . . . He has a *talent* for all things, but no positive *genius* for
> *adaptation*, and still less for that metaphysical art in which
> the souls of all *mysteries* lie. "Caleb Williams" is a far less
> noble work than "The Old Curiosity-Shop;" but Mr. Dickens
> could no more have constructed the one than Mr. Godwin
> could have dreamed of the other. [11.63–64]

Dickens wrote a gracious response to Poe's rather daring
criticism of his narrative approach, in that he refers to Godwin's own exposition of how he had sought to preserve the
intensity and unity of *Caleb Williams*. It should be noted that
he might have read this explanation in Godwin's preface to
Bentley's 1832 edition of *Fleetwood*, a novel first published in
1805. This was Godwin's first statement. However, Dickens
might also have read it in the pages of the very popular
Literary Gazette, the periodical of his good friend, William
Jerdan.[20] Poe's attention having been called to Godwin's truly
startling literary avowal, he could have read it himself in several sources, a few of them more available to him than the
English journal. One of them, by its omissions, may have been
responsible for a subsequent error in Poe's second presentation
of Godwin's statement. We may discount, perhaps, the chance
that he might have seen it reprinted in the Paris edition of
Caleb Williams, published by Baudry, in English, in 1832.
He might have noticed it in the *Baltimore Literary Monument*,
of August, 1839. More likely, after the interview with Dickens,

he looked it up in the well-indexed and widely read *Museum of Foreign Literature,* of Philadelphia, which devoted its pages to reprints of foreign articles and reviews. Strangely enough, the *Museum* published the London *Literary Gazette's* reprint of the *Fleetwood* preface with no explanation of its being a preface to a novel other than *Caleb Williams.*[21] Poe makes this error as to the novel which bears the preface when he refers to Godwin's account in 1845 and erroneously calls it a preface to *Caleb Williams.*

Clearly Dickens had stimulated him to considerable thought about Godwin's method of plot construction; Poe contributed a "Chapter of Suggestions" to the annual *The Opal,* of 1845,[22] in which he says: "Godwin . . . has left a preface to his 'Caleb Williams,' in which he says that the novel was *written backwards,* the author first completing the second volume . . . and then casting about him for sufficiently probable cause of these difficulties, out of which to concoct volume the first" (Harrison, 14.189). We have seen that the *Museum* could have misled him about the source of Godwin's statement, but only a careless reading of the letter of Dickens (which refers to the "last volume") and also of the published account could have made him think that the first edition of *Caleb* was in two rather than three volumes. Since Godwin's preface actually did make a fine magazine article, in the *Literary Gazette,* I am inclined to believe that Poe is still working only with Dickens's letter at this time, for he starts his *Opal* chapter with this statement: "An excellent magazine paper might be written upon the subject of the progressive steps by which any great work of art—especially of literary art—attained completion." Godwin specifically had told how he had "employed his metaphysical dissecting knife" for the "involutions of motive," both of his characters and of himself as novelist. It was a preface of respectable length, remarkable for the very objective application of that candor which had been a basic principle of *Political Justice.* Poe's *Opal* chapter drives home again Godwin's superiority over Dickens:

Some authors appear, however, to be totally deficient in constructiveness and thus, even with plentiful invention, fail signally in plot. Dickens belongs to this class. His "Barnaby Rudge" shows not the least ability to *adapt*. Godwin and Bulwer are the best constructors of plot in English literature.

Poe could scarcely have linked Godwin with the prolific Bulwer on the basis of *Caleb Williams* alone. Obviously he had in mind other novels of Godwin, such as *St. Leon* and *Mandeville*.

Later in 1844, he reviewed the New York pirated edition of *Ellen Middleton* by the interesting popular novelist and Catholic philanthropist, Lady Georgiana Fullerton. In his two-paragraph review in the *Democratic Review* of December, 1844 (Harrison, 16.34), Poe asserts of her work that it has "imagination . . . of a lofty order. . . . There is much, in the whole manner of this book, which puts me in mind of 'Caleb Williams.'" There is no further explanation of this apparently far-fetched comparison, occurring to none of the other critics of the work whom I have read. However, a careful reading of the work itself with Godwin in mind convinces one of Poe's amazing perceptiveness. The contemporaries of this very aristocratic lady—Puseyite in outlook in this strongly theological novel and only two years away from her future conversion to Catholicism—could not dream of such a connection. Yet how Godwinian is the declaration of Henry Lovell, who believes that he controls Ellen's fate through knowledge of her being the accidental cause of the death of her detested young cousin!

> Ellen, I must be the blessing or the curse of your life. Never shall I be indifferent to you. You have refused, in ignorance, in madness . . . to be my wife. You shall be my victim.

Likewise, after he permits her marriage to his cousin: "You lose your victim, but you gain a friend." Signs of *Mandeville's* striking ending appear in Ellen's penitent "tears which wash away that fiery mark which has branded so long" her brow, that "mark set on Cain's brows." This is the *smorfia*, of *Mandeville*, which Shelley thought to be one of the strongest effects

of the novel.[23] There is no room to show other very real traces
of Godwin in a writer who was well read in the fictions of
Scott, Byron, and Maria Edgeworth, in Shelley's poetry, and
very likely, in Godwin's novels.[24]

The next reference, unimportant in itself, serves to show
how insistently in Poe's mind ran the theme of Godwin's
supreme role as an English novelist. In the "Marginalia" of
the *Democratic Review,* also of December, 1844 (Harrison,
16.48), we find a curiously bland quotation about Godwin:
" 'With all his faults, however, this author is a man of respectable powers.' Thus discourses, of William Godwin, the *London
Monthly Magazine,* May, 1818." The very insipidity of the
statement convinces one of Poe's entrenched "Godwinolatry,"
since he unquestionably coud have found a more entrancing
space-filler for his "Marginalia." Poe is quoting the penultimate sentence of a long sketch of Godwin, originally published
in the *Monthly Magazine* (15.299–302), as Number VI of its
"Contemporary Authors" series; it is largely favorable to Godwin's originality and "intrepidity," characteristic praise from
the organ of the old "Jacobin," Sir Richard Phillips, Godwin's
publisher. The last part takes exception to Godwin's faults of
style, a not uncommon complaint among the contemporary
journals, and concludes with the statement quoted by Poe. The
quotation makes a tacit assumption that his readers either start
out with a prepossession in favor of Godwin or else have read
the entire preceding, largely sympathetic article. Poe very
possibly did not see it in the *Monthly,* which he misnames the
"London Monthly," but rather in another of the popular American reprint magazines, the *Atheneum, or the Spirit of the
English Magazines,* published at Boston (3.349–352 [August,
1818]). One suspects that many of the references to the contemporary reviews in Poe's critiques and "Marginalia" come
from the two magazines mentioned, although none of his
biographers have made this point.[25] Perhaps his regular failure
to indicate pages is some slight evidence of that secondary
type of extraction.

The importance that Poe attached to Godwin's works may be surmised from his mentioning him three times during the one-year of publication of the *Broadway Journal*. Of these instances one is at the beginning and another at the end of the weekly series. The first item is in Poe's review of "*Poems* by Sir Edward Lytton Bulwer, edited by C. Donald Macleod," in the New York reprint of 1845. Having been initialled by Poe in the Halsey copy, this article was listed by Harrison in his bibliography of Poe's writings (16.372) but carelessly omitted from the text of the *Complete Works*. My citation comes from the *Broadway Journal* of February 8, 1845 (1.81):

> As a novelist, then, Bulwer is far more than respectable— although he has produced few novels equal and none superior to "Robinson Crusoe"—to one or two of Smollet's [*sic*]—to one or two of Fielding's—to Miss Burney's "Evelina"—to two or three of the Misses Porter's—to five or six of Miss Edgeworth's—to three or four of Godwin's—to the majority of Scott's—to one or two of D'Israeli's—to three or four of Dickens'—to the "Ellen Wareham" of Mrs. Sullivan, or to the "Ellen Middleton" of Lady Georgiana Fullerton.

Now Poe is definite about Godwin's "three or four" novels (in fact, there were six acknowledged by Godwin, plus three early anonymous works). Poe places him in the best company of British authors, including several with whom he will again be linked in 1849. Clearly, he is among the immortals of English fiction, even though the last two names on the list might cause considerable misgiving today. Poe's placement of Godwin directly before Scott might imply his awareness of Godwin as a writer of historic fiction, at least in *St. Leon*, a book which he had previously mentioned in the review of the *Lives of the Necromancers*. Perhaps the fourth novel in Poe's mind, beside *Caleb Williams* and *Mandeville*, is *Cloudesley* of 1830, which has several historic elements.

Godwin enters next into a brief review in the August 9 issue of the *Broadway Journal* (2.74–75), which has been collected by Harrison (12.223–224); it is a discussion of the novel *Ettore Fieramosca, or The Challenge of Barletta, an Historical Ro-*

mance of the Times of the Medici, by Massimo D'Azeglio, as translated from the Italian by C. Edwards Lester, the consul at Genoa. Lester had recently returned to New York City with two works of art that were being displayed at the time with considerable acclaim.[26] After asserting with his usual air of authority and lack of authentication that the novel has been frequently designated by Italian and British critics as "the best romance of its language," Poe declares it to be "vivacious" but "defective" in lacking "autorial comment." Again he confirms this by the standard of Godwin:

> [It is] that which adds so deep a charm to the novels of Scott, of Bulwer, or of D'Israeli—more especially to the works of Godwin and Brockden Brown. The book before us is feeble, too frequently, from its excess of simplicity in form and tone. The narrative proceeds as if *to narrate* were the author's sole business. The interest of mere incident, is all.

A careful check in the book itself reveals the justice of Poe's criticism, unless we admit as "autorial" some comments with no psychological depth, which are furnished by D'Azeglio on a few pages.[27]

Poe's third allusion to Godwin in the *Broadway Journal* of December 27 is one of the last items that he prepared for the magazine, which lasted for only one more issue, probably under the editorship of Thomas Dunn English. Poe here is reviewing the New York reprint of George Gilfillan's *First Gallery of Literary Portraits,* published in America under the title of *Sketches of Modern Literature and Eminent Literary Men: Being a Gallery of Literary Portraits,* in "Appleton's Literary Miscellany. Nos. 6 and 7" (*BJ,* 2.387). The article, which has not been collected by Harrison,[28] deserves complete quotation, especially since Poe himself inserted into the copy that he gave to Mrs. Whitman the marks for special emphasis which are printed in my text below:

> This is in all respects a valuable work—containing some of the most discriminative criticism we have ever read. We refer especially to a parallel between Shelley and Byron.

The portraits are those of Shelley, Jeffrey, Godwin, Hazlitt, Rob. Hall, Chalmers, Carlyle, De Quincy [*sic*], John Foster [*sic*], Wilson, Edward Irving, Landor, Campbell, Brougham, Coleridge, Emerson, Worsdworth [*sic*], Pollok, Lamb, Cunningham, Elliott, Keats, Macaulay, Aird, Southey, and Lockhart.

Perhaps the most original and judicious of these sketches is that of | Godwin—a very remarkable man, not even yet thoroughly understood.|

Poe's singling out of Godwin is only partly a consequence of the prominence accorded Godwin in Gilfillan's work.[29] The "discriminative criticism" of Gilfillan concerning Godwin declares that he founded a small but distinguished school of writers in England and America. (One wonders whether Poe included himself in this group.) Godwin renounced his more "obnoxious" views before his death in 1836, but will live as a novelist rather than as a philosopher. Surely Poe must have agreed with the characterization of Godwin's fictional personae as "quiet, curious, prying, morbid," and misanthropical. The second paragraph in Poe's review extols the sketch of Godwin, after he had begun his review with praise of the sketches of Godwin's son-in-law, Shelley, and his friend Byron. As if to highlight Godwin even more for Mrs. Whitman, recipient of the two-volume magazine, Poe side-lines the whole second paragraph of his review and picks out, as for a portrait caption, the last ten words. This is surely a new intensity in his fervor for Godwin.

It was not very long afterward, April, 1846, that Poe expressed a like adulation of Godwin in one of his major critical works. Poe used his indirect rendering of the passage from Dickens's letter on Godwin, which he had put into his *Opal* "Chapter of Suggestions" in 1844, for the opening of "The Philosophy of Composition." It is amusing to find Poe inserting into his putative quotation from "a note now lying before me," a sentence with a few changes which is derived from his own free rendering of the same note in the earlier publication.

This was allowable since he had not acknowledged earlier that he was citing the note from Dickens but had pretended to be citing from Godwin's preface itself. My discussion requires excerpting the first two paragraphs:

> Charles Dickens, in a note now lying before me, alluding to an examination I once made of the mechanism of "Barnaby Rudge," says—"By the way, are you aware that Godwin wrote his 'Caleb Williams' backwards? He first involved his hero in a web of difficulties, forming the second volume, and then, for the first, cast about him for some mode of accounting for what had been done."
>
> I cannot think this the *precise* mode of procedure on the part of Godwin—and indeed what he himself acknowledges, is not altogether in accordance with Mr. Dickens' idea—but the author of "Caleb Williams" was too good an artist not to perceive the advantage derivable from at least a somewhat similar process. Nothing is more clear than that every plot, worth the name, must be elaborated to its *dénouement* before anything be attempted with the pen. It is only with the *dénouement* constantly in view that we can give a plot its indispensable air of consequence, or causation, by making the incidents, and especially the tone at all points, tend to the development of the intention. [Harrison, 14.193]

The first paragraph obviously almost duplicates Poe's earlier comment save that here it is attributed to Dickens, not to Godwin. It should be compared with Dickens's real statement (see above and Harrison, 17.107), to determine how free was Poe's rendering of the note, despite his initial statement. Most important is his making Dickens say "second volume" instead of "the last volume first," which implies at least three volumes. Dickens, however, erred greatly in stating that Godwin wrote the book *backwards*. Poe has by now become disenchanted with Dickens, as letters to Lowell in the spring of 1844 show: for example, "There is an article on 'American Poetry' in a late number of the London Foreign Quarterly, in which some allusion is made to me as a poet, and as an imitator of Tenny-

son. . . . Dickens (*I know*) wrote the article—I have private
personal reasons for knowing this."[30] When Lowell attributed
the review to John Forster, the close friend and future biographer of Dickens, Poe stubbornly maintained: "I still adhere
to Dickens as either author, or dictator, of the review."[31] This
little episode in disenchantment probably was responsible for
Poe's remark, in 1846, that Dickens seems to misrepresent
"the *precise* mode of procedure on the part of Godwin." Poe
is correct, since Godwin specifies it very clearly:

> I devoted about two or three weeks to the imagining and
> putting down hints for my story, before I engaged seriously
> and methodically in its composition. In these hints I began
> with my third volume, then proceeded to my second, and
> last of all grappled with the first. I filled two or three sheets
> of demy writing-paper, . . . with these memorandums. They
> were put down with great brevity yet explicitly enough to
> secure a perfect recollection of their meaning, within the
> time necessary for drawing out the story at full. . . . I then
> sat down to write my story from the beginning.[32]

There is a suggestion in Poe's comment on what Godwin "himself acknowledges" that he has once looked at Godwin's statement of procedure; indeed, his further comment on elaborating
a plot "to its dénouement" before "anything be attempted with
the pen" supports this view. Probably he did not have the
preface of Godwin's work before him while writing "The
Philosophy of Composition" and accordingly devised a somewhat indirect allusion while correcting Dickens in favor of
Godwin at the very beginning.

This essay Poe regarded as his best "specimen of analysis."[33]
Subsequently, critics have agreed with him, especially because
of the clear statement of the need for securing unity through
limiting the length of a work; he had, however, approached
the idea earlier (Harrison, 10.122 and 11.106). What critics
have failed to note is the possibility that not only the whole
process of backward composition for the "Raven" can be
traced to Godwin's avowal about *Caleb Williams* but even
Poe's emphasis upon unity of effect. Godwin's preface to *Fleet-*

wood, of 1832, asserted the advantage of "carrying back" the invention from the conclusion to the beginning. "An entire unity of plot would be the infallible result; and the unity of spirit and interest in a tale truly considered, gives it a powerful hold on the reader which can scarcely be generated with equal success in any other way" (p. viii). To be sure, Poe need not have derived the commonplace idea of the importance of unity of plot from any specific source, but Godwin's preface may have reinforced his conviction and statement.

There is another parallel between the two worthy of attention. After Godwin adds, to the account indicated above, his references to the dedication of spirit in which he wrote *Caleb Williams*, he apologizes for his "most entire frankness. I know that it will sound like the most pitiable degree of self-conceit. But such perhaps ought to be the state of mind of an author, when he does his best."[34] Similarly, Poe deprecates the evasive concealment of authors, who prefer the public to think of composition as "a species of fine frenzy," and he assumes it is perfectly decorous "to show the *modus operandi* by which one of my own works was put together" (Harrison, 14.195).

Of further specific allusions to Godwin after this major exploitation there were to be two. The first occurs soon after "The Philosophy of Composition," in a letter to Evert A. Duyckinck, of April 28, 1846, asking whether he or Cornelius Mathews might furnish him with autographs of a number of eminent persons including Godwin and "Mrs. Godwin."[35] By this last he probably meant Mary Wollstonecraft rather than the relatively obscure second Mrs. Godwin, formerly Mrs. Clairmont. Ostrom suggests that his request was part of his preparation for the "Literati" papers which appeared in *Godey's Magazine*, in May to October, 1846, since the first ten names listed were those of Poe's series. This does not, however, explain the inclusion of those of the deceased Godwin and his wife. Apparently, Poe intended a separate autograph series or a series of literati of the past, among whom Godwin would naturally assume a place.

One final reference to Godwin in 1849, the last year of Poe's life, is chiefly a repetition of the first allusion that he inserted into the *Broadway Journal* of 1845, when he was reviewing Bulwer Lytton's poems. Now Poe dips into the review for a long entry in the "Marginalia" of the *Southern Literary Messenger* of May, 1849. The two and a half pages in Harrison's edition (16.156–159) are almost entirely reprinted from the earlier piece with minor changes, mainly to provide transitions; one difference is Poe's elevating Godwin and his literary colleagues *above* Bulwer, as a novelist, and in associating Godwin with a slightly different set of names. Poe writes: "As a novelist, then, Bulwer is far more than respectable although *generally* inferior to Scott, Godwin, D'Israeli, Miss Burney, Sue, Dumas, Dickens, the author of 'Ellen Wareham,' the author of 'Jane Eyre,'" and several others. Poe has tried to abridge the original review and yet preserve its substance; hence, possibly, the elimination of De Foe, Smollett, Fielding, and Maria Edgeworth. Yet, in those that he includes can be found a significant gauge of how Poe's taste has evolved over a period of four years. For the worthies of eighteenth-century English fiction he has exchanged three new names: Eugène Sue, Dumas, and Charlotte Bronte, only the last of whom offers any real compensation, we are likely to think. We are glad to see Lady Georgiana Fullerton depart and notice that Scott leads the list, one place ahead of Godwin, while Dickens fits between Dumas and Mrs. Sullivan, author of "Ellen Wareham."

One final point about Poe's great respect for Godwin might be made of an oddly consistent pattern of negative evidence. In all his references to those eminent in philosophy and political economy, Poe unfailingly exempts Godwin from the strictures that he addresses to the utilitarians and the perfectibilitarians, showing that he regarded Godwin as primarily a writer of fiction; even his *Lives of the Necromancers* has some of the qualities of fictive tales. Thus, despite the fact that after writing *Political Justice* Godwin was virtually identified with the theory of perpetual progress, Poe, in 1835, scorns as "human-perfectibility" spokesmen Turgot, Price, Priestley, and Condorcet

(Harrison, 2.38, "Lionizing"). An allusion is made to the "wild doctrines" of the same four, again without Godwin, in "The Landscape Garden" of 1842 (4.259; also 6.176). Ideas of "universal equality," "wild attempts at an omni-prevalent Democracy," and the propriety of the term "improvement" for the "progress of our civilization" are all deprecated in "Monos and Una," of 1841 (4.200–212), and likewise the idea "of human perfectibility" in the letters of July 2, 1844, to Lowell and of July 10, 1844, to Chivers.[36] Also, in "Monos and Una," he calls the utilitarians "rough pedants," following this in 1847 with scorn for Mill as a logician and for his "mill-horse," Bentham ("Mellonta Tauta," 6.204). Previously he had called both of them "the most preposterous" among "*a priori* reasoners upon government" ("Marginalia," 1844, 16.37). Poe's intense admiration of aristocracy and its chivalric and medieval provenance was also revealed in his unflattering reference to men like Bentham as "worshippers of Mammon" in the age of "joint-stock companies" (14.104).

In short, Poe seems entirely to ignore Godwin's social criticism, even as presented in *Caleb Williams:* his condemnation of false notions of honor, the advantages over the poor and obscure given by wealth and landed property, and the demoralizing cruelty of legal punishments. Poe's references to Godwin and remarks about his work show clearly that he considered Godwin as a craftsman, whose handling of the plot and atmosphere entitled him to respect. Godwin's use of suspense, morbid psychology, and alienated heroes provides a strong bond between two major writers. It is a bond which is deserving of more thought than has hitherto been given to it.

8

POE AND THE "MAGIC TALE" OF *ELLEN WAREHAM*

EARLY IN 1835 Poe became a "magazinist," as he proudly termed himself, pouring out almost one hundred reviews for the *Southern Literary Messenger* in less than two years. This was the start of his career in criticism, the aspect of literature for which he was best known in his own lifetime.[1] During the half century after his death his reputation as writer of tales and poems superseded the fame, or rather notoriety, derived from his keen and often blunt reviews of the second-rate literature that came to his desk.[2] We can now largely agree with Edmund Wilson: "Perhaps more than any other writer, French or English, of the first half of the century, he had thought seriously and written clearly about the methods and aims of literature. He had formulated a critical theory, and he had supplied brilliant specimens of its practice."[3] Poe's proclivities and experience also led him to rank the short story and the short poem above the long narrative in prose and the epic in poetry. His stress upon "unity of effect" made the aesthetic or psychological response preeminent over the moral.

Even his early criticism indicates his firm advocacy of the superior merits of the short literary work of a non-didactic tendency. Poe faced a dilemma, of course, since the majority of the books sent him for reviewing were novels, which would have to be damned out of hand on the basis of this critical touchstone. In 1836, then, he states his position of compromise. Since I intend later to trace Poe's views of one novel throughout his entire career, as a gauge of his taste in this genre, I must first examine this basic statement:

The novel certainly requires what is denominated a sustained effort—but this is a matter of mere perseverance, and has but a collateral relation to talent. On the other hand—unity of effect . . . is indispensable in the "brief article," and not so in the common novel . . . admired for its detached passages, . . . without reference to any general design—which, if it even exist in some measure, will be found to have occupied but little of the writer's attention, and cannot . . . be taken in at one view, by the reader.[4]

Incorporated into his review of Dickens's *Watkins Tottle,* this comment implies the secondary quality of the novelist's genius and of the novel as an art form. Yet, as critic, Poe must still formulate for himself standards for judging those "detached passages" or episodes and whatever of "general design" does exist in the whole work. In effect, most commentators on Poe's writings have been so concerned with his tenets of unity and antimoralism that they have neglected to look for his other standards for determining merit in fiction. I have already indicated that his praise of Godwin was deeply rooted in an admiration for the power to "construct" an effective plot, but this is really another way of saying that the unification of the various elements in the novel brings it closer to the short story as a guarantee of its artistic success. But this still begs the question of evaluating the "detached passages" and the delayed effect of a long narrative. Perhaps a very brief survey of Poe's criticism of novels will reveal empirically a few of his implied standards.

In his August, 1836 review of Ingraham's novel, *Lafitte: The Pirate of the Gulf,* Poe asserts that we should not judge an historical novel only by reference to its "historical truth," praises its "vigor" and some of the "admirably colored" descriptive pieces, and offers the generalization that "the most simple, is the best method of narration" (Harrison, 9.106–116). In the same issue of the *Messenger* he objects to a "glaring improbability" in a "*rencontre*" as the worst feature in James S. French's novel *Elkswatawa* and praises it for its well-drawn

characters (9.118–122). The next issue of the magazine carries
Poe's review of Simms's novel about metempsychosis, *Sheppard Lee,* the "jocular" manner of which he finds unsuitable.
The book fails, Poe says, because of the awkward handling of
the effect of six reincarnations upon the same almost "unchang-
ing" character (9.137–138). In the same month, Poe reviewed
Mrs. Lydia Child's historical romance, *Philothea,* the chief
merit of which is to reveal "antique manners, costume, habits,
and modes of thought." Bulwer's *Last Days of Pompeii,*
however, does more, by "commingling" with the "exciting"
destruction of the city "human passions wildly affected thereby" (9.153–154; see also, 8.222). In January, 1837, Poe sounds
several of the same notes in his evaluation of *George Balcombe*
by Beverley Tucker: "*the best* American novel" with "invention, vigor, almost audacity of thought—great variety of . . .
intrigue, and exceeding ingenuity and finish in the adaptation
of its component parts" (9.264–265).

In his middle period of criticism, reviewing another novel
by Simms, *The Damsel of Darien* (1839), Poe objects to the
"grossness of thought" and the exaggeration of expression
(10.53). Many of his previous themes are stressed in his long
review of Bulwer's *Night and Morning.* "The interest of plot
. . . is by no means a popular interest." Moreover, "a good tale
may be written without it," such as *Gil Blas, Pilgrim's Progress,* and *Robinson Crusoe.* Length by itself does not entitle
a work to respect; only "the unity or totality of *effect*" is
"worth the attention of the critic." In reading the fashionable
"wire-drawn romances . . . the pleasure we derive (if any)
is a composite one, and made up of the respective sums of
the various pleasurable sentiments experienced . . ." (10.122).
In the same review, Poe pointedly notes a marked distinction
between narrative value and dramatic value; for example,
drama requires frequent shifts in scene and a marshalling of
events in terms of time because of the absence of a suitable
"*commenting* power." In his comments of 1841 on *The Old
Curiosity Shop,* Poe objects to the "ultra-accident" of the rela-

tionship between Kit's master and the old church bachelor
as well as to the painfulness of Nell's death, but he praises
the "originality" of the "admirably drawn characters" (10.151–
152). Concerning Ainsworth's *Guy Fawkes,* also in 1841, he
objects to the poor motivation of the plot and the use of "accidental or irrelevant circumstances" which negate the implied
plan of the whole book. His insistence upon the "autorial
comment," previously seen in his comments on Godwin (chapter vii), again leads him to object to the "merely narrated"
escapes in another of Ainsworth's novels, *Jack Sheppard.*

During the year 1842, in his review of *Barnaby Rudge,* as
we have seen, he praises *Notre Dame de Paris* for showing
how to gain "force" through respect for the "unity of place,"
and he disparages Dickens's attempt to maintain interest
through an appeal to "curiosity" (11.58). His first notice of
Twice-Told Tales again asserts the superiority of the tale over
the novel and the long poem and objects to three elements in
much of the contemporary fiction: "Rosa-Matilda effusions"
or sentimentality, "blue-blazing melodramaticisms," and an
attempt to copy "low life."[5] His promised follow-up review of
Hawthorne's work has become the *locus classicus* for the idea
of the merit in the poem or tale that can be read at one sitting;
again the novel is relegated to an inferior category (11.106–
108). In his 1843 criticism of Cooper's *Wyandotté,* Poe objects
to the lack of "plot" or design in this episodic novel but admits
that "the absence of plot can never be critically regarded as a
defect" in this genre (11.209–210). He also objects to the
"revolting and supererogatory" killing of three characters and
approves the "collateral interest" given by the Revolutionary
War setting as well as the "skill and truth" used in depicting
the love of two characters (11.212).

The last five years of Poe's life provide critiques not markedly different in their views on the novel. In 1845, for example,
in evaluating *The Wigwam and the Cabin* by Simms, Poe
appears more partial to the Southern novelist because he is
supreme in "vigor, in movement, in the power of exciting

interest, and in the artistical management of his themes," especially in *Martin Faber*.[6] In the next year, 1846, "The Philosophy of Composition" offers the famous analysis of the writing
of "The Raven"; again Poe deprecates the long literary work
but exempts "certain classes of prose composition, such as
'Robinson Crusoe,' (demanding no unity)" from the single-
sitting limitation (14.196). During his last year, in one of the
"Marginalia" entries of May, 1849, Poe specifically makes a
rare distinction between the novel and the tale: "In the tale
proper there is no space for development of character or for
great profusion and variety of incident—mere *construction* is,
of course, far more imperatively demanded than in the novel.
Defective plot, in this latter, may escape observation, but in
the tale, never" (16.171). It is superfluous to stress that Poe's
manifest incapacity to develop character is the chief basis for
this confident dictum; it also implies that Poe was now considering the motivation and revelation of character as equivalent
to "mere *construction*," at least in the novel.

These instances show that Poe paid his respects to other
criteria than the "unity of effect" and the deliberate artistry
needed in "constructing" a narrative. The virtues of the novel
also included vigor and force, truth in fiction depicting the
past, simple and straightforward narrative but always with the
observational comment of a perceptive and broadly cultured
author, delicacy in the language used by the characters and
purity of style in that used by the author, and reticence in
presenting the passions, which must, however, be described
accurately. There was little in this list to which a critic of the
eighteenth century could take exception.

I now propose to examine Poe's implicit application of these
criteria to a novel mentioned often by him and yet having the
charm for all of us today of being totally unfamiliar. No commentator on Poe has even identified by title the larger work
which contains the novel. Eventually we shall find it necessary
to seek the causes for Poe's inordinate partiality to a popular
work of the time which has now justly disappeared from con-

sideration, even in the histories of literature. In Poe's early
criticism one finds three references to a "tale" or novel entitled *Ellen Wareham,* edited by Lady Dacre; Poe published a
fourth and a fifth statement about the same work in 1844, a
sixth in 1845, and a seventh during the last year of his life. All
these comments, uniformly laudatory, prepare one for a masterpiece of the order of *Vanity Fair* or *Sense and Sensibility.*

His first statement consists of a brief announcement of a
second collection of "tales," which Lady Dacre is alleged to
have edited rather than written, according to Poe. It occurs
among the "Critical Notices and Literary Intelligence" of the
August, 1835 *Southern Literary Messenger* (*SLM,* 1.715–716).[7]
Since it is uncollected by Harrison, I shall give the comment
in toto:

> Lady Dacre, who wrote the *Tales of a Chaperon,* has pub-
> lished *Tales of the Peerage and Peasantry.* The work is
> ostensibly *edited* by Lady Dacre, but there can be no doubt
> of her having written it. Every lover of fine writing must
> remember the story of Ellen Wareham in the Tales of a
> [C]haperon. Positively we have never seen any thing of the
> kind more painfully interesting, with the single exception of
> the Bride of Lammermuir. The Tales in the present volumes
> are *The Countess of Nithsdale, The Hampshire Cottage,*
> and *Blanche.*

The extravagance of this praise of her earlier work (of 1833)
may be gauged by the fact that in the December, 1835 issue
of the *Messenger* (*SLM,* 2.43) Poe terms the *Bride of Lam-
mermuir* "that most pure, perfect, and radiant gem of fictitious
literature."

It is likely that his August notice of the *Tales of the Peerage
and the Peasantry* was based simply upon an advertisement of
the English edition in one of the monthlies that Poe was then
digesting for the *Southern Literary Messenger,* for in the
December, 1835 issue of the magazine he includes a full
review of the New York reprint of the three-volume work,
which begins: "We had been looking with much impatience

for the republication of these volumes, and henceforward we shall look with still greater anxiety for any thing announced as under the *editorial* supervision of Lady Dacre."[8] It must be explained that *Recollections of a Chaperon* had also been published as "edited" by Lady Dacre with no authorship indicated. In reality, both collections were by her daughter, Mrs. Arabella Jane Sullivan, but Lady Dacre's name carried much more weight in the social and literary world. She had been born Barbarina Ogle, the daughter of Admiral Sir Chaloner Ogle: he was an eccentric who early taught her the Italian which she was to use for her famous translations. After the death of Barbarina's first husband, Valentine Henry Wilmot, wealthy lawyer and secretary to Lord Chancellor Camden, she married Thomas Brand, Baron Dacre, in 1819. Readers of Byron biography know him as one of the referees in the settlement of Lady Noel's estate, which greatly enriched Byron. A few years later Lady Dacre was separated from her husband and devoted herself to her art work, her writing, and the education of her daughter, Arabella Jane Wilmot. Arabella, who was married to the handsome and genteel Frederick Sullivan, produced these two sets of tales, edited by her mother, Lady Dacre.[9]

The preface to the American edition of *Recollections of a Chaperon* seems to have given Poe the impression that Lady Dacre wrote them, for the rest of the first paragraph of his December, 1835 review can allude only to the earlier set of volumes (1833); nothing in the preface to the *Tales of the Peerage* supports Poe's inference:

> But why, Lady Dacre, this excessive show of modesty, or rather this most unpardonable piece of affectation? Why deny having written volumes whose authorship would be an enviable and an honorable distinction to the proudest literati of your land? And why, above all, announce yourself as editor in a title page, merely to proclaim yourself author in a preface?[10]

His reading of the preface must have been hasty, for the *Quarterly Review* notice of the book repeatedly alludes to Mrs.

Sullivan as the author and asserts that Lady Dacre's "editorship has been confined to a preface."[11] We know from the family papers that Mrs. Sullivan had relied upon the *Quarterly* to resolve the mystery of authorship.[12] I cannot check the preface to the American edition of *Recollections,* for the book seems to be unprocurable.[13] The British Museum copies of the 1833 first edition and the 1848 and 1853 reprints contain a pseudo-preface, which is part of the fictitious text and purports to be written by the chaperon herself—a widow with seven daughters. There is no mention of Lady Dacre as the author.

In reality, none of Lady Dacre's writings consisted of prose fiction. She was the acknowledged author of translations of Petrarch's poems (1815, 1818, 1819, and 1836), which had received high praise and had been reprinted, in part, by Ugo Foscolo in his *Essays on Petrarch* (1823), dedicated to Lady Dacre. *Blackwood's Edinburgh Magazine* thought hers the best translation of Petrarch in its review of Foscolo's book.[14] In her two-volume *Dramas, Translations and Occasional Poems* (1821) she reprinted four of her own plays, including *Ina,* which was produced in the Drury Lane Theatre on April 22, 1815. This had the distinction of an epilogue by Thomas Moore, on which he had lavished some wit and attention; the failure of the April 22 performance is humorously told by Byron in a letter to Moore, of the next day. This drama, the only work (save for a play for children) which Lady Dacre did not publish privately, went into three editions in 1815. Byron speaks of it as having "good language but no power."[15]

There is little evidence of this "good language" or of any merit at all in Arabella Jane's fiction. Her mother's aptness of diction in *Ina* and in her many letters in *A Family Chronicle* is completely missing. Poe would disagree sharply with my view. Concerning *Winifred, Countess of Nithsdale,* one of the *Tales of the Peerage,* he writes: "A thrilling and spiritual story, rich with imagination, pathos, and passion," every part of which contributes to "the unity of effect" achieved by the "fair authoress." He asserts: "There can be no doubt that Lady

Dacre is a writer of infinite genius, possessing great felicity of expression, a happy talent for working up a story. . . ." His last and climactic paean here concerns Arabella's earlier work:

> No person, of even common sensibility, has ever perused the magic tale of *Ellen Wareham* without feeling the very soul of passion and imagination aroused and stirred up within him, as at the sound of a trumpet.
>
> Let Lady Dacre but give up her talents and energies, and especially *her time* to the exaltation of her literary fame, and we are sorely mistaken if, hereafter, she do not accomplish something which will not readily die. [Harrison, 8.75]

The modern reader's appetite for this work is whetted even further by his meeting it five more times in widely spaced Poe criticisms. In the review of Bulwer Lytton's *Rienzi*, in the February, 1836 *Messenger*, he is told that "Lady Dacre has written *Ellen Wareham*, a more forcible tale of Passion" than Bulwer's (*SLM*, 2.197; Harrison, 8.223). After many years, Poe took up the critical touchstone of this novel again, both at the beginning and end of 1844. In the January issue of *Graham's Magazine* (24.46) is a review of *Ned Myers; or, A Life Before the Mast'* (1843)—an article which has not been collected by Harrison, although unmistakably Poe's. Here Poe explains the reason for his persistent attribution of the *Recollections* to its "editor," showing an extremely personal motivation in the matter. Since the review has not been reprinted, it will be necessary to give a rather long excerpt:

> The words "*edited* by J. Fenimore Cooper" in the title-page of this volume, have, no doubt, a suspicious appearance. It has been the fashion, of late days, for authors to speak of themselves, modestly, as editors of even original works. We all remember the magnificent "Recollections of a Chaperon" *edited* by Lady Dacre—and then (a case more in point just now) there was the "Narrative of Sir Edward Seaward," *edited* by Miss Porter—a work of deeper interest, and of a far more *vraisemblant* character than even "Robinson Crusoe," upon which it is modeled. The merit of originality is,

of course, De Foe's and Miss Porter is but an imitator at best; but, setting aside all reference to the credit due to the respective *authors,* and regarding only the two *books,* we should have no hesitation in saying that "Sir Edward Seaward's Narrative" is, in every respect, superior to "Robinson Crusoe's." In the same manner, "Arthur Gordon Pym"—another series of sea-adventures purporting to be *edited* only by Mr. Poe, was in reality his own composition—the supposititious hero having existed in imagination alone. Bearing these, and other similar works in mind, the reader will naturally be induced to suspect Mr. Cooper, who professes to *edit "Ned Myers,"* of having, in fact, composed it himself. . . . After all, its chief charm lies in the details of the everyday matters. . . .

Professor Mabbott early had concluded that this review was Poe's on the basis of the reference to *Pym,* while Professor Hull assigned the entry to Poe largely because of its reference to *Recollections of a Chaperon.*[16] Clearly it was the manner in which Poe had presented *The Narrative of Arthur Gordon Pym* to the public—"edited" by Poe, the real author—that led him to the assumption about Lady Dacre. Poe, by the way, may have been correct about *Ned Myers,* sometimes included in the canon of Cooper's works. On the other hand, it is not printed in the collected works of Cooper and seems to cause some disagreement among Cooper scholars.[17] One would judge that Poe had some justification for his views about Cooper's use of details; as he says later in the review, the marine aspects of the work were convincingly close to those in *The Pilot.*[18]

At the end of 1844, in the *Democratic Review* of December, Poe makes a fifth allusion to *Ellen Wareham* in his notice of Lady Georgiana Fullerton's *Ellen Middleton.* The fact that this novel too had a heroine called Ellen—Poe's favorite name —and a titled author may have triggered Poe's comparison: "Who is Lady Georgiana Fullerton? Who is that Countess of Dacre, who edited 'Ellen Wareham,'—the most passionate of fictions—approached in some particulars of passion, by this?"

(Harrison, 16.34). Lady Dacre, one might add, never called herself by that very unusual, almost unEnglish title of "countess." (The *DNB* styles her "baroness.") It is clear that the passionate nature of the plot and possibly of the heroine was somehow associated in Poe's mind with the "blue blood" of each of the authors.

The two ladies and Bulwer Lytton, as a writer, are still associated in Poe's mind for his sixth reference, a few months later. In his magazine, the *Broadway Journal* of February 8, 1845, Poe is reviewing the New York edition of Bulwer's *Poems*, edited by Macleod. The article is not printed in the text of Harrison's edition, although it is correctly listed in his bibliography of Poe's writings (Harrison, 16.372). Poe writes: "As a novelist then, Bulwer is far more than respectable— although he has produced few novels equal and none superior to . . . three or four of Godwin's, to the 'Ellen Wareham' of Mrs. Sullivan, or to the 'Ellen Middleton' of Lady Georgiana Fullerton."[19] Apparently he had discovered finally that Lady Dacre is not the author of *Ellen Wareham,* but his admiration is undiluted. He still associates the novel with *Ellen Middleton* as similar in genre and quality.

The link between Bulwer and the novel must have lingered in Poe's memory throughout the next four years, for in May, 1849, the "Marginalia" of the *Messenger* included a seventh comment: "As a novelist, then, Bulwer is far more than respectable; although *generally* inferior to Scott, Godwin, D'Israeli, Miss Burney, Sue, Dumas, Dickens, the author of 'Ellen Wareham,' the author of 'Jane Eyre,' and several others." Poe is now disinclined to impute the book either to Lady Dacre or to her daughter, Mrs. Sullivan, but he compensates for depriving the author of her original nobility by placing her among even more eminent authors than in 1835–36. This is, by the way, Poe's only reference to Charlotte Bronte and Fanny Burney.

No library catalogue or bibliography will produce the novel, *Ellen Wareham,* as such, for the interested reader, since it is the last of the five stories in Mrs. Sullivan's *Recollections of a Chaperon* and occupies the third volume by itself in the first English and American editions. The titles of the other stories or novelettes have some significance for evaluative purposes: *The Single Woman of a Certain Age; Milly and Lucy; Warren, or the Piping Times of Peace;* and *An Old Tale, and Often Told.* His comments on both of Mrs. Sullivan's collections of tales, but especially on *Ellen Wareham,* are obviously part of what Harrison calls "this mass of criticism . . . lavished on volumes that have succumbed into oblivion" (8. ix). I intend briefly to pluck the book out of that merciful oblivion in order to ask what could have led Poe to his commendation. Despite the fact that the *Recollections of a Chaperon* went into two editions after the 1833 publication (both the 1849 and 1853 reprints are listed as No. 114 of Bentley's "Standard Novels"), it is a very scarce work in libraries today.[20]

First, however, I must devote a few words to a remarkable coincidence: William Evans Burton—the owner of the *Gentleman's Magazine* of Philadelphia, which Poe joined as editor in May, 1830—had adapted *Ellen Wareham* for the London stage in 1833. In its first edition it bore the subtitle "A Domestic Drama in Three Acts," and upon being reprinted in 1858 it was called *Ellen Wareham, the Wife of Two Husbands.*[21] Indeed, Billy Burton, as he was jovially known both as actor and magazine journalist, had even taken the role of Dick in the play at some time in his long stage career. It was being played in the London theaters, back in May, 1833—in fact, in five at the same time.[22] It must be admitted, however, that this may not have been totally a tribute to Burton's adaptation, for the novel had also been adapted by J. B. Buckstone for performance at the Haymarket Theatre as early as April 24, 1833, with the famous Mrs. Yates as Ellen.[23] There is no doubt that Burton, setting much store by his reputation for acting in comic roles and also for his version of *Ellen Wareham,* expected to be well received when he came to America in 1834.[24] The play itself had not been acclaimed when it opened at the American Theatre in New York City, November 6, 1833, in one version or other.[25]

Burton's subsequent career in the theater and in Philadelphia publishing need not concern us, but it is significant that in a draft of his letter to Burton, of June 1, 1840, bitterly complaining of his treatment and apparent dismissal after a year of arduous service on the magazine, Poe mentions Burton's "design to give up your journal, with a view of attending to the Theatre" (Harrison, 1.167). This led to the merger of Burton's magazine with Graham's *Casket*, which provided Poe with his next position as editor and with the outlet for several of his masterpieces. Poe undoubtedly knew about Burton's adaptation of *Ellen Wareham*, which was produced by Burton himself in Philadelphia at the Arch Theatre on July 3, 1837, and at the Chestnut Street Theatre on June 11, 1840, virtually the date when Poe was complaining in the above letter about his "attending" to the drama rather than to the magazine.[26] There is further evidence that Poe must have seen the play in Philadelphia. He was familiar with theatrical people there, such as Richard Penn Smith (1799–1854), well known for his plays and his many adaptations of English and French works.[27] Quinn speaks of a tradition that Poe associated with actors in Philadelphia and postulates that Burton secured Poe regular admission to the Walnut Street Theatre, during 1839–1840, before the break in their cordial relations.[28] Certainly Poe's knowledge of the play and of the melodrama of the novel's plot would have kept alive more vividly his early memories of the tale which became almost a touchstone for genuine passion throughout Poe's criticism. Its rarity today will justify, I trust, my enabling the reader to savor its "magic" quality.

Ellen Wareham is the daughter of a half-pay captain, retired to a resort town, where he hopes that the balls and visitors will help him to marry off his three daughters: Caroline, Ellen, and Matilda. At seventeen Ellen captures a dull but prosperous merchant, Mr. Cresford (we are never told his first name), and they have two children within five years. Her older sister Caroline marries Lord Coverdale. Unfortunately, Cresford,

while traveling on the Continent, is "detained" by Napoleon
in 1803, and within a year Ellen receives an announcement of
his death in the prison at Verdun. She has met Algernon Hamilton, Esq., through the Coverdales, and he begs her to grace
his large Elizabethan mansion of Belhanger as his wife. After
waiting two years and two months, she makes him and herself
happy, and within a proper time these two become three, plus
Cresford's children. Ellen admits to herself that she had never
really loved the crass and unimaginative Cresford. Picture her
consternation to discover, five years after her second marriage,
that he has just been released from imprisonment in Germany,
to which he had escaped from France through the ruse of a
mock funeral. (Could this have suggested to Dickens Barsad's
escape in the *Tale of Two Cities*?)

Algernon is equally shocked: "Striking his forehead, he
rushed out of the room, darted down the stairs, out of the
house, and plunged into the most retired part of the park,
where he wildly paced the ground, beating his bosom, and
almost dashing his head against the trees." Ellen immediately
leaves her second husband, and returns to her father to await
the arrival of Cresford, who now shows himself to be a demon.
Although his business partners too had believed in his death,
he is irrationally convinced that Ellen knew the truth about
his survival. At the confrontation scene he says to Ellen herself
with masterful irony: "She has given the loose to her profligate
fancies, under the specious veil of marriage. Well done, your
sanctified hypocrite! The mourning wife of Ephesus with a
vengeance!" Then "he laughed an appalling withering laugh.
. . . His eyes glared, with the fire of madness."[29]

The relentless Cresford insists that Ellen be prosecuted for
bigamy, and he challenges Hamilton to a duel, which is refused. Although Hamilton's lawyer defends Ellen and although
the friend who was to deliver a message from Cresford years
ago is proved to have died en route to England, Ellen is
judged guilty *but* fined merely a shilling. Still, since she is
legally married to Cresford, she continues to live with Papa,
until her first husband, in his mad fury and ambition, drives

his repossessed business into bankruptcy and himself into the grave. The deathbed scene is most affecting, for no proper wife of that period could fail to pray for the life of her legal spouse. After another decent interval of mourning, Ellen remarries Algernon and regains happiness.

This is the "magic tale" of *Ellen Wareham,* whose author, says Poe, knows more about "the springs of the human heart . . . than *any of her female contemporaries.*"[30] And this is the reviewer to whom James E. Heath wrote, in 1839, "Your dissecting knife, if vigorously employed, would serve to rid us of much of that silly trash and sickly *sentimentality* with which puerile and conceited authors, and gain-seeking booksellers are continually poisoning our intellectual food." (Harrison, 8.xi). Poe is generally thought to have been shaping his taste in his early criticism. His praise of *Ellen Wareham* matched his praise in February, 1836, of Henry F. Chorley's *Conti the Discarded,*[31] which Edward H. Davidson excerpts as a fine example of the whole period's delight "in fashionably exquisite, nubile young women in erotic poses of death."[32] He also praised Chorley in September, 1836, for his papers on music (Harrison, 9.145). Yet, as Poe became more mature in judgment, he outgrew his reverence for the third-rate dilettante and in November, 1844, says of Chorley: "The author speaks of music like a man, and not like a fiddler. This is something—and that he has imagination is more. But the philosophy of music is beyond his depth" (Harrison, 16.8). In the first review there may have been a tinge of Poe's early idolatry of British literary circles and also a hope that a man as powerful on the *Athenaeum* as Chorley might help to advance his own career as author. Moreover, even in February, 1836, Poe was quite capable of administering the axe, or rather the tomahawk, to Morris Mattson's *Paul Ulric: or the Adventures of an Enthusiast*—"four hundred and forty-three pages of utter folly, bombast, and inanity" (Harrison, 8.179); perhaps this severity came from his fear of the "absurdities with an inundation of which our country is grievously threatened."

Yet, in his continuing praise of *Ellen Wareham,* this piece of literary claptrap, Poe allows himself to be misled by a host of factors which cannot be precisely defined but merely suggested. He thought that he found in the work a unity of effect, although only its "passionate" nature is specified; one suspects that it aroused Poe's gallant sense of pity for the poor wronged female. He also hints at verisimilitude of details, the last quality that we find in this book. It is true that being only one volume long, unlike the typical three-decker Victorian novel, it may tell its sad story with a little more superficial directness and simplicity, qualities which Poe praised in the novel. A sense of force and vigor may result from this relative conciseness, in which the "dead-alive" theme, so near to Poe's morbid interests, shapes the whole direction of the plot. Poe may also have given the author credit for her "construction of plot" through entering Ellen into a loveless marriage and sending Cresford into the dangers of a business mission on the Continent during Napoleon's wars.

There are other factors, I suspect, basic to his praise. I have mentioned his reverence for authors of nobility, which actually led to his misconception about the writer of the work. Yet, Poe himself issued an effective and well-founded warning to the American readers of British books in one of the "Marginalia" of 1849:

> Irreparable ill is wrought by the almost exclusive dissemination among us of foreign—that is to say, of monarchical or aristocratical sentiment in foreign books; nor is this sentiment less fatal to democracy because it reaches the people themselves directly in the gilded pill of the poem or the novel. [Harrison, 16.79]

Certainly he failed to heed his excellent advice in considering this "gilded pill." A lady offering this tale of woe would naturally receive more than her just tribute from the susceptible writer of "Annabel Lee." In general, Poe's unfailing commendation of *Ellen Wareham* is proof of the wide variety of his literary judgments and of his yielding at times to the fashions of the period.

9

POE AND THE RIVER

IN 1827 EDGAR Allan Poe published his first volume, *Tamerlane and Other Poems,* in Boston. Two of the poems, reprinted on successive pages in his 1829 volume, *Al Aaraaf, Tamerlane, and Minor Poems,* very helpfully highlight the theme of this chapter, namely, that Poe usually and significantly attaches a distinctive complex of associations in his writings to each of three aspects of nature: the sea, the river, and the lake. In illustration I cite "The Lake":

```
1   In spring of youth it was my lot
2   To haunt of the wide world a spot
3   The which I could not love the less—
4   So lovely was the loneliness
5   Of a wild lake, with black rock bound,
6   And the tall pines that towered around.

7   But when the Night had thrown her pall
8   Upon that spot, as upon all,
9   And the mystic wind went by
10  Murmuring in melody,
11  Then—ah, then I would awake
12  To the terror of the lone lake.
        .   .   .   .   .   .   .   .   .   .   .
18  Death was in that poisonous wave,
19  And in its gulf a fitting grave
20  For him who thence could solace bring
21  To his lone imagining—
22  Whose solitary soul could make
23  An Eden of that dim lake.[1]
```

Surely this demonstrates the attraction lurking for Poe in the dark waters of a remote lake, with its "black rock" and "black

wind," creating "a dirge of melody," and with its poisoned
wave and its solitude, according to Poe's variations.[2] The fatal
fascination of the mountain lake or tarn, as Poe calls it, subsequently appears in his creative works.

The preceding page of the 1829 volume (p. 63) carried "To
the River":

> Fair river! in thy bright, clear flow
>   Of labyrinth-like water,
> Thou art an emblem of the glow
>   Of beauty—the unhidden heart—
>   The playful maziness of art. . . .

This was revised for the 1845 edition of his poems, even more
pointedly, to "Fair river! in thy bright, clear flow / of crystal,
wandering water. . . ." The darkness of the lake water and of
its shores is in sharp contrast with the glinting purity of the
flowing stream.

But what attitude does Poe take toward the sea—to add
the third type of waterscape? In his earliest volumes of
poetry, there is no single poem using the sea as a theme, but
some gauge is furnished by the 1829 "Fairy-Land," containing these lines:

> O'er the strange woods—o'er the sea
> Over spirits on the wing
>
> . . . .
> With the tempests as they toss,
> Like—almost any thing—
> Or a yellow Albatross.
>   [pp. 70–71]

The fatal bird of the *Ancient Mariner* indicates the trend of
Poe's sea-borne thought in his poetry and his fiction. The sea
shares the emotive overtones of the lake in being a source and
symbol of disaster to man. Usually it is described as rough,
stormy, dangerous. Even when calm, it has its sinister side, as
I shall show through a survey of Poe's poetry and tales which

will consider his major treatments of waterscapes and several minor allusions.

Poe's third collection of poetry in 1831 provides a death-ridden seascape, "The City in the Sea." The sunken metropolis, replete with shrines and palaces and time-worn towers, is tributary to Death. "Light from the lurid, deep sea / Streams up the turrets silently," through the "melancholy waters"; "open graves / are on a level with the waves."[3] In this poem the sea is "hideously serene," although in Poe it is usually hideously agitated. The tranquillity if not the basic theme reminds one of Shelley's sunken buildings in Baiae's Bay.[4] More usually, as in his poem "To F—" of 1835, there is a "tumultuous sea . . . throbbing far and free / With storms." In "The Valley of Unrest" of 1831 a wind makes the trees "palpitate" as do "the chill seas / Around the misty Hebrides."[5] In 1827 the dreamer-poet, in "A Dream Within a Dream," had stood "amid the roar / Of a surf-tormented shore" and could not save the golden sand "from the pitiless wave," thereby showing how early was his rooted attitude of fear and distaste for the ocean.

These early instances express Poe's characteristic attitudes concerning water scenes. In the small body of Poe's poetry they can all be charted. *Al Aaraaf* of 1829 is full of the beauty of river scenery, highly artificial and dependent upon Thomas Moore, Chateaubriand, and others, as the poem is. There are the "Valisnerian lotus thither flown / From struggling with the waters of the Rhone" and the "Nelumbo bud that floats for ever / With Indian Cupid down the holy river" (p. 17). By contrast, note the destructive marine element of "The wave / Is now upon thee," that is, "beautiful Gomorrah" (p. 27). A footnote explains that more than two cities were "engulphed in the 'dead sea.'" There is a "lone lake that smiles, / In its dream of deep rest" (p. 32), to be sure, but also in "Romance" of 1829 appears a "shadowy lake" which does not smile and which produces a general drowsiness (p. 57). Quite consistently, in *Al Aaraaf* Poe mentions "springs that lie clearest / Beneath the moon ray" (p. 31), the "melody of woodland rill" (p. 13),

"fountains . . . gushing music" and "bright waterfalls" (p. 28).
By contrast:

> The crowd
> Still thinks my terrors but the thunder cloud
> The storm, the earthquake, and the ocean-wrath—
> [Ah! will they cross me in my angrier path?]
> [p. 20]

In his celebrated poem "To Helen" (1831), the beauty of the
love object is indeed compared with "those Nicéan barks of
yore, / That gently, o'er a perfumed sea" bear the "weary, way-
worn wanderer" to his native shore. But this gentleness is obviously uncharacteristic, for the next stanza asserts that he was
"on desperate seas long wont to roam" (Harrison, 7.46). In the
1831 "The Sleeper," "the lake / A conscious slumber seems to
take, / And would not, for the world, awake"—a slumber in
short that resembles death (7.51).

In *Graham's Magazine* of June, 1844, appeared "Dream-
Land" which virtually epitomizes my thesis:

> Seas that restlessly aspire,
> Surging, unto skies of fire;
>
> .   .   .   .
>
> Lakes that endlessly outspread
> Their lone waters, lone and dead,—
> Their still waters—still and chilly
> With the snows of the lolling lily.
> [Harrison, 7.89]

A repetition of the section provides the variant phrase, "sad
and chilly," before mentioning the "swamp / Where the toad
and the newt encamp,— / By the dismal tarns and pools /
Where dwell the Ghouls." But he writes of the "river / Murmuring lowly, murmuring ever," even among the "grey woods."
In "The Raven," finally completed and published in 1845, we
twice find the night's "Plutonian shore," the second time associated with "the tempest" (Harrison, 7.94–100, stanzas 8 and
17). In "Eulalie" of the same year he speaks of his soul as "a

stagnant tide" as in one of his lakes (7.91), and in 1847
"Ulalume" presents a "dim lake" and the "dank tarn of Auber"
as its characterizing natural scenery (7.102). In "Annabel Lee"
of 1849, Poe's last year, the wind that "chills and kills" Annabel
seems to come from the sea, on whose shore the speaker builds
the sepulchre (7.117–118). It seems to me that these allusions
serve to present the sea as generally cold and dangerously
violent, the lake as lifeless and melancholy, and the river as
freely flowing and useful to life.

Poe's fiction, I believe, makes the point even more clearly.
In his mind the reader can quickly catalogue the short stories
according to these three themes. The first is "Ms. Found in a
Bottle," which was one of the "Tales of the Folio Club," offered
for a prize to the *Baltimore Saturday Visiter* of 1833. At the
beginning Poe describes an East Indian "simoom"—his error
for *typhoon*[6]—which hurls "a wilderness of foam" and water
upon an unwary ship and drowns or sweeps off everyone except the narrator and an old "Swede." After five days of
miraculous speeding directly south, they are completely
wrecked in a "supernatural sea" by a weird black boat, full-
rigged, which crashes into their hull; it proceeds with the
narrator fortuitously on board. This Flying Dutchman tale,
compounded of old legends and the *Ancient Mariner*, ends
when a polar whirlpool engulfs the vessel, leaving behind the
narrator's manuscript in a bottle. The entire story describes the
menace of the waves, the war of wind and ocean, and the
horrors of the polar ice. It is obviously a preliminary study for
the strange *Narrative of Arthur Gordon Pym,* part of which
was serialized in the *Messenger* of 1837 before it appeared as
a book in 1838. Here Poe adds the violent outrage of sea-going
man to that of marine nature, including a villainous crew that
butchers the officers and their loyal following, maroons the
captain, and ultimately destroys even itself. The island aborig-
ines pretend to be ingenuous and affable while harboring
beastly plans of slaughter.[7] The sea provides additional horrors
of parching heat and vicious sharks. Finally, as in the shorter

tale, the narrator and his single companion, Peters, with the native Nu-Nu set out into the Antarctic Ocean in a fifty-foot canoe; their trip ends when in warm and luminous water, before a mysterious cataract, they encounter a giant white human figure.

Written perhaps as early as 1833, although published only in 1841, was "A Descent into the Maelstrom," with many elements of the hostile sea which echo those of the other two narratives.[8] In this masterpiece the dangerous Norwegian current is rendered more deadly by a terrible hurricane that increases the force of the rising whirlpool and engulfs the boat of the fishermen after a faulty watch has led them to miscalculate the ebb and flow of the "Ström." The wily survivor, who has cast himself overboard on a barrel, sees his brother sink with the boat into the funnel-shaped water trap, to be battered by the rocks below the surface. The horror of this nautical experience turns the fisherman's hair white and evokes a shiver of sympathy from the most sophisticated reader.

Far different in tone and intention is Poe's early grotesque tale "King Pest: A Tale Containing an Allegory," dating from the September, 1835 *Southern Literary Messenger*. It is full of references which show clearly the association of death and the sea. Two seamen, lanky Legs and short Hugh Tarpaulin, of the schooner *Free and Easy*, flee from The Jolly Tar tavern, without paying their reckoning, into the plague district of medieval London. They take refuge in the wine cellar beneath an undertaker's shop, where six weird survivors of the plague are conducting a bacchanal. Finally a "fatal hogshead" is overturned and inundates the room, much like a great sea wave pouring into a ship's hold. Some revelers are drowned and one floats away in a coffin. Earlier in the story, Poe provides the following dialogue: Says the host, King Pest the First, "We are here this night . . . to examine, analyze, and thoroughly determine the . . . wines . . . and by so doing to advance not more our own designs than the true welfare of that unearthly sovereign whose reign is over us all, whose dominions are

unlimited, and whose name is 'Death.' "[9] To this Hugh Tarpaulin adds, "Whose name is Davy Jones," while he pours out
a "skull of liqueur" for himself (Harrison, 2.180). Evidently
for Poe death is intimately connected with the sea.

This same association occurs later in "The Oblong Box,"
published in *Godey's Lady's Book* of September, 1844. The
plot is grotesque but ingenious, preserving a mystery for the
narrator and the readers until the end. Only then do we discover that the young artist, Cornelius Wyatt, in a large box
had kept the body of his recently deceased wife, which he was
trying to convey home to New York from Charleston without
agitating the passengers. The Captain alone, knowing about
the salt-packed corpse, understands the strange conduct of the
young man. When the ship founders in a storm, Wyatt, seeking
to rescue the box, throws himself into the waves strapped to
the coffin, which immediately sinks. The hurricane wrecks the
ship off Cape Hatteras, and the jolly boat brings the survivors to safety at Ocracoke Inlet three days later (Harrison,
5.284–285).

These same two locations (near which Poe spent the year
1828–29 as a soldier on Fort Moultrie) are oddly although
indirectly connected with the very last story that Poe wrote:
"The Light-House," also implicitly about a deadly storm at sea.
It is an unfinished tale, which remained unpublished during
the nineteenth century, preserved on four sheets of manuscript
paper.[10] The fragment seems to stress the lighthouse-keeper's
diary, his large dog, and the vulnerability of the lighthouse,
180 feet high but with a "hollow interior at the bottom," which
is "twenty feet below the surface of the sea"; the whole is built
on a "chalk" island. The cellarage feature goes counter to the
standard accounts of lighthouses that Poe must have seen, such
as that of the famous Eddystone lighthouse, which was twice
demolished (1703 and 1799).[11] As for the shoals off the coast
of South Carolina, with which he was familiar, as early as 1798
there were lighthouses on Ocracoke Inlet and at Hatteras.[12]
A secure one was finally established in 1870, by odd coinci-

dence corresponding to Poe's putative building in "The Light-House."[13] Poe's "hollow interior," although in rock, suggests the futile attempts to sink a caisson in the outer Diamond Shoal off Cape Hatteras.[14] The problem of ensuring safety in coastal or rock-strewn waters apparently seemed important to Poe, for in the *Broadway Journal* of March 22, 1845, he is the probable author of the comment on H. L. Raymond's "able article on our light-house system . . . the most important one in the magazine. The subject is very justly handled, and the improprieties of our system forcibly exposed" (*BJ*, 1.183). In August Poe also noted the erection of a lighthouse on the Goodwin Sands (*BJ*, 2.11). I suspect that Poe's attention was directed in 1848 or 1849 to the subject of lighthouses again through the widespread interest in the new screw-pile type of construction, devised by Alexander Mitchell, with examples being built just then in Delaware Bay and on Minot's Ledge off Boston Harbor.[15] The story itself shows Poe's characteristic handling of scientific details for narrative purposes and also his interest in the predominantly hostile nature of the sea.

Far different is the lake setting of "The Fall of the House of Usher" of 1839, a silent tarn, whence comes "a pestilent and mystic vapor." This symbolizes the decadent atmosphere within Roderick's mouldy castle with its hints of incest, murder, and sadism. (The word *tarn* may have crept into Poe's works from its use by Coleridge, one of his favorite poets,[16] in "Christabel" [line 306] or in "Dejection: An Ode" [line 100].) The "black and lurid tarn" is what strikes the narrator of "The Fall of . . . Usher" when first he views the entire scene. At the end he flees across the causeway, after seeing Roderick's sister, bloody from the struggle to escape from her tomb, bear down in her death agonies the last of the House of Usher. He watches the fissure in the building widen to a distintegrating gap which sends the castle into "the deep and dank tarn" at his feet.

A curiously melancholy lake occurs in an earlier tale (1835), the long balloon hoax of "Hans Pfaall," purporting to be the

journal of a Rotterdam artisan who learned the equivalent of
aeronautics, made a trip to the moon, and then sent home his
journal via a moon dweller. The piece was a somewhat grotesque study for Poe's "Balloon Hoax" of April 13, 1844. Only
one vivid passage need occupy our attention. As the aeronaut
approached the moon his "fancy revelled in the wild and
dreamy regions of the moon. Imagination . . . roamed at will.
. . . Then I came suddenly into still noonday solitudes, where
no wind of heaven ever intruded. . . . Then again I journeyed
far down away into another country where it was all one dim
and vague lake, with a boundary line of clouds. . . . And out of
this melancholy water arose a forest of tall eastern trees, like a
wilderness of dreams." As the trees sink into the water and mix
with their shadows, the narrator thinks: "This, then, is the very
reason why the waters of this lake grow blacker with age, and
more melancholy as the hours run on."[17] Then, he resolutely
puts "appalling horrors" out of his mind.

Even earlier than "Hans Pfaall," although first published in
the *Baltimore Book* of 1839, was Poe's odd "fable" first called
"Siope" but published as "Silence: A Fable." This had been
included among the "Tales of the Folio Club" of 1833.[18] It is
worth mentioning here only because the entire setting is oddly
reminiscent of the dream sequence in "Hans Pfaall." As if to
confirm this relationship Poe excluded from his 1840 reprint
of the *Tales* a passage which specifically relates the scene to
"one of those vigorous dreams which come like the Simoom
upon the brain of the sleeper . . . among the forbidden sun-
beams . . . which slide from off the solemn columns of the
melancholy temples in the wilderness" (Harrison, 2.380). The
fable takes place "in a dreary region in Libya, by the borders
of the River Zäire," the old name of the river Congo.[19] There
are many links between the lake in "Hans Pfaall" and the
whole dreary atmosphere of this mood piece. Here Poe is really
talking about a lake, almost an inland sea like the Dead Sea,
for perversely and unnaturally the waters "flow not onwards
to the sea, but palpitate . . . with a tumultuous and convulsive

motion. For many miles on either side of the river's oozy bed is a pale desert of gigantic water-lilies. . . . And I stood in the morass among the tall lilies" (2.220–221).

More direct evidence is provided by "The Island of the Fay," published in *Graham's* in June, 1841, which is generally assumed to reflect Poe's excursions into the Ragged Mountains near Charlottesville. It is usually overlooked that the major part of this sketch is a description by Poe of one of the plates, engraved by John Sartain from an original by John Martin.[20] Here Poe speaks of a bosky island in a small lake surrounded by "trees dark in color and mournful in form and attitude, wreathing themselves into sad, solemn, and spectral shapes that conveyed ideas of mortal sorrow and untimely death." A tiny boat is being paddled by a woman, whom Poe imagines to be a fairy, representing the cycle of the years—a last survivor of her race and a symbol of all life, drawing closer to death with each circumnavigation of the island. It is impossible to disregard Poe's faylike wife, Virginia, who at this time was showing unmistakable signs of her fatal consumption.

The theme of the fairy dying in a watery setting was again exploited by Poe in "Eleonora," written also during that critical year of 1841, when he occasionally took his stricken wife on outings up the Susquehanna and its tributary, the Wissahickon. His use of river scenery in this tale well illustrates his characteristic attitude of pleasure in running water—living water, as the French would have it. By stressing the beauty of the river valley, he develops the lovely and idyllic relationship of the narrator and Eleonora, significantly in the tale his junior by five years and also his cousin. Through their paradise runs a river "narrow and deep" and so clear that they can see "the pearly pebbles." It produces soft grass and radiant and odoriferous flowers, as well as fantastic tall trees. But when she is fifteen and they have "drawn the God Eros from that wave," she speaks only of the end of humanity and of herself—a kind of *Liebestod*. The author promises never to marry after her death, an event which strips the valley of its natural charm and

causes him to leave for a strange city. There he marries Ermengarde and is visited by the forgiving spirit of Eleonora (for
treatment, see chap. iii).

George Woodberry aptly pointed out that a passage from
"Eleonora" echoes one in the "Journal of Julius Rodman,"[21] the
unfinished story of an expedition of 1792 up the Missouri
River, which Poe almost compiled, one might say, from many
travel accounts by Zebulon Pike, Lewis and Clarke, Captain
Bonneville via Irving, and Alexander Mackenzie. These date
from the next two decades, of course, but Poe's six installments,
May–June, 1840, in *Burton's Gentleman's Magazine* were
presented as being entirely authentic. As Quinn comments,
Rodman-Poe is at times rhapsodic and uniformly praises the
river scenery (*Poe*, p. 293). The implicit primitivism of "The
Journal of Julius Rodman" has a correspondence with one
passage in "The Colloquy of Monos and Una," printed in
Graham's Magazine, August, 1841. The two souls of the title
are discussing not only their own death but also "Earth's dotage" and that "ruin" which was "the price of highest civilization." By contrast, men knew "happiness" during those "holy,
august and blissful days, when blue rivers ran undammed . . .
into far forest solitudes, primaeval, odorous, and unexplored"
(Harrison, 4.200–212).

Another prose piece of this middle period parallels "Eleonora" in its river valley source of inspiration. I refer to his
sketch of 1844 at first entitled "Morning on the Wissahiccon"
and later "The Elk." This short composition was first printed
in the annual *The Opal*, with a full-page illustration of an elk
in reference to its rather gratuitous and irrelevant ending. Poe
first discusses the major attractions of America, among which
he lists such river views as the Hudson, Niagara, Harper's
Ferry, the Ohio, and the Mississippi, all worthy of a visit from
a foreigner who has seen the "arrowy Rhone." This is a slight
topographical indication of Poe's support of American prod-
ucts which was to link him to the "Young America" movement,
so prominent in the *Broadway Journal* of 1845.[22] In "The Elk"

he indicates the river valley of "Louisiana" as one of our Edens and speaks in favor of fine river landscapes that can be visited on foot. "River scenery has, unquestionably, within itself, all the main elements of beauty, and time out of mind, has been the favourite theme of the poet."[23] This is indeed Poe's credo. Now he wishes to hymn a rivulet, the Wissahickon (modern spelling), which empties into the Schuylkill, about six miles west of Philadelphia. The unusual loveliness, he says, had been pointed out by Fanny Kemble in her *Journal* of 1833–34 (published in 1835), which Poe had reviewed and publicized in the *Southern Literary Messenger* of August and December, 1835, and February, 1836. In the sketch Poe gives the reader specific directions for reaching the small stream with its picturesque gorge and varied picnic spots, either by taking a skiff or by "clambering along the banks." He describes its "pellucid water," lolling "in gentle flow," with "richly herbaged land" breaking up the steep banks and the dense foliage.[24] He has seen it, recently, from a skiff at midday, when he imagined that he saw an elk, relic of days of yore, on top of a cliff, but it proved to be a tame animal belonging to a nearby villa. The piece has been highly praised by Quinn and Hervey Allen for its idyllic qualities; it is assumed to reflect his rambles with Henry Hirst, author of *The Coming of the Mammoth*,[25] and with the eccentric novelist and Rosicrucian, George Lippard.[26] Quinn also thinks that it recalls picnics with Virginia during her intervals of tranquil health.

I must mention that most of the elements described in "The Elk" can also be found in a sketch on the Wissahickon "by a Philadelphian," which Poe as editor had undertaken to publish in the *Messenger* of December, 1835. The earlier article, by B. Matthias, provides several striking coincidences of details.[27] For example, in one paragraph of the earlier piece we find a noisy "laboring mill," the "desolating depredations and officious interference of the march of civilization," occasional "pic-nic parties," a reminder of the long vanished "Indians on the summit of this very hill"—but the "savage no longer strolls" and "the active deer no longer bounds." This becomes in Poe, I believe, "My imagination revelled in visions of . . . the 'good old days' when the Demon of the Engine was not, when picnics were undreamed of, when 'water privileges' were neither bought nor sold, and when the red man trod alone, with the elk, upon the ridges" (Harrison, 5.161). I suspect that the elk seen at the end is a pure figment of Poe's imagination and not a pet from the Spring Bank Asylum on the Wissahickon, traced by Quinn through Weygandt and other historians of the locality.[28] Poe was not disregarding his personal memories of rambles and boating up the stream; but a man with so absorptive a memory could, perhaps unconsciously, utilize remembered details from the writings of others to organize and even express his own observations, especially under the grim demands of datelines.

Another tale with flowing water as part of the setting was soon published in *Godey's Lady's Book,* April, 1844. Here too is an admixture of personal experience woven into a context closely derived from Poe's reading and imagination. More ingenious and narrative than "The Elk" is "A Tale of the Ragged Mountains." Set near Charlottesville, the tale is assumed to derive from his college-period ramblings, like "The Island of the Fay." Although he describes the mountain ravines with some pleasure, no river is mentioned until the hallucinatory aspects of the tale are developed. Then the narrator finds himself in India, where at first he is soothed by a spring of water and next delighted by the vista of an oriental city bordering a "majestic river." He describes the colorful temples on the streets sloping to the water and the bathing places along the bank and even the solitary "graceful maiden," going to fill her pitcher. At last he beholds a grim attack on "a gay palace, that overhung the river" with a keen interest that ends when a poisoned arrow strikes him on the temple. Eventually Oldeb, the narrator, dies from a poisonous leech, applied to his temple, a fate like that of his double of palindromic similarity, Bedloe. Many details, of course, come right out of Macaulay's essay on Warren Hastings (see chapter ii), but Poe enhances the river, which he calls "gently-flowing" and "magnificent" (Harrison, 5.169–170).

There are three somewhat equivocal river allusions in three of Poe's tales of different periods. The earliest, "Four Beasts in One," published in the March, 1836 *Messenger* but dating from 1833, has a reference to the real Syrian river, the Orontes; the tale accurately mentions its being "rapid" and having innumerable falls before it comes to the plain of Antioch, scene of this "Tale of Jerusalem," as it was formerly and somewhat inaccurately called. Given the chosen *mise-en-scène*, Poe's use of the river here shows no basic attitude. Similarly innocent of "tendency" is Poe's use of the James River as setting for "The Premature Burial," when he mistakes the berth of the sloop for a coffin (Harrison, 5.272–273). In "The Mystery of Marie Rogêt," published in 1842, Poe's many references to the river Seine might appear at first to indicate another viewpoint. Poe had drawn a parallel, through his many footnotes, between the murder of Marie, a young Parisienne, and the real slaying of Mary Cecilia Rogers of New York, August, 1841. The Hudson River and its environs, where she was last seen and her corpse found, are equated with the Seine. A gruesomely detailed passage tells how long cadavers will float or remain submerged and how soon they will decompose (5.25–27). Yet Poe is not inventing a menacing or dangerous river setting, but simply using an instrument for his plot borrowed from the original account. I attach some slight significance to his gratuitous presentation of loathsome details of drowning. Poe was peculiarly fascinated by this type of death, as "The Pit and the Pendulum" shows. Minor evidence of Poe's antipathy for the sea may be found in his stressing one small alleged clue in the original murder account and clinging to it as reality years later. The man who was the last person seen with Mary Rogers appeared to be a naval officer (Quinn, p. 358). In Poe's tale this became the "sailor's knot" (5.11), and all signs "point to a seaman" as the murderer (5.60). Even in 1848 he wrote to

Eveleth: "The 'naval officer' who committed the murder (or rather the accidental death arising from an attempt at abortion) *confesse*d it."[29] This follows his footnote in the 1845 edition of the story in his *Tales* (Harrison, 5.1). It was either a slight hoax on Poe's part or an indication of his belief that unexplained deaths are likely to be produced by seamen if not by the sea.[30]

"The Landscape Garden" in the *Ladies' Companion* of October, 1842, is a preparatory study leading to the most completely developed treatment of the loveliness of river scenery. Here Poe, chronically impecunious himself, presents us with young Ellison, inheritor of a fabulous income, which enables him to reshape a vast natural setting, grandly but artistically. In 1847, Poe again took up the unfinished task of Mr. Ellison in "The Domain of Arnheim," published in the March issue of the *Columbian Lady's and Gentleman's Magazine*. After four years of searching for a site for his new Fonthill, the millionaire finds an ideal tableland, traversed by a river. The approach—a gorge with pellucid water—shares elements with the gorge of the Wissahickon. As in "Eleonora," there are delightful alabaster pebbles and rich vegetation, ever more luxuriant as the river widens between the gentle slopes. A lavish imagination and purse richly vary the entire landscape; this is indeed "the playful maziness of art," mentioned in Poe's 1827 "To the River."

The imaginary idyll beside the stream still needed one more element—a female presence. Two years later and four months before his death, in the *Flag of Our Union* of June 9, 1849, Poe published "Landor's Cottage, a Pendant to 'The Domain of Arnheim'" as he called it. Now he moves Ellison's domain —and entirely removes Ellison—from its original location, vaguely Monticello plus Philadelphia, to one of the "river counties of New York." Different memories are fused together in this document from a rather chaotic period in Poe's life, for he speaks of a "Virginia mountain wagon" and of "velvet grass" such as "we seldom see out of England." The girl Eleonora of his early river tale is transformed into Annie, that is, Mrs. Annie Richmond, one of the several ladies being courted at this time, while Landor's cottage is clearly now the Fordham cottage of Poe. The approach has become a carefully constructed, "pittoresque," infinitely varied river route. Poe borders the valley with precipitous granite cliffs, like those of the Wissahickon, and gentle, carefully tailored slopes. The profuse vegetation includes trees that never could survive in the Hudson region, and inevitably Poe devotes space to the clear, pebble-strewn rivulet, bubbling its way past the cottage. The details make us certain that the unseen person who calls, "Annie, darling," from the interior will turn out to be Muddy Clemm. Nor do we have any need for the proposed sequel to glean "some particulars of Mr. Landor himself," Mr. Landor-Poe, so soon to be at rest in Baltimore.[31]

Many supporting suggestions and statements about the theme could be drawn from Poe's large body of criticism and literary theory. Perhaps one will suffice—his review of *Passaic, a Group of Poems, touching that river, with other musings* by Flaccus (or Thomas Ward), published in *Graham's Magazine* of March, 1843 (20.195–198; Harrison, 11.160–174). First Poe quotes "an entire page of even remarkable beauty," from which I select a few lines: "Beautiful Rivers! that adown the vale / With graceful passage journey to the deep / . . . yes, from your birth / Has beauty's shadow chased your every step: / . . . From deep mysterious wanderings your springs / Break bubbling into beauty" (11.161–162). But Poe is dissatisfied with what follows after "so fine a beginning." Flaccus, then, "instead of confining himself to the true poetical thesis, the Beauty or the Sublimity of river scenery, . . . descends into mere meteorology" (11.163).

I should now like to correlate Poe's treatment of waterscapes with two areas of inquiry: the background experiences inclining him toward this type of emphasis and the manifestations of partiality toward rivers in his own life. As a boy in Richmond, Virginia, from 1811 to 1815, and upon his return from

England in 1820, up to 1826, Poe must have had many agreeable experiences on the broad James River. Pleasure boats used the river and numerous commercial vessels came up to Richmond to discharge their cargoes and load up with Virginia goods. Agnes Bondurant in *Poe's Richmond* and Hervey Allen in *Israfel* give a good picture of what the river meant, first to the small child and then to the adventurous youth ripened into a young sportsman by English games and standards.[32] We know about his boating along the river and swimming for six miles against what he calls "one of the strongest tides ever known in the river" (Ostrom, 1.57). Poe compared himself in swimming prowess with Byron, asserting his superiority over his early poetic idol. A clear, flowing river must always seem more attractive to a good swimmer than a weed-grown stagnant lake. But, of course, this is no explanation. One broad factor must have been Poe's opportunities to observe various types of streams as well as the ocean in all its moods. We can authenticate the unpleasantness of his voyage to England, June 22 to July 28, 1815, from the letters of the Allan family (Quinn, pp. 64–65). The sea was rough and the niggardly captain kept them inadequately supplied with essentials.

Once in Scotland in August, Poe seems to have stayed for an undetermined period in Irvine with John Allan's sisters, Mary and Jane.[33] It is by no means certain that he went to the old Kirkgate school in this seaport on the river, with picturesque stone houses and a bridge celebrated even then.[34] Local history, of course, is firm in this matter and also records a family sailing trip to the island of Arran where Poe, it is said, saw a "tarn" to be used in "The Lake."[35] Perhaps Poe's reference to Ben Nevis in western Scotland (Harrison, 2.170) may be a trace of a trip up from Oban to the head of Loch Linnhe, to see the highest British peak. By the end of September, Edgar was accompanying the Allans to London, via Glasgow, Edinburgh, and Newcastle; according to Hervey Allen much of the approach was by a sea voyage that provided "notable scenery."[36]

He was back in Richmond, Virginia, in 1820 to continue his pleasant "riverside" life. In 1825 he moved with the Allan family to their new home, Moldavia; there he occupied a northeast corner room from which he had a panoramic view of the river down the hill. During 1826, while a student at the University of Virginia, he engaged in rambles through the valley of the Rivanna River, which Quinn finds reflected in portions of *Tamerlane* (*Poe*, p. 98) and which we have also found in two tales, "The Island of the Fay" and "Tale of the Ragged Mountains." In Richmond again after his quarrel with Allan over debts incurred at college, Poe chose to work his way by ship to Boston, under the pseudonym of Henri Le Rennet, and enlisted as Edgar A. Perry. (It must be borne in mind that even after the advent of the railroad, much ordinary travel would proceed via shipboard on the ocean, rivers, and canals.)

From Boston harbor "Edgar A. Perry," on November 8, 1827, sailed aboard the *Waltham* for a ten-day trip to Fort Moultrie on Sullivan's Island, South Carolina. This was to form the setting for "The Gold-Bug" and the terminus for the voyage in "The Balloon-Hoax." Poe's biographers generally ignore the storminess of this November passage. Only Henry Campbell Davis in his "Poe's Company Tempest-Tossed" has paid attention to the freezing gales during the early part of the trip, which caused the *Waltham's* officers to tender a printed card of thanks to Captain Webb for "his nautical abilities . . . in extricating the vessel . . . from most imminent danger."[37] Hervey Allen gives the best account of the subtropical oceanic atmosphere which surrounded Poe from 1827 until his transfer in December, 1828, to Fortress Monroe, Virginia, but he treats it rather as an idyllic period of rambles and relaxation in an army resort area; omitted are the hurricanes which Poe included, for fatal effect, in "The Oblong Box" and, by implication, in "The Lighthouse."[38] While serving in Virginia he was promoted to the rank of sergeant major and was honorably discharged on April 15, 1829. His appointment to West Point came in March, 1830.

In June, 1830, he was living in the academy on the Hudson, at that noble river's most spectacular stretch. His enchantment was indicated in a letter of November 6, 1830, to John Allan, who had recently been in New York without seeing Edgar: "I was indeed very much in hopes that the beauty of the river would have tempted yourself and Mr and Mrs Jas Galt to have paid us a visit" (Ostrom, 1.39). Clearly, to Poe this river had become one of the "lions," worthy of a tourist visit. Yet the discipline and general atmosphere of West Point became stultifying to the young poet, who contrived his own court martial and dismissal in February, 1831.

Not long afterwards, he had recourse to the home of his aunt, Maria Clemm, in Baltimore. The city is situated on the Patapsco River, where it enters Chesapeake Bay amid "romantic scenery," as Washington Irving called it.[39] Certainly Poe could indulge his riparian proclivities during this obscure period of his life, before his return to Richmond in 1835 to edit the *Messenger*. He settled in Richmond for two years, married to Virginia with Mother Clemm keeping house. Early in 1837 we find the family removed to New York, where Poe managed to complete his sea tale of Arthur Gordon Pym and very little else. The shift to Philadelphia in the summer of 1838 marked the beginning of his most creative period. In that city Poe's varied residences included a little house on Coates Street near the present Fairmont Park, which is bounded by the Schuylkill on one side. It is across from the famous reservoir which was to figure in one of Poe's last ramblings in 1849. I have cited Horace Wemyss Smith previously for evidence of Poe's frequent visits to the old Smith homestead where he used to read or gaze out over the river scene, near the Wissahickon.

The Poe-Clemm family returned, in 1844, to New York City on shipboard from Perth Amboy, the cheapest route possible. Poe found a succession of dwelling places for the ailing Virginia and her mother. Many of them had river views, probably to provide purer air for his wife's weak lungs and to indulge his partiality. The house at 130 Greenwich Street then had a clear prospect of the Hudson. After other changes of residence, he took rooms in the Brennan farmstead, at about 84th Street in the Bloomingdale section of Manhattan. A large storage room in the attic with windows looking out on the slopes descending to the Hudson provided an ideal view for the artist at work. (The prominence of the site had induced General Washington to make his headquarters in that very building.) Closer to the water's edge was a high rock, known as Mount Tom, on which "Poe would often sit, write, and dream." Sometimes he would go down to the river, accompanied by a few of the ten Brennan children.[40] Despite the beauty of the location, late in 1844 he moved his family to the more convenient No. 15 Amity Street, to escape the cold of the winter in the Bloomingdale country-side and to put him into closer touch with journalist circles.[41]

Early in 1846 the Poes spent a brief period in a dwelling at the foot of East 47 Street, in the Turtle Bay area, again for Virginia's benefit.[42] During this period he often rambled along the East River shores of Manhattan, whose conversion from forest and meadow to residences and commercial buildings he lamented in *Doings of Gotham*.[43] When he moved out into West Chester County, to Fordham, now in the Bronx section of the city, he seemed far from water perhaps, save in Landor's imagination, as we have seen. Yet from a nearby ledge he could see beyond the meadows and even the distant East River over to the Long Island Hills. Thanks to Mrs. Whitman, there is vividly preserved for us Poe's view of another river prospect, that of the Harlem:

> At Fordham a walk to High Bridge was one of his favourite and habitual recreations. The water of the Aqueduct is conveyed across the river on a range of lofty granite arches. . . . On the top a turfed and grassy road, used only by foot-passengers . . . makes one of the finest promenades imaginable [showing] the winding river and the high rocky shores at the western extremity of the bridge. . . .[44]

Virginia died in the Fordham cottage on January 30, 1847, and after this Poe's life became a constant search for the ade-

quate income and the ideal woman, the two in one if possible.
He can be followed, biographically, up to Boston for lectures
and visits to Mrs. Annie Richmond; to Richmond, Virginia, for
lectures and visits to Elmira Royster, now the widow Shelton;
and to Providence, where he almost married the widow Mrs.
Sarah Whitman. One visit was to John Sartain, the engraver
of "The Island of the Fay." Sartain, now a magazine publisher,
had bought "Annabel Lee," which he issued in 1850, although
he was not the earliest to publish it. Poe had embarked by
steamboat from Brooklyn for Richmond but stopped at Philadelphia for business on July 2nd or 9th, 1849. While there he
yielded once again to taking the "one drink too many" and
threw himself upon Sartain's hospitality in a state of terror or
dementia and without any of his luggage. He begged Sartain
to take him to the Schuylkill River; wearing the engraver's
slippers, he accompanied Sartain in an omnibus along the river
to his old strolling-haunt, the Fairmont area. On a bridge
overlooking the stream and the reservoir, Poe told a lurid tale—
probably false—about his recent imprisonment for drunkenness and about a radiant dream figure, very like Virginia. He
spent several days in Philadelphia, during which he was aided
by old friends such as Lippard and Charles Chauncey Burr,
before proceeding to Richmond.[45] Several months later, after
lecturing and wooing, he was returning to Philadelphia, probably by boat, and inexplicably found his way to Baltimore
and to death, early in October, 1849. In his alleged last words
some biographers find traces of a "phantom ship" bearing
him into darkness.[46]

I have made no assumption about fundamental or psychological causes for attitudes implicit in Poe's waterscapes.
Certainly it would be misleading to offer an explanatory motivation that would require one to select and emphasize only a
few of the many instances[47] or that would reduce the varied
work of this complex and extremely mutable author to a single
pattern, misleading in its simplicity.[48] Poe was one of the many

who like the possibilities for change, for movement, and also for mere drifting—if only in imagination—provided by a stream which can carry voyagers away from the intolerable present. Not for him the monotonous and sometimes violent stretches of ocean or the unfathomable depths of the lake. The clear waters of the running stream were the ideal scene for Poe; and, on occasion, in his poetry and his prose, if not in his life, they carried him to brilliant success.

10

POE IN "VON KEMPELEN AND HIS DISCOVERY"

"VON KEMPELEN AND His Discovery" represents the culmination of Poe's efforts in the field of the literary hoax. Written and published during 1849, his last year of life, it contains many themes and references of the utmost significance in his emotional and intellectual career. Yet, it has been studied perhaps the least of his tales and has received almost no critical attention.[1] It should be rewarding, therefore, to trace the origin of this story of gold-seeking—a subject which inspired his "Gold Bug" and probably his last poem, "Eldorado."[2] Gold-seeking is a theme which symbolizes Poe's life-long difficulty in adjusting to ordinary economic realities and to the need for distinctions between the mystic world of dream fulfillment and that of practical necessity.

The hoax was apparently motivated by Poe's awareness of the frenzied rush to California for gold, 1848–49. Poe had set himself the goal of procuring funds to start the "Stylus," but, as always, was distraught by the need for providing basic essentials for himself and Mother Clemm. His letter of January 21 (?), 1849, to Annie L. Richmond, written "in all my adversity," pointedly remarks: "I am beginning to grow wiser, and do not care so much as I did for the opinions of a world in which I see, with my own eyes, that to act generously is to be considered as designing, and that to be poor is to be a villain. I must get rich—rich. Then all will go well—but *until* then I must submit to be abused."[3]

On February 14, 1849, he was to write to Frederick W. Thomas, the editor of the *Louisville Chronicle:* "I shall be a *littérateur,* at least, all my life; nor would I abandon the hopes which still lead me on for all the gold in California."[4] Poe placed considerable hope in this, the last of his hoax-tales, if we may judge from the letter which he wrote to Duyckinck a month later, March 8, 1849, asking him to print it in the highly reputed *Literary World.* (It was actually published by the far less celebrated but more responsive *Flag of Our Union,* of Boston, on April 14, 1849, with "Eldorado" following it, on April 21.) Part of Poe's letter to Duyckinck gives insight into his intentions:

> I mean it as kind of "exercise," or experiment, in the plausible or verisimilar style. Of course, there is *not one* word of truth in it from beginning to end. I thought that such a style, applied to the gold-excitement, could not fail to effect. My sincere opinion is that nine persons out of ten (even among the best-informed) will *believe* the quiz (provided the design does not leak out before publication) and that thus, acting as a sudden, although of course a very temporary, *check* to the gold-fever, it will create a *stir* to some purpose. . . . I believe the quiz is the first deliberate literary attempt of the kind of record. . . . In my "Valdemar Case" (which *was* credited by many) I had not the slightest idea that any person should credit it as a thing more than a "Magazine-paper"—but here the whole strength is laid out in verisimilitude. [Ostrom, 2.433]

Poe had always shown a leaning toward "diddling" or fooling the public; Since "man is an animal that diddles,"[5] the literary man and the magazinist must diddle via his tales.

In June 1835, Poe had published the hoax tale "The Unparalleled Adventure of One Hans Pfaall," full of details to give verisimilitude. Poe delved ardently into other sources in search of these facts, and thus was able to sidetrack the reader away from the main source of his story.[6] Invariably, he seems to enjoy teasing the reader with hints of his real sources, dropping here a name, there a title, as if to savor his triumphant deception through having left so many ungathered clues.[7]

Even earlier, in the *Baltimore Saturday Visiter* of October 12, 1833, Poe had published the first of his tales of sea horror, "Ms. Found in a Bottle," conceived entirely in the spirit of the hoax. Similar was the *Narrative of Arthur Gordon Pym of Nantucket,* which was issued as a book, in 1838, "edited" by Poe. In *Pym* the hoax is a double one, for the account is a literary invention and contains long passages borrowed from other sources without acknowledgment.[8]

When Poe returned to New York, he was ready for a full-blown, well-publicized deception, intended to raise his credit and make his fortune. He soon arranged to publish, in the *New York Sun* of April 13, 1844, a documentary tale, disguised as a news account, which has come to be known as "The Balloon-Hoax." It was issued with the cooperation of the sympathetic editor, Richard Adams Locke (Harrison, 15.126–137). The broadside or "Extra page," in the midday issue, as Poe tells it, was preceded by an early morning "Postscript." The full title helps to explicate Poe's particularity of method:

> Astounding News by Express, *via* Norfolk! The Atlantic Crossed in Three Days! Signal Triumph of Mr. Monck Mason's Flying Machine!—Arrival at Sullivan's Island, Near Charleston, S.C., of Mr. Mason, Mr. Robert Holland, Mr. Henson, Mr. Harrison Ainsworth, and four others, in the Steering Balloon, "Victoria," after a Passage of Seventy-Five Hours from Land to Land! Full Particulars of the Voyage! [Harrison, 5.224]

The "Postscript," reprinted by W. K. Wimsatt, Jr.,[9] who believes that Poe wrote it, shows the careful planning of the whole "jeu d'esprit," to use Poe's own words in his footnote added later (Harrison, 2.103). One wonders whether the editor knew that Poe filched over one-fourth the text of his tale from two pamphlets. The first was Thomas Monck Mason's *Account of the Late Aeronautical Expedition from London to Weilburg, Accompanied by Robert Holland, Esq., Monck Mason, Esq., and Charles Green, Aeronaut;*[10] the second, probably also by Mason, was entitled, *Remarks on the Ellipsoidal Balloon, pro-*

*pelled by the Archimedean Screw, described as the New Aerial
Machine* (London, 1843).[11]

A third area of literary hoaxing besides the sea tale and the
"airy" tale was that of mesmerism, a subject then popular
among the "prescientific" educated public of the western
world.[12] Poe's first major use of the topic was in the fantastic
dialogue between Mr. Vankirk and "P" (Poe), entitled "Mesmeric Revelation." It had five printings in 1844 and 1845 before
it was published by the London *Popular Record of Modern
Science* as a true document on November 29, 1845, entitled
"The Last Conversation of a Somnambule." The popularity
of the tale led Poe to write "The Facts in the Case of M. Valdemar," which appeared in the *American Review* of December,
1845. Poe was proud of the even greater acclaim granted this
story in dialogue. Whimsically Poe gives Valdemar the designation "M." for "Monsieur," although he lives in Harlem, New
York, and writes under the "nom de plume" of Issachar Marx.
Here we find the same startling presentation of oddly specific
and sometimes very plausible details as in "Von Kempelen and
His Discovery." Here too Poe garrulously states his intention
to present a clear view of the *"facts"* to counter the "garbled"
accounts circulating since "the year 1839" concerning Valdemar. Because of its verisimilitude and gruesome ending, involving the "putridity" of the awakened corpse, "Valdemar"
had success in England. There it was republished both as an
article in the *Morning Post* and as a pamphlet, "Mesmerism 'In
Articulo Mortis.' "[13] The stir over both these printings led to
the well-known letter about the "admired disorder" from Elizabeth Barrett Barrett (Ostrom, 2.318–320). When Poe decided
to write another hoax, demanded, he thought, by the gold rush,
he hoped for a similar reception from the public. A tale touching the purses of everyone should engender even more excitement than a tale of mesmerism.[14]

A summary of the tale will perhaps indicate why the public
was less apt to be easily gulled in this case. Since it is not well
known and I must treat of specific aspects, the order of its

items must first be given. In first referring to the treatment of the "discovery" by Arago, "Silliman's Journal," and Lieutenant Maury, Poe, as narrator, disclaims that he will attempt any scientific treatment of the subject; he intends merely to speak of Von Kempelen, who is a "slight personal acquaintance," and of the results of the process. In a long passage, he denies that the discovery is "unanticipated," finding hints in an apocryphal "Diary" by Sir Humphry Davy, for which he invents bibliographical data. However, he discredits an account in the *Courier and Enquirer* concerning an earlier "invention" by Mr. Kissam of Brunswick, Maine, and is somewhat amazed that the eminent "chemist" Professor Draper has deigned even to discuss Mr. Kissam's pretentions. Returning to Davy's "Diary," Poe quotes a sentence to prove that it was only a "rough notebook," intended to be burned. The quoted passage, plus others, says Poe, may have given Von Kempelen the hint for a discovery which may be a "service or disservice to mankind."

Next he speaks of an account in the *Home Journal,* taken from an original item in the Presburg "Schnellpost," translated with many errors, he says. This account has misled the *Literary World* into thinking Von Kempelen a native of Presburg.[15] Poe personally knows him, he says, and declares him to be from Utica, New York, of Presburg descent, his family having been "connected, in some way, with Maelzel." He inserts a putative editorial note, that the original inventor of the chess-player was a Von Kempelen. He then denies the charge that Von Kempelen is a "misanthrope" and mentions being a fellow resident at Earl's Hotel in Providence, Rhode Island, where Von Kempelen gave no evidence of his thaumaturgic capacities. The strange truth of this entire story, says Poe, is like the startling truth of the California "discoveries."

An account is now given of Kempelen's brush with the police officers of Bremen, where the transmutation was detected; their search of his rooms where he was caught in the deed; his destroying the crucibles and refusing to answer their questions; their finding a large trunk of pure gold; and their being unable to analyze a substance which, with lead and antimony, seems to constitute his "philosopher's stone" ingredients. Poe alludes to a report by Arago on the magic properties of bismuth. Finally, he speculates that the results of the "analysis" will affect migration to California. Meanwhile, in Europe the price of lead and of silver has risen considerably. Despite the "corroborating" details and, as we shall see, the importance and relevance of the proper names, it is, indeed, a "tired" kind of hoax, which defeats its purpose by presenting too much of the familiar from which readers could check on its authenticity. In the choice of these references, Poe reveals a large number of his deep-rooted attitudes and preoccupations.

Von Kempelen, the name of the discoverer, goes back to Poe's early study of "Maelzel's Chess-Player," of April, 1836. Poe's exposé has been beautifully exposed, in turn, by W. K. Wimsatt, Jr., as being entirely derived from Brewster's *Letters on Natural Magic*, a foreshadowing of the truth having been given by Woodberry.[16] Indeed, Poe's dependence upon Brewster's material in 1836 was so flagrant as to justify the belief that he intended it originally as a kind of hoax. The ignorance of the public and the failure of anyone to note the pretensions of his claim may then have led him to persist in presenting it as a piece of original ratiocination. At any rate, Poe knew very well that the inventor of the deceptive automaton, operated through a concealed player, was "Baron Von Kempelen," a "nobleman of Presburg in Hungary" (Harrison, 14.11, 12, 29, 35), where it was first exhibited before being taken to Paris, Vienna, and other cities; finally Maelzel bought it for exhibitions in Europe and the United States. The personality of Maelzel himself must have appealed strongly to Poe. For one thing, he turned several other ingenious devices into gold for himself, without any real claim to the originality that was imputed to him: the metronome, the principle of which he borrowed without authorization from Winkel of Amsterdam; and the Panharmonicum, which was sold in the United States for a fantastic sum.[17] Poe later lists Maelzel as an inventor of a

chess-player in "The Thousand and Second Tale of ScZehera-
zade" in the February, 1845, issue of *Godey's Lady's Book*.

In this tale of 1849 he uses Presburg as the erroneously
imputed origin of Von Kempelen. In itself this would have
been astute, since the city was once renowned as a center of
the study of the occult sciences. For the same reason, in
"Morella" (1835), Poe gave the enchantress a "Presburg education."[18] But this connection was too recherché and Poe provides
another, more significant reason for mentioning Presburg. He
speaks of a "brief account of Von Kempelen which appeared
in the 'Home Journal,' and has since been extensively copied;
Poe adds: "several misapprehensions of the German original
seem to have been made by the translator, who professes to
have taken the passage from a late number of the Presburg
'Schnellpost' " (6.248–249). The title *Schnellpost* is a key to one
of the sources of the whole tale and gives us insight into the
literary method entailed by the persistent memory of Poe. The
name, meaning "fast courier," had actually been used from
1826–1829 by the *Berliner Schnellpost für Literatur, Theatre
und Geselligkeit*. This journal may have been the source for
the title and format of a New York German-language semi-
weekly paper, started January 4, 1843, and continued, in various forms, into 1849. The New England *Dial* of January, 1844,
affirms its high quality, praising especially "the very well
selected paragraphs from all the German newspapers, com-
municating important news not found in any other American
papers, from the interior of the continent of Europe."[19]

Copies of this New York *Deutsche Schnellpost für Euro-
päische Zustände, öffentliches und sociales Leben Deutsch-
lands* came to the desk of Poe as associate editor of the
Broadway Journal. After he had wrested control of the magazine from Briggs, he began the issue of July 12, 1845, with a
message to the public: "The editorial conduct of 'The Broadway Journal' is under the sole charge of Edgar A. Poe—Mr. H.
C. Watson, as heretofore, controlling the Musical Department"

(*BJ*, 2.1). In this number he inserted four paragraphs translated from the *Schnellpost* with the following headnote:

> The publication or [*sic* for of] Alexander von Humboldt's "Cosmos," has engaged the attention of the most distinguished public writers in Germany. The late number of the "Deutsche Schnellpost" contains a critick [*sic*] of the work from Berlin, addressed to the editor of a newspaper in Cologne.
>
> The following is a true translation of it.—Eds. B. J.[20]

This is indeed taken from an article in the New York *Deutsche Schnellpost* of July 2, 1845.[21] Poe had been able to arrange for a very rapid translation of this eulogy of Humboldt's book. Later he dedicated *Eureka* to the scientist, "with very profound respect," and showered praise upon him in the work that Poe was confident would be his own major "poem."[22] The encomia lavished upon *Cosmos* by the Berlin correspondent may even have prodded Poe into making his own study of cosmology, as he implies in *Eureka* (Harrison, 16.186–187).

Poe could not forego mentioning once more a paper whose name gave a tone of cosmopolitanism to the *Broadway Journal;* on August 30 he includes a reference in his "Editorial Miscellany," uncollected by Harrison: "We forgot to say, last week, that the 'Schnell Post,' published in New-York, has, by a ministerial edict, been forbidden to be taken at the Cabinets de Lecture of Leipsic. The *exact* reason for the prohibition does not yet appear."[23] This tidbit of news must have come from the *Schnellpost* itself. Five years later he would use the name in his story of Von Kempelen, and just as the German paper brought him and his readers news of the cosmological "discoveries" of Humboldt, so the "Presburg Schnellpost" would bring word of Von Kempelen's discovery.

One of Poe's reasons for writing hoax tales was the sheer exuberant humor of his inventiveness, which frothed up into tales of magical flights and voyages but always with enough corroborative details to induce a hesitant acceptance—of part of the story at least. To supply these details Poe ransacked his richly laden memory, sometimes dropping no hint of the jokes that he gave out so freely to the public—jokes often unnoticed to this day. Several place names in "Von Kempelen" illustrate this. A single paragraph gives us three traceable bits of word play. In Bremen, "when the great excitement occurred about the forgery on the house of Gutsmuth and Co., suspicion was directed towards Von Kempelen, on account of his having purchased a considerable property in Gasperitch Lane, and his refusing, when questioned, to explain how he became possessed of the purchase money" (Harrison, 6.250). This corresponds to one of the "Marginalia" items, published in *Godey's Lady's Book*, August, 1845 (Harrison, 16.71). Significantly listing well-known geographers, Poe writes, apropos of John Henry Mancur's *The Palais Royal:* "Here is a book of 'amusing travels,' which is full enough of statistics to have been the joint composition of Messieurs Busching, Hassel, Cannabitch, Gaspari, Gutsmuth and company." Two of these writers of geography textbooks are used in "Von Kempelen" with changes. "Gutsmuth and company" becomes "Gutsmuth and Co." in the tale and Gaspari becomes "Gasperitch Lane." The first, in fact, was Poe's error for Johann Christoph F. Gutsmuths (1759–1838), whose fourteen works on geography and children's education are listed in Michaud's *Biographie Universelle*. Poe was under no obligation to be accurate about the name of "Gutsmuth and company" in the tale, nor did he have to preserve the spelling of the surname of Adam Christian Gaspari (1752–1830), when this German geographer and statistician becomes part of "Gasperitch Lane." But the unGermanic nature of Poe's spelling, "—itch," shows that the misspelling, in the above list, of the surname of Johann Gunther Friedrich Cannebich ("Cannebitch" in *Godey's*) springs from Poe's poor grasp of the German tongue.

Later, in the same paragraph of "Von Kempelen" Poe uses two other names of interest: Von Kempelen always gave "his

watchers the slip in the neighborhood of that labyrinth of narrow and crooked passages known by the flash-name of the
'Dondergat.'" Here we find Poe coining a new word; "flash-
name" seems not to exist independently. Since *flash* has so
many meanings, such as "of the lightning" and "sham" and
"quibbling," it seems appropriate for the word *Dondergat*—
literally "thunderpass or thunderchannel"—which combines
the German forepart with *gat* from the Old Norse, used as a
marine term in English. He had used the common *Donder* in
"The Devil in the Belfry" (1839), where it also provided a
humorous combination in "Dundergutz" (Harrison, 3.248).
The last place name in the paragraph is Poe's pure invention,
I believe. The seven-story building which houses Von Kempelen's aurific establishment is "in an alley called Flatzplatz,"
a name which Griswold seems to have altered in his edition
of the tale to "Flätplatz."[24] The whole is a "jeu d'esprit," for
the knowing readers, but Poe could scarcely have expected
many such; he seemed not to care greatly, since his mind threw
off these bubbles of humor so freely.

To make his hoax credible, however, Poe presents some
genuine scientific personalities, well known at that time
although a trifle obscure today. With at least one of them—
Draper—Poe was personally involved, and he was possibly
involved with Maury as well. Arago, i.e., François Arago, chief
savant and Perpetual Secretary of the Academy of Science in
France at the time, need not concern us long; his fame was
international and sound, as the seventeen volumes of his collected works could demonstrate. In his *Scientific Notice of
Comets,* translated into English in 1833, Poe may have found
a hint for his "Conversation of Eiros and Charmion," in which
he postulates a comet which has exhausted the air of nitrogen,
leading to the combustion of the world.[25]

Lieutenant Maury, as Poe terms him, the second scientist
mentioned at the beginning of the tale, was one of the pioneers
in the application of scientific knowledge to navigation. With
good reason two biographers call Matthew Fontaine Maury

"Pathfinder of the Seas."[26] At the time of the gold rush, Maury's name would naturally occur to Poe, since the use of his charts was cutting the travel time between New York and San Francisco from 150 to 133 days.[27] Much earlier Poe had reviewed for the June, 1836, *Southern Literary Messenger* Maury's work, *A New Theoretical and Practical Treatise on Navigation.* There is almost a coincidental symbolism in the conclusion of Poe's flattering review:

> We are pleased to see that science also is gaining votaries from its [the Navy's] ranks. Hitherto how little have they improved the golden opportunities of knowledge which their distant voyages held forth, and how little have they enjoyed the rich banquet which nature spreads for them in every clime they visit![28]

Soon after, Maury briefly became the superintendent of the Federal gold mine at Fredericksburg in 1836. Between 1838 and 1841 he won far-flung renown with a series of articles which decried the Navy Department's inefficiency.[29] Influential posts in Washington were given to him in 1842, a place as head of the Depot of Charts and Instruments, for example. Upon the death of Thomas W. White, he became editor of the *Messenger* for the first eight months of 1843. His major endeavor was to organize the vast body of information in old logbooks owned by the Navy Department for the benefit of mariners; thus in 1847, he published his *Wind and Current Chart of the North Atlantic* and, in 1848, the ten-page "Abstract Log for the Use of American Navigators."[30] The latter ingeniously offers a free copy of the 1847 book to navigators who put specified data into tightly corked bottles for later checking by Maury's office. The plan may well have been suggested by Poe's early "Ms. Found in a Bottle," of October 19, 1833, which was to be reprinted five times before 1848.[31] It is a resource also mentioned in the "Balloon-Hoax" (5.234). Although biographers of Poe have little to say about Maury, the two must have continued to be well aware of each other into 1849.[32]

The third name, that of Sir Humphry Davy (1778–1829), helped to lend authenticity to Poe's hoax, since no scientist in the English-speaking world was better known. In fact, Poe included a testimonial to his fame in the "Pinakidia" of the August, 1836 *Messenger*. Item 134 tells of the correct routing to Davy of a letter sent from Rome solely addressed "Alla sua Excellenza Seromfidevi" in London (Harrison, 14.64–65). Perhaps the reason for using his name was Davy's remark on gold-making which was added to one of the later editions of Isaac Disraeli's *Curiosities of Literature*, conspicuously placed at the end of the article on "Alchymy": "Sir Humphry Davy told me that he did not consider this undiscovered art an impossible thing but which, should it ever be discovered, would certainly be useless."[33] Poe could also have seen the same statement, quoted from this source, as a footnote to the first page of an early chapter in Bulwer's *Zanoni*, a novel which he did not review, as Harrison believed, but which he undoubtedly knew.[34] Surely Davy was worthy of being included in the tale, but Poe devotes a surprising amount of space to the passages from Davy's alleged "Diary," purportedly including technical as well as purely personal material (Harrison, 6.245–248). Part of the actual material used by Poe comes from Davy's *Researches,* as we shall see. There is, however, a slight question in my mind about the origin of Poe's term "Diary," from which he pretends to excerpt two passages, the first of which the "Ed.," i.e., Poe himself, has omitted because "The 'Diary' is to be found at the Athenaeum Library." As usual with Poe, there is a thin strand of truth from which this absurdity can hang, for Poe certainly had used the Baltimore Athenaeum Library many years before. One wonders whether any work corresponding to this could have been found therein. Its catalogue of 1827 lists only one by Davy, *The Elements of Agricultural Chemistry,* but others might have been added in the 1830's.[35]

Apart from the library collection, his reference to a "Diary" may have been derived from the two-volume *Memoirs of the*

Life of Sir Humphry Davy, Bart, by John Davy, Humphry's
brother, published in 1836 and republished in a much abridged
form as volume one of the nine-volume set of Davy's *Collected
Works* (1839–1840). Oddly enough, in the 1836 edition of the
Memoirs, on page 83, following one of the two pages scrupu-
lously indicated by Poe for the "Diary" (pp. 53 and 82), I
find a passage which bears tangentially on "Von Kempelen"
and even more closely upon the ideas that he had recently
embodied in *Eureka.*

> Or, is even the highest perfection and aggregated power of
> the human mind a mere nothing compared with the immen-
> sity of intellectual combinations belonging to the universal
> mind, a mere image in a dream in relation to the whole living
> and acting Universe? On all these subjects man is profoundly
> ignorant; yet some processes analogous to creation seem to
> have been recent. [2.83]

On page 53 of this 1836 edition there is no link at all with "Von
Kempelen," but in the revised *Memoirs* of 1839 is to be found
a rather significant item: "He undertook an investigation of the
effects of the gases in respiration. Of these, the nitrous oxide
was one of the first he experimented upon. Its agency he found
to be of a very novel and wonderful kind, contrary to all expec-
tations, and almost exceeding belief" (1.53). The link is this,
that a little further on in "Von Kempelen" Poe gives a passage, allegedly from the same "Diary," concerning Davy's
"researches about the protoxide of azote" (Harrison, 6.247).
Poe then criticizes the ungrammatical style of the sentence
which deals with the effect of a gas upon respiration, but he
excuses it on the grounds that the "MS. so inconsiderately published, was merely a *rough note-book,* meant only for the
writer's own eye." Now, the passage which Poe quotes has
been traced to one in an actual work by Davy—actually the
work alluded to on page 53 of the *Memoirs.*[36]

To appreciate a series of very characteristic Poe jests, one
must see the original in Davy and the corresponding passage
in Poe. The brackets were inserted by Poe in the following:

In less than half a minute, the respiration [being continued, these feelings] diminished gradually, and were succeeded by [a sensation] analogous to gentle pressure on all the muscles. [Harrison, 6.247]

Davy's passage reads:

Having previously closed my nostrils and exhausted my lungs, I breathed four quarts of nitrous oxide from and into a silk bag. The first feelings were similar to those produced in the last experiment; but in less than half a minute, the respiration being continued, they diminished gradually and were succeeded by a sensation analogous to gentle pressure on all the muscles, attended by a highly pleasurable thrilling, particularly in the chest and the extremities. [*Collected Works*, 3.272]

Poe has provided his wary reader with all the clues for understanding the joke, for "azote" was the name given to nitrogen by Lavoisier and the "protoxide" of azote is therefore nitrous oxide, which occurs in the full passage before Poe's excisions were made. The title of the early and famous work by Davy, from which it comes, is *Researches, Chemical and Philosophical, chiefly concerning Nitrous Oxide and its Respiration* (1799). Poe is merely preserving the description of the physiological effect of nitrous oxide, that is, laughing gas. Faced by such delightfully hidden jokes, one wonders whether Poe ever had the satisfaction of hearing anyone, even one of the many literary ladies of his circle, comment on his humor. I fear that too often his jests were made solely for his "private world."

I believe it possible to trace the origin of his distortion of Davy's respectable sentence about laughing gas and respiration; it will require our looking into the pages of the *Broadway Journal* of December 20, 1845.[37] In this issue, the next to the last published under Poe's direct editorship, appears a review of three books for young people, all called *First Lessons*, the first being in *English Composition* by Union College President E. Nott and the second in *Political Economy* by Columbia College Professor John M'Vicar. Poe devotes his entire review, however, to the anonymous third book. Since this item is uncollected by Harrison, I shall give it here:

> *First Lessons in Chemistry, for the Use of Schools and Families. By Uncle Davy. Sixth Edition.*
> These little works have been received with great favor, and it would be difficult to conceive any similar Lessons better adapted to the instruction of very young persons. The two volumes first mentioned are guaranteed by the names of the authors. The last (by Uncle Davy) may be by Humphrey [*sic*] Davy, or his ghost, for anything that we know to the contrary, but with a fund of accurate chemical information it contains some unusually loose grammar. On the very first page, for example, we read:
> "Heat means the substance, that, when enough of it gets into anything, it makes that thing feel hot."
> We will put this sentence (punctuation and all) against anything written by Thomas Carlyle.
> These three valuable little volumes are published in New York, by Saxton & Miles.[38]

This has all the touches of Poe's reviewing method and style, such as plucking an example from the beginning of the book— probably the only part given any real attention, the sarcastic reference to the anonymity of the author; the unnecessary attack upon Carlyle, one of his pet aversions, here so remotely drawn in; and finally the objection to "loose grammar." Surely this item from one of Poe's last issues of the *Broadway Journal*, stored up in that marvelously allusive and capacious memory, led to the grammatical jesting of "Von Kempelen" with its effervescent humor rising from below the surface.

Sandwiched in between Poe's allusions to Sir Humphry Davy, we find a puzzling reference to Professor Draper, "eminent" as "a chemist." This can be explained only through delving into Poe's relationship with George W. Eveleth, a medical student in Maine, and also into one of the forgotten minor controversies of the period. There is no question about the identity of Professor Draper—John William Draper (1811–1882), then teaching at New York University and distinguished in chemical and physical research. In "Von Kempelen" there is, I believe, an allusion to Poe's support of Draper when an attack was made upon his *Treatise on the Forms Which Produce the Organization of Plants* (New York, 1844). In the *North American Review* of January, 1845, the writer of a review of four new scientific works maintained that Draper's bold theory about the decomposition of carbonic acid through light in "vegetable digestion" has no substantial basis. On the other hand, there is a great deal that is "trite and elementary" —the mere condiments to the soufflé, he says. Draper must have relied too much on material prepared as lectures to medical students.[39] The attack was soon noticed by the writer of paragraphs, i.e., Poe, in the *New-York Daily Mirror,* portions of which often appeared in the *Weekly Mirror,* both being under the direction of N. P. Willis and George P. Morris. In an article not collected by Harrison, Poe defends the New Yorker, Draper, against the much scorned organ of the New England literary group, the *North American Review.* On January 20, 1845, in the *Daily Mirror* and February 1, in the *Weekly Mirror,* Poe, the "paragraphist," gives an account of the attack and speaks of the eminence of Draper, who had been praised by Brewster, Herschel, and Moser and was famous for experiments far above the skill of schoolboys. The "coarse allusion to medical students" makes Poe "suspect . . . something connected with the rivalries of medical colleges" or the "gratification" of some personal feeling.[40]

There ensues a break in Poe's published references to Draper until the Von Kempelen story, but a private letter contains a statement shockingly at variance with the first one of 1845 and linked to Poe's reference to Draper in the story. It occurs in the last of thirteen letters that Poe wrote to Eveleth, the medical student in Brunswick, Maine, the place mentioned in "Von Kempelen" as the residence of "Mr. Kissam" (6.246–247). The seven letters sent by Poe between April 16, 1846, and June 26, 1849, are among the richest and most varied of his whole correspondence. John Ward Ostrom has been able to present Poe's side of the exchange more accurately than James Southall Wilson and Thomas Ollive Mabbott were able to do in 1922 and 1924.[41] Unfortunately, however, the absence of Eveleth's letters makes it necessary still to consult the earlier compilations.

The warm letters between the callow medical student in Maine and the widely known literary figure have always seemed an indication of Poe's extreme graciousness. At the same time it has been difficult to understand Poe's remark in an undated letter printed by Rufus W. Griswold in his memoir, in which he calls Eveleth "a Yankee impertinent who, knowing my extreme poverty, has for years pestered me with unpaid letters." Wilson believes this to be a Griswold forgery.[42] Yet the tone that Poe covertly takes toward Eveleth in the tale is very similar. I must explain, first, that Eveleth's letter to Poe of February 17, 1849, from the Maine Medical School in Brunswick, is a discussion of Eveleth's reading of *Eureka,* the work which Poe thought to be his masterpiece.[43] Eveleth asks Poe whether his notion about the origin of the rotation of the heavenly bodies is his own or that of Laplace.[44] He encloses a "bit in which is my expression of it. . . . I wrote it some 2 or 3 months ago and offered it for insertion in Silliman's American Journal. I forwarded it to Professor Draper of your city for comment." Eveleth then transcribes Draper's reply which speaks about two "introductory lectures, on phosphorus and oxygen, sent to Eveleth." Next Draper mentions fugitive pieces that he wrote for the *Southern Literary Messenger* when Poe was editor: "I have not any personal acquaintance with him, and do not know what is his prospect with the magazine you refer to. From the circumstance that it is very rarely mentioned here, I should doubt its success." This skepticism about the never-to-be founded *Stylus,* which represented a journalistic Eldorado for Poe the last two years of his life, might almost explain Poe's vituperation of Draper in his reply to Eveleth,

June 26, 1849. It would not, however, explain his 1848 reference to him in *Eureka,* unless Poe were inventing the insulting
application. Concerning Draper, Poe wrote to Eveleth:

> The chief of the very sect of Hog-ites to whom I refer as
> "the most intolerant and intolerable sect of bigots & tyrants
> that ever existed on the face of the earth." . . . A merely per-
> ceptive man, with no intrinsic force—no power of generaliza-
> tion—in short, a pompous nobody. He is aware (for there
> have been plenty to tell him) that I intend *him* in "Eureka."[45]

Certainly, Draper seemed unaware of the *Eureka* animadver-
sion when he wrote Eveleth in February, 1849. Draper's scientific and social eminence might have been precisely the cause
of Poe's animosity at a time when he was contemplating the
ruin of his own life and sensed his impending death. I believe,
however, that some other personal animus must lie buried in
an unknown phase of Poe's life.

Surely it might seem "impertinent" for the young medical
student to attempt to rival Poe's *Eureka* glory with his own
cosmological theory, as his letter of February 17, 1849 shows.
Hence Poe goes out of his way in "Von Kempelen" to ridicule
"a Mr. Kissam, of Brunswick, Maine," who claims the "invention" of the gold-making apparatus and formula. The very
name has its symbolic scorn for a humble admirer who has
become too ambitious. Poe piles on the ridicule: "How hap-
pens it that he took no steps, *on the instant,* to reap the immense benefits which the merest bumpkin must have known
would have resulted to him individually, if not to the world at
large, from the discovery?" He "subsequently acted so like a
baby—so like an owl—as Mr. Kissam *admits* that he did." Kissam's claim, Poe says, has "an amazingly moon-hoax-y air"
(6.247). This is perhaps a covert allusion to the gullibility
Eveleth had displayed in two other letters: that of January 5,
1846, expressing a belief in the truth of "The Facts in the Case
of M. Valdemar" (which Poe contradicted) and, more recently,
that of January 19, 1849, in which Eveleth speaks again of the

"Valdemar" story and also of Poe's "Balloon-Hoax," both of which have "ingenious management and . . . a coloring of truth."[46] As if to resolve any doubts about the application of this section to Eveleth, Poe concludes by being "profoundly astonished at finding so eminent a chemist as Professor Draper discussing Mr. Kissam's (or is it Mr. Quizzem's?) pretensions to this discovery in so serious a tone." May not his spirit have been wounded to find an intellectual leader in New York writing to a mere Eveleth in Maine and not to Poe?[47]

The matter concerns also the entire orientation of Poe to experimental and theoretical science. What should we assume, for example, from Poe's mention of Davy's "dislike to quackery" directly before his being "morbidly afraid of *appearing* empirical" (6.248)? We have seen, in this attention to Maelzel and the real Von Kempelen, his interest in technical advancement, as represented by modern mechanical devices. In "Mellonta Tauta," also of February, 1849 (Harrison, 6.197–215), a long trip in the year 2848 on board a balloon—named perhaps symbolically after the "Skylark" of the ameliorist Shelley—is the occasion for a gossipy discussion of progress. It is not clear that technology has really improved the life of man. Similarly, in his "Scheherazade" of February, 1845 (6.78–102), Poe had listed a long series of "marvels," including scientific developments such as "The Electrotype" which has "the faculty of converting the common metals into gold" (6.98). The whole is given more in the spirit of a magic show than with a sense of any possible benefit to the lives of men. The invention of the "Electro Telegraph" is satirically equated with that of the bustle at the end of the tale. In April, 1845, in his tale "Some Words with a Mummy" (6.116–138), Poe humorously maintained that modern inventions are inferior copies or postludes to the glories of Egypt and makes a poor joke about the present lack of advance in that "which the Bostonians call the Great Movement or Progress" (6.136). Poe's social sense may be gauged by his admiration of Southern aristocracy and slavery.[48] Even in "Von Kempelen" no practical result seems worth mentioning save a probable shift in the migration to California, the fluctuations in the price of other metals, and for the fortunate discoverer the ability to purchase considerable property for his own benefit. Characteristic of Poe's approach is his showing the police as chagrined at not having pocketed a few slugs of gold while taking the chest of "brass" to the station.

How much more social-minded is the use of magical goldmaking in the first Rosicrucian novel, Godwin's well-known *St. Leon,* which may have been a source for the theme of "Von Kempelen."[49] The Baltimore Athenaeum Library contained a copy of the 1801 Alexandria reprint. Poe mentions *St. Leon* in the first sentence of his December, 1835, review of Godwin's *Lives of the Necromancers:* "The name of the author of Caleb Williams, and of St. Leon, is, with us, a word of weight . . ." (Harrison, 8.92). There are several interesting parallels between the two works: the search by the police of the goldmaker's premises and the lengthy interrogation in the police headquarters, the alarm felt by neighbors at the sudden acquisition of wealth as displayed in his purchase of property, the pointed references to the misanthropy of Von Kempelen and of Bethlem Gabor in *St. Leon,* and the extensive portion of *St. Leon* which is set in Presburg (spelled thus in both works).[50] Moreover, there are even hints for the plot in the references to Rosicrucianism in Godwin's *Lives of the Necromancers.*[51]

Godwin's influence may have merged with that derived from other literature of the period, rife with the twofold Rosicrucian theme: the search for the elixir of life and for the philosopher's stone. As a simple example, there is Coleridge's *Ancient Mariner,* which Poe cites at least nine times, and which he unquestionably used in his "Ms. Found in a Bottle."[52] Poe alludes to the *Juif Errant* of Eugene Sue in the "Domain of Arnheim," and he lengthily reviews *Sheppard Lee,* the novel of his unrecognized friend, William Bird, with its playful use of metempsychosis, in 1836 (Harrison, 9.126–139). Indeed, at the end of the review he objects to the author's "jocular manner" and reliance upon a dream explanation of the successive avatars of the hero? (For Poe's use of metempsychosis see chap. iii.)

In the "Discovery" Poe gave Von Kempelen only one attribute for his would-be hoax, the aurific power, and endeavored to corroborate this with a wide range of details. Besides citing the names of scientific celebrities, he sought to establish the earmarks of a real event through glib references to famous periodicals. This may have been a blunder, since too many readers would have been able to check their own memories of recent issues. Biographical interest lies for us today in the titles that Poe chose. The first mentioned is "Silliman's Journal," a rash stroke, since Silliman's *American Journal of Science and Arts* was a prominent publication in America and certain to be familiar to many readers of the tale.[53] Next he speaks of a paragraph from the "Courier and Enquirer" which is "now going the rounds of the press" in connection with his "Kissam" insertion. This mention confirms my belief that he is covertly referring to Eveleth and his cosmological discovery, for the *Courier and Enquirer* of New York had favorably reviewed Poe's *Eureka* lecture on cosmology, of February 3, 1848.[54] This was one of the two reviews which Poe sent to Eveleth, February 29, 1848, as items which approach "the truth," the other being that from *The Express*. He specifically begs Eveleth to return the clippings (Ostrom, 2.360–362).

Similarly, a reference to the "brief account" of the discovery, in the "Home Journal" plunges one into the *Eureka* matter and other aspects of Poe biography. The *Home Journal* had printed a "very complimentary notice of the forthcoming lecture" (Ostrom, 2.359). Nathaniel P. Willis had founded the *Journal* in February, 1846, and was to show the greatest friendliness to Poe in its pages, even to excess, in Poe's opinion, as when the *Journal* published an appeal for aid to the Poes as Virginia lay dying, at the end of 1846 (Ostrom, 338–339). (Poe had reciprocated Willis's many acts of solicitude in his earlier "Literati" picture of the man, May, 1846.) May there not be a definite trace of this very notice of the *Journal* concerning Virginia's anguish in Poe's pretense in the "Discovery" that "in the brief account of Von Kempelen" the *Home Journal* has misapprehended the "German original":

> "*Viele*" has evidently been misconceived (as it often is), and what the translator renders by "sorrows," is probably "*leiden*," which, in its true version, "sufferings," would give a totally different complexion to the whole account. . . . [Harrison, 6.248–249][55]

In relation to the gold-making achievement this insertion makes no sense at all, but it poignantly illustrates the obsessive force of the last grim days of Virginia's life, filled with "viele leiden." It also serves to confirm more substantially the transmutation of Poe into the successful gold-maker, Von Kempelen.

The next periodical mentioned, *The Literary World*, was also highly significant in Poe's life. As I indicated at the beginning of this chapter, Poe had offered his "Discovery" to the editor, Evert A. Duyckinck, March 8, 1849, and had apparently been refused.[56] This magazine had just reprinted "Ulalume," on March 3, 1849, from the *Providence Daily Journal* of November 22, 1848.[57] In his letter of June 26, 1849, to Eveleth, Poe pointedly asks whether he has ever seen *The Literary World*. In the last or else the penultimate letter of his life, that of September 18, 1849, to Maria Clemm, Poe says in a postscript: "Be sure & preserve all the printed scraps I have sent you & keep up my file of the Lit. World" (Ostrom, 2.461).

There is another amazingly specific reference in the tale, which also conceals significant personal experiences. Twice Poe disclaims misanthropy for Von Kempelen, a quality not ill-applied to the deteriorating Poe himself.[58] The passage is important:

> Von Kempelen, however, is by no means "a misanthrope," in appearance, at least, whatever he may be in fact. . . . To have seen and conversed with a man of so *prodigious* a notoriety as he has attained, or *will* attain in a few days, is not a small matter, as times go. . . . Altogether he looks,

speaks and acts as little like "a misanthrope" as any man I
ever saw. We were fellow-sojourners for a week, about six
years ago, at Earl's Hotel, in Providence, Rhode Island.
. . . He left the hotel before me, intending to go to New
York, and thence to Bremen; it was in the latter city that
his great discovery was first made public; or, rather, it
was there that he was first suspected of having made it.
[Harrison, 6.249–250]

All students of Poe, at the mention of Earl's Hotel, i.e., the
Earl House in Providence, will recall the painful circumstances
involved in the courtship of Mrs. Helen Whitman, in 1848.
There is no need to rehearse the course of letters to and from
the attractive, wealthy widow of Providence, Poe's visits and
attempt at suicide by laudanum, his refusal to withdraw his
suit despite the opposition of her family and friends, her sign-
ing away her property as part of the marriage agreement, and
finally her rejection of him the day of the marriage because of
an alleged drinking episode at the bar of the Earl House.[59]
A few excerpts from the correspondence will indicate how
heavily the fact of Mrs. Whitman's affluence and respectable
position in Providence society may have weighed with Poe. In
his first letter, of October 1, 1848, he would be "proud" to
"beseech" her for her love, "were I wealthy, or could I offer
you worldly honors . . ." (Ostrom, 2.389). On October 18 he
writes, with a rather obvious denial of his knowledge of that
affluence: "That you are quite independent in your worldly
position (as I have just heard)—in a word that *you are com-
paratively rich while I am poor,* opens between us *a gulf* . . ."
(Ostrom, 2.397). After her friends have managed to make this
gulf impassable at the last moment, Poe follows up the shock-
ing separation with a letter of January 21, 1849, while he is
writing the "Discovery." He asks Mrs. Whitman for an explanation of certain allegations concerning her termination of the
marriage proceedings and refers to the settlement by which he
took her without her property: "So far I have assigned no reason for my declining to fulfill our engagement—I had none but

the suspicious & grossly insulting parsimony of the arrange-
ment into which you suffered yourself to be forced by your
Mother" (Ostrom, 2.420–21).

The well-attended lecture on "The Poetic Principle" was
held in the Earl House, on December 20, 1848 (Ostrom, 2.391
and 413); his drinking bout at the hotel bar gave Mrs. Whitman's friends and family a reason to cancel the marriage. Can
we doubt that his inclusion of the name "Earl's Hotel" in the
tale is significant?[60] It appears to me likely that the termination of the affair had something to do, also, with Poe's use of
the terms "notoriety" and "misanthrope" as applied to Von
Kempelen.[61]

At this time of dire "adversity," as Poe called it in January,
1849, the need for material gain was very much on Poe's mind
and entered into fantasies which find expression in letters as
well as tales: "I am so busy now, and feel so full of energy.
Engagements are pouring in upon me every day." Ostrom comments on the sad lack of evidence to support this euphoria
(2.417–420). It seems clear that at this period thoughts of
"Eldorado" were unusually urgent.[62] In "Von Kempelen and
His Discovery" Poe ingeniously merges the profitable practice
of Rosicrucian magic with the search for California gold. But
the period is no longer suitable for Poe's fantastic trickery. In a
kind of apt symbolism, the same periodical, a week later, published the poem concerning the self-described "gallant knight":

>   And o'er his heart a shadow
>   Fell as he found
>   No spot of ground
>   That looked like Eldorado.

11

POE AS "MISERRIMUS"

IN 1748 THOMAS Morris, a nonjuring canon of Worcester
Cathedral, died at the age of eighty-eight; he commemorated
a life replete with disappointments through the single word
"Miserrimus" inscribed on his gravestone in the cathedral.[1]
Those who saw the epitaph many years later surmised the
worst about the buried man, and three speculative sonnets
about him were written from 1828 to 1830, one by William
Wordsworth.[2] My concern will be to trace the use of the title
"Miserrimus," first as used for the poem by Wordsworth; next
by his friend Reynolds, for a morbid novel praised by Poe; and
finally by Richard Stoddard, for derogatory verses upon Poe
after his death. In the unwinding of this curious thread, a new
explanation will be offered for the strange utterance of the
name "Reynolds" by the dying Poe. His grave, prepared just
one hundred years after that of the unhappy Thomas Morris
was, for a long time, to be equally unmarked through a peculiar accident. Surely these verifiable connections of the British
and American memorials with the four authors have an arresting implausibility, characteristic of Poe's most fantastic tales.

Wordsworth's attention was drawn to the epitaph at Worcester Cathedral when he visited it briefly in December, 1827.
Early in 1828 he was invited to contribute poems to Heath's
opulently illustrated new annual, *The Keepsake*, edited by
Frederick Mansell Reynolds.[3] For the November publication
of the book, the poet set to work on a sheaf of poems, one of
which was the sonnet on the Worcester gravestone. It is one of
the "Miscellaneous Sonnets," always printed with the wrong
date and with an incorrect capitalization of an important word:

A Gravestone upon the Floor in the Cloisters
of Worcester Cathedral

"*Miserrimus*," and neither name nor date,
Prayer, text, or symbol, graven upon the stone
Nought but that word assigned to the unknown,
That solitary word—to separate
From all, and cast a cloud around the fate
Of him who lies beneath. Most wretched one,
Who chose his epitaph?—Himself alone
Could thus have dared the grave to agitate,
And claim, among the dead, this awful crown;
Nor doubt that he marked also for his own
Close to these cloistral steps a burial-place,
That every foot might fall with heavier tread,
Trampling upon his vileness. Stranger, pass
Softly!—To save the contrite, Jesus bled.[4]

Clearly Wordsworth assumed the iniquity of the interred, to
judge by the italicized "who" and the phrases, "dared the grave
to agitate," "awful crown," and "trampling upon his vileness."
Soon after the November publication of *The Keepsake* a Worcestershire antiquarian sent him a corrective paper "spoiling
. . . the Poem altogether," Wordsworth wrote in a letter of
December 20, 1828, but his amazement was great that the
"ejection" of Morris could have produced "so emphatic and
startling an Epitaph—and in such a place, just at the last of
the steps falling from the Cathedral to the Cloister." The 1857
edition was the first to print the information about the non-
juror, but only as a "conjecture" which had been dictated by
Wordsworth to Miss Fenwick.

This delay is an important link in the chain, for it explains
why Reynolds in 1832 still held the mistaken notion that the
epitaph concerned a criminal. Wordsworth could have clari-
fied the matter, but early in 1829 he became so irritated with
the editor over publication matters that their relations were
strained (*Letters*, 3.378 and 385). Hence Reynolds used Words-

worth's original conception about the man for his own novel
Miserrimus, which had one printing in 1832 and two in 1833.
The epigraph for the novel follows the *Keepsake* poem: "On a
gravestone in Worcester Cathedral is this inscription—Miserrimus with neither name, nor date, comment nor text." The
first sentence sufficiently illustrates his view of the character:
"The hand of the fiend was on me at my birth."

William Godwin, creator of several similarly somber and
obsessed characters, played an interesting role in the development of Reynolds's tale. Godwin's journal for June 16, 1828,
records a significant fact: "Wordsworth and F R call." It may
have been in Godwin's house that the two discussed Wordsworth's sonnet on the theme. The unpublished journal lists
other meetings between Godwin and Reynolds at this period.[5]
Consequently it is not surprising that Reynolds inscribed the
book to Godwin.

A summary of Reynolds's plot might be useful for several
comparisons: The chief character in this first-person narrative is the unnamed, inexplicably vicious son of a prosperous
farmer. At boarding school he bullies a fellow student and
stabs a peacemaker. Expelled, the narrator returns to his
family, to be softened by the rustic environment. At eighteen
he falls in love with the daughter of a wealthy newcomer to
the districts and expects her to marry him. The suitor meets
her brother—his chief school rival—and provokes a challenge
to a duel. Despite the pleading of his fiancée, he meets and
kills the young man the next day. After sending her a stinging
letter of reproach, he leaves for the Orient where he amasses
a vast fortune. A few years later he returns, to discover that
the girl's family is being dispossessed. He restores their estate
and the unhappy girl writes him a note expressing mingled
gratitude and detestation. Then she plunges into a river in a
suicide attempt which he manages to thwart. Although still in
love with her, he asks for her hand simply to torment her to
death. At the sight of the black draperies of the church, of
two inscribed coffins, and of the newly erected monument

memorializing her marriage to her brother's "murderer," she succumbs to brain fever and dies after one week. After wandering for years the now penitent husband is telling the story of "Miserrimus" before entering his unmarked tomb.

The mark of *Caleb Williams* and *Mandeville* is certainly strong upon the work, as the reviews of the period were quick to observe, usually in its favor. Said *The Court Journal* reviewer about the "unpublished" first edition of 1832: "On the Worcester Cathedral engraving, the author has grounded a Godwinian novel. . . . Some portions of the story are such as Goethe himself, in some fit of morbid enthusiasm, might have embodied in poetical prose." *The Metropolitan Magazine* characterized the first 1833 edition as an "impassioned work of a man of talent . . . to be compared with the best pages of Godwin" and written in his "earnest and all-absorbing manner."[6] There were dissenters of course. *The Gentlemen's Magazine* could not consider any Godwinian novel without taking up the old anti-Jacobin cudgel. It termed the work "a posthumous libel, . . . one of the most extravagant rhapsodies of the ultra-romantic or, it may be said, stark-mad school, . . . the disgusting offspring of a depraved imagination." This review may have been responsible for Reynolds's finally checking on the background of the interred "unknown" and regretfully indicating his error about the malefactor in the second edition of 1833.[7]

For the sake of explaining an odd mistake about its author made by Poe, I must mention the third and last novel of Reynolds, the purposeful companion to *Miserrimus* in its generally morbid tone and theme: *The Parricide: a Domestic Romance* (1836). The very beginning quickly established it as of the school of Godwin and of Poe: "I record the events of a long life of self-indulgence, anarchy, passion, and truculence, of which every minute has been a tempest, and every thought a wound. . . . Yes, I am myself alone. . . . [no] guilt is equal to my guilt."[8] The London market had apparently been glutted with this type of fiction, for the work created no stir at all. The oddity is that another writer of the same surname, George

William MacArthur Reynolds, in the early 1840's, saw fit to issue his own earliest novel, a sensational and paltry work called *The Youthful Impostor,* under the new name of *The Parricide: or, The Youth's Career of Crime.* This duplicity of title and author, so to speak, may have led Poe into writing of *Miserrimus* as being by "G. M. W. [*sic*] Reynolds" in Novemvember, 1844, and "by the author of *Pickwick Abroad,*" i.e., G. W. M. Reynolds, in January, 1846.[9]

Poe's error is understandable when we note that neither the British nor the American editions of *Miserrimus* gave the name of the author. However, there is no doubt that Poe knew the book well. There are five references to it in the body of his criticism and definite traces, I believe, in his creative work. The late poems "Annabel Lee" and "The Bells" show the influence.[10] The first has the perhaps prescient lines concerning his deceased Virginia and his own approaching death: "And so, all the night-tide, I lie down by the side/ Of my darling— my darling—my life and my bride." In *Miserrimus* the narrator, after dragging the suicide from the stream, in vain he thinks, writes of a similar necrophiliac frenzy:

> I threw myself by her side, and insanely kissed her lips, her eyes, and her forehead. The blood began to dance in my veins like burning alcohol, and the pent-up passion of years burst their unnatural confinement. I wound my arms around her unresisting form . . . and yet I felt as though I only grasped a vision, a vacancy. . . . None, but those who may have possessed passions as ungovernable as mine, can picture the savage, the fierce delight, which I derived from this clandestine embrace of what I then conceived to be the living and the dead! [Philadelphia edition, pp. 113–114]

The passage shows the strong, Poeësque quality of the text. As for "The Bells," the reader will remember that each of the four sections starts with an injunction to "hear" the different types of bells. Part II begins: "Hear the mellow wedding bells,/ Golden bells!/ What a world of happiness their harmony foretells!" Reynolds has the dying bride remark, "Hear that village bell: how many vain associations it suggests!" (*Miserrimus,* p. 193). Poe, if influenced by the book, detailed the "associations" in immortal verses.

Poe's tales are full of themes that may have been confirmed, if not actually implanted by elements in the book. For example, the eyes of Ligeia, full, black strange—"Those shining, those divine orbs!"—have their counterpart in this novel. In *Miserrimus* we are first told, "Her *eye* was the organ of her eloquence" (p. 25). Toward the end, the narrator speaks of the "extraordinary loveliness of those singular eyes. Liquid, mild, and pellucid as the fawn, yet dark and penetrating, they could flash with the fire of love, or, as I too well knew, with the fire of hate. . . . They beamed a melancholy, at once timid, submissive, deprecating, which might have touched the heart of a fiend" (pp. 161–165). The stress upon cruelty for its own sake, as in "The Tell-Tale Heart," "The Black Cat," and "The Pit and the Pendulum," is paralleled in the motto of *Miserrimus:* "Plus on aime une maîtresse, et plus on est près de la haïr," and in such sentences as: "That very impetuosity of character and feeling which is the source of all passionate love, is also a mine of combustible which any spark may explode into a conflagration of evil" and "Perhaps of all passions, cruelty is that which is most strengthened by indulgence; the more it attains, the more it desires" (pp. 136 and 176).

There is no need to underscore the "William Wilson" aspect of the beginning of *Miserrimus,* in which the narrator finds his vindictiveness at school thwarted by a fellow student, whom he kills for revenge years later. "The morbid desire of vengeance" (p. 139) also motivates "The Cask of Amontillado" and "Hop Frog." May not *Miserrimus* have contributed to one of the most powerful effects in "The Masque of the Red Death" through its description of the funereal bridal draperies of the church: "The walls, pews, ceiling, and floor, were covered with black crape; there was not a portion of the interior which revealed the material of which it was composed. . . . Numerous flambeaux, impregnated with a sickly perfume, were scattered about. . . . The windows too had all been carefully covered with hangings of the same lugubrious hue. . . . [There was] the strange glare of the red light of the torches" (pp. 173–174). This is very much in the spirit and language of Poe.

Poe showed his awareness of the book by associating it, in four critical references, with *Martin Faber* by William Gilmore Simms. From 1844 to 1849, the year of Poe's death, there are five separate articles which mention the work of Reynolds. In the first, the "Marginalia" of the *Democratic Review* (November, 1844), he merely notes: "The author of '*Miserrimus*' might have been William Gilmore Simms (whose '*Martin Faber*' is just such a work) . . ." (Harrison, 16.62–63). Poe was not the first to imply a relationship of the two novels; the critics of 1833 jumped to the conclusion that Simms was a borrower if not an outright plagiarist. In fact, in the second edition of *Martin Faber, the Story of a Criminal,* Simms enlarged his first preface into a defense, indicating that the charge was based upon fortuitous correspondences of date, size, format, theme, narrative method, and American publisher. But his was an eminently moral work, showing how "evils" spring from "errors," he protested. Moreover, his story was developed from a tale of eight or ten pages, first published in the *Southern Literary Gazette* in 1828 and elaborated in 1829 and 1832 into the novel. "The sterner, darker features of the story . . . were all conceived in the first instance."[11] Simms repeated the account in a long letter of December, 1846, to Griswold.[12]

Poe greatly admired *Martin Faber,* whose author he calls "the Lopez [*sic*] de Vega of American writers of fiction." In the rest of this review of Simms's *The Wigwam and the Cabin* in 1845 he notes that *Martin Faber* "has been said to resemble '*Miserrimus*'—and in fact we perceive that the independent minds which originated the two stories have much in them of similarity—but as regards the narratives themselves, or even their tone, there is no resemblance whatever. '*Martin Faber*' is the better work of the two" (Harrison, 12.248). In his third reference, an adaptation of the same review for *Godey's Lady's*

Book of January, 1846, Poe mentions the allegation of imitation again and ascribes *Miserrimus* to the "Author of 'Pickwick Abroad.'" Yet he now grants "the absolute identity of *effect* wrought by both." *Martin Faber* "is a more forcible story," more poorly received only because it is not the work of an Englishman (Harrison, 13.93–95).

The fourth and fifth instances of reference to *Miserrimus* are connected with Laughton Osborn's *The Confessions of a Poet, by Himself*. In *Godey's Lady's Book* for May, 1846, among the "Literati" Poe includes this author, whose work he terms: "fiction of *power* without rudeness. Its spirit, in general, resembles that of 'Miserrimus' and 'Martin Faber'" (Harrison, 15.46). With a few changes in wording this judgment is included in the "Marginalia" of the *Southern Literary Messenger* of April, 1849. Considering Poe's contemptuous remarks about Osborn's work in the same magazine in April, 1835 (Harrison, 8.2–3), Griswold insidiously suggests that Osborn's wealth and social standing helped to elevate Poe's opinion.[13] Actually Griswold chose to overlook a very neutral reference which Poe made concerning another book by Osborn, in April, 1849.[14] Quite possibly a more mature Poe, rereading *Confessions of a Poet*, formed a different judgment on the basis of changed critical standards. He declares that it is "a book remarkable for its artistic unity. . . . [No] better novel of its kind has been composed by an American. To be sure, it is not precisely the work to put in the hands of a lady, but its incidents are striking and original, its scenes of passion nervously wrought, and its philosophy [full of] . . . suggestiveness and audacity. . . . Its spirit, in general, resembles that of Reynolds' 'Miserrimus.'" Its protagonist, described as "self-willed and violent" from his earliest years, fights with his relatives and associates, and finally commits suicide; the *Confessions* are intended to warn men through his "foul example." Poe was perfectly correct in linking the work with *Miserrimus* in this, one of his last printed pieces (Harrison, 16.142).

We come now to the importance of the name Reynolds in

the last unhappy days of Edgar Allan Poe. Many biographers
have followed him all along the course of his trip from New
York to Richmond, before the extremely puzzling last stage in
Baltimore, between September 27 and October 3, 1849. There
is no need for me to consider whether he was "cooped" and
drugged the evening before the local Baltimore election of
October 3, to serve as a voting "repeater." Certainly he was
taken, moribund, to the Washington College Hospital on that
day and placed under the attending physician, Dr. John J.
Moran. Found in a state of coma, he later became violently
delirious. Before his death, the morning of October 7, he was
visited by Neilson Poe, his third cousin, and possibly by others.
Self-interest and self-deception can be suspected of most
"observers" who furnished accounts of Poe's death. Credence
is usually given to the letter which Dr. Moran wrote, on November 15, 1849, to Poe's mother-in-law, Maria Clemm. After
describing Poe's delirium and general incoherence, Moran
remarked: "At the end he began calling for one 'Reynolds'
which he did through the night until three on Sunday. Then
he became feeble and quiet, moved his hand, said, 'Lord, help
my poor soul!' and expired."[15] Almost every biographer has followed a clue given by Woodberry and has taken this to mean
Jeremiah N. Reynolds, who had deeply stirred Poe's interest
through his involvement with Polar and Pacific exploration.[16]

There are several discrepancies, however, in the picture of
Poe as the voyager "into trackless seas and yawning chasm . . .
[confronting] that shrouded human figure, very far larger . . .
than any dweller among men" (Pym). Most biographers seem
willing arbitrarily to discard other portions of Moran's testimony delivered then and repeated, with variations, in the
succeeding years. Two further interpretations of the name
Reynolds are possible, if indeed Poe did utter it. First, let me
grant that a very strong case for its being J. N. Reynolds can
be made; it certainly has been made by Aubrey Starke and
Robert F. Almy.[17] Both are cautious scholars and rely chiefly
on Poe's reviews of Reynolds's rather few works and on the

opportunities that the two men had for meeting. It is true that
Poe lavished praise on Reynolds's letter to the "Committee on
Naval Affairs" (Harrison, 9.84–90) and his "Address" delivered
in the House of Representatives, April 3, 1836 (9.306–314),
from which he also derived phases of *The Narrative of Arthur
Gordon Pym.*[18] Poe was then ignoring his jocular remarks of
December, 1835, about Reynolds's preface to the Latin "life"
of Washington by Francis Glass: that "meeting with" it was
"an episode of the purest romance" and that "Mr. Reynolds
was quizzing" the public (8.103–107). Poe's growing respect
for the role of Reynolds in promoting a United States explora-
tory expedition led to his inclusion in the early "Autography"
in the *Messenger* of February, 1836. However, there is no
respect indicated for Reynolds's "common mercantile hand"
(Harrison, 15.159). The second series on autography, in *Graham's Magazine* of December, 1841, again expresses scorn for
his "clerk's hand," as well as praise for his "exertions to get up
the American South Polar Expedition" (Harrison, 15.243–
244). In the same magazine, September, 1843, Poe again
speaks of the "scandalous chicanery practiced . . . to thrust
from all participation in the enterprise the very man who gave
it origin and who cherished it to consummation." Finally, Poe
praised Reynolds in like vein in the June 4, 1844 issue of the
Columbia Spy of Pottsville, Pennsylvania.[19]

Nevertheless there is nothing in these articles to prove that
Poe knew J. N. Reynolds personally. Indeed, the tone of his
handwriting analysis suggests that he did not even know him
as an acquaintance. Almy says cautiously, "Poe could have
met Reynolds in New York" and "It seems to me that the
inference—and it must remain an inference—has considerable
plausibility." Starke is also cautious, speaking of the "many
opportunities for their meeting—but never proved."

I am led to draw a different inference, which may be equally
plausible, from the importance of the novel of F. M. Reynolds
in Poe's criticism and creative work. Since the last reference to
the American occurs in 1844 and to the English novelist in

1849, I propose the novelist as the person in Poe's dimming consciousness in Baltimore, for Poe was obviously aware of his own state of keen misery in the hospital. If we give credence to Moran's letter, the final statement, "Lord, help my poor soul," may be illustrative of Poe, "miserrimus," who had written an article about *Miserrimus* and its author only the preceding April. Of course, the account of Dr. Moran may be rife with erroneous memories or impressions. Harrison judiciously considers the elaboration of the letter in Dr. Moran's *A Defense of Edgar Allan Poe . . . an Official Account of His Death* (Washington, 1885) and states: "Romantically interesting but not convincing. Judge Neilson Poe, his third cousin, who was at the hospital constantly until he died, asserted that he never regained consciousness."[20]

Since it is a question of selecting and emphasizing the facts, we must make Poe's death call more complicated by noting a third possibility for the name Reynolds. One of Dr. Moran's memoranda of 1875 seems unequivocal: "I had sent for his cousin, Neilson Poe, having learned he was his relative, and a family named Reynolds, who lived in the neighborhood of the hospital. These were the only persons whose names I had heard him mention living in the city. Mr. W. N. Poe came, and the female members of Mr. Reynolds's family" (*Works of Poe*, 1884 edition, l.cxx). No one seems to have followed up this promising lead from the chief Baltimore witness. Just what is meant by "I had heard him mention living in the city"? If Poe was in a coma or delirious all the time, he could have mentioned nothing intelligible, although the doctor's letter of 1849 also implies clear, substantial speech from Poe. I should add that the *Baltimore Directory for 1845* lists sixteen persons named Reynolds.[21] Therefore, after mentioning these possibilities, we must finally leave unsettled the question of which Reynolds Poe intended at the end, if he called out at all.

To continue my present account, the word *miserrimus* occurs one more time in connection with this unhappy man. There is no need to underscore the role played by Rufus Wilmot Griswold in the systematic depreciation of Poe's virtues and merits, particularly as a critic; this was the field in which Griswold had personally suffered at the hands of Poe.[22] But the mantle of "dean of Poe's memoirs" seemed to fall upon the increasingly well-known critic, poet (or poetaster), and compiler, Richard Henry Stoddard. Like Griswold he had suffered from the whip in the hand of Edgar Allan Poe, critic and editor. From 1872 he seemed to enjoy recounting the story of how, as a young man, he had submitted to Poe's *Broadway Journal* of 1845 his "Ode on a Grecian Flute," which, he admitted, was "influenced by Keats but not copied from anyone." When he had waited many weeks, he personally called upon Poe, who assured him that it would be printed. Soon the *Journal* noted that the verses had been mislaid, and next asserted: "We decline to publish the 'Ode on a Grecian Flute' unless we can be assured of its authenticity." The "indignant" Stoddard went to the office to demand an explanation from Poe who "gave me the lie direct, declared that I never wrote it, and threatened to chastise me unless I left him at once." At a later date on a rainy day he had his last glimpse of Edgar Allan Poe, "pale, shivering, miserable." Years afterward, concerning his failure to share an umbrella, Stoddard piously added, "I can never forgive myself."[23] This account was to be retold frequently as though the upward swing of Poe's reputation could bear with it the fame of a popinjay like Stoddard.[24]

Stoddard, however, wisely and consistently left out of later memoirs of Poe the verses with which he had concluded his highly sarcastic, deprecatory article in 1853.[25] There he found only a few of Poe's poems with "the seal of immortality"; most of his work was "unreadable." In criticism "he had a singular power of analysis," but was the master of the "dyspeptic school," which "confuses right and wrong, faith and morality, and leagues itself with darkness." Stoddard insidiously excused Poe for "vices," such as drunkenness, which were the result of his "genius's" being unrecognized. Stoddard's memorial poem restates his basic view: "In Poe's writings there is [*sic*] despair,

hopelessness, and the echoes of a melancholy . . . but no-
where . . . conscience." As was Stoddard's habit in criticism,
the verses conclude the article, with the note: "Upon hearing
of his death. Faulty they certainly are, but they say what
should be said on such an occasion."[26] Here are the lines which
do no service to the reputation of either Poe or Stoddard:

                    Miserrimus
              He has pass'd away
              From a world of strife,
        Fighting the wars of Time and Life;
        The leaves will fall when the winds are loud,
        And the snows of winter will weave his shroud,
        But he will never, ah never know
                  Anything more
                  Of leaves or snow!

              The summer tide
              Of his life was past,
        And his hopes were fading, fading fast;
        His faults were many, his virtues few,
        A tempest with flecks of heaven's blue;
        He might have soared to the gates of light,
                  But he built his nest
                  With the birds of night.

                  He glimmer'd apart
                  In solemn gloom,
        Like a dying lamp in a haunted tomb;
        He touch'd his lute, with a magic spell,
        But all its melodies breath'd of hell,
        Raising the afrits and the ghouls,
                  And the pallid ghosts,
                  Of the damned souls.

                  But he lies in dust,
                  And the stone is roll'd
        Over his sepulcher dark and cold;
        He has cancel'd all he has done, or said,
        And gone to the dear and holy dead!
        Let us forget the path he trod,
                  And leave him now
                  With his Maker—God!

Stoddard clearly had the gravestone of Worcester Cathedral in mind, having learned of it from either the novel of Reynolds or the sonnet of Wordsworth.[27] Although he omitted any ascription to Poe after the first printing of the poem, he included "Miserrimus" in two collections of his own poetry.[28] Incidentally, a casual glance into Stoddard's early poems corroborates Poe's accusation of 1845, for they are often heavy with the freight of borrowed phrases and themes.[29] With regard to the value of the poem, Stoddard is strangely straightforward, for in his *Recollections* he wrote: "Within a day or two after the death of Edgar Allan, I penned a copy of careless verses which had more success than they deserved." The incredible, petty spitefulness of the man is shown in his newly adding to the Grecian flute story his "consolation" that Poe's ancestors were ignoble by comparison with the eminent early Stoddards. Stoddard also asserts that Poe was constitutionally "unveracious," but his statement that Griswold and Thomas Dunn English were extremely friendly to Poe makes one wonder about his own honesty.[30] He also alluded to the verses in an article in *The Independent* of February 1, 1894: "I scribbled some verses in his memory; and . . . [Mrs. Osgood] was good enough to think some of it not unworthy of its theme. She died a few weeks later" (Harrison, 1.244). If true, was this a judgment upon a woman whom Poe had publicly and privately adulated?

I know of only one American comment on Stoddard's "Miserrimus"—that of the eccentric Oliver Leigh, or "Geoffrey Quarles," in his little book *Edgar Allan Poe*. He scornfully quotes, "His faults were many / His virtues few."[31] Eugene Lemoine Didier in *The Poe Cult* devotes a chapter to "Poe and Stoddard," chiefly summarizing the Grecian flute story and indicating its monetary rewards to Stoddard. He makes no allusion to "Miserrimus."[32] It is strange that few Americans took issue with the cleverly scattered canards of Stoddard, possibly because of his increasing power in the field of publishing. Even Sarah Whitman, whose *Edgar Poe and His Critics* was expiation for her weakness toward the poet as suitor in

Providence, 1848–1849, is deliberately silent about Stoddard's
continuation of Griswold's contumelious role. In her work he
figures only as one of the "Literati" in Mrs. Osgood's happy
drawing room.[33] Even Harrison, usually ardent in Poe's defense, calls Stoddard "a keen admirer of Poe's genius, but an
unsparing foe to what he considers . . . Poe's moral delinquen-
cies and mendacity" (Harrison, 1.241). It apparently required
the physical as well as psychical distance afforded by England
to see the role of Stoddard. Ingram, in his *Life of Poe*, cites a
neat statement of the case from the *Quarterly Review*: "The
last addition to the Poe biography is an 'Original Memoir'
by R. H. Stoddard, a gentleman of New York, who denounces
Griswold and then proceeds simply to surpass him in his own
line; raking together such a mass of irrelevant gossip as we
never read before."[34] With this we shall leave Stoddard.

One final word is needed for the object of his pity. It is not
necessary to emphasize the terrible melancholy of Poe's life,
relieved by brief moments of pleasure amid his bevy of literary
ladies or at childlike play with the cat and birds during Virginia's long decline. The title, if not the sentiment, "Most
wretched of men" certainly applies to Edgar Allan Poe. Yet
chance—certainly not justice—seemed determined to render
his grave as unmarked and unknown as that of Thomas Morris
in 1748. After the small funeral party, consisting chiefly of
Baltimore relatives, saw Poe's remains interred, his grave was
marked only by a fragment of sandstone numbered "80" to
designate the lot; this was placed by the kindly sexton George
W. Spence.[35] Several years later Judge Neilson Poe ordered a
proper stone for the grave, but this was utterly destroyed at
the monument works by a railroad train which apparently
jumped the track. The state of the grave was indicated in the
October 7, 1865 resolution of the Public School Teachers' Association: "The mortal remains of Edgar Allan Poe are interred
in the cemetery of the Westminster Church without even so
much as a stone to mark the spot." Ten years later the efforts
of their "committee of five" bore strange fruit in the ornate

granite and marble monument built by "Col." Hugh Sisson, whose establishment had never replaced the original grave-stone. The stilted suggested inscriptions and the fulsome trib-utes given at the unveiling[36] make one feel that perhaps the most appropriate epitaph for Edgar Allan Poe would, after all, be a simple "Miserrimus."

12

POE'S IRON PEN

THERE IS GENERAL agreement that "The Fall of The House of Usher" of September, 1839, is "Poe's finest short story."[1] Naturally, the list of recondite titles of obscure works, furnished by Poe in this Gothic tale, has engaged the attention of many commentators; they can all be authenticated, although not always in the form used by Poe, except for the "antique volume" called "The Mad Trist" of Sir Launcelot Canning.[2] This is the interior tale which, when narrated, serves as the textual accompaniment of the Lady Madeleine's efforts after seven or eight days of interment to free herself from her tomb; finally she returns to her twin brother, to destroy him in her death throes. Ethelred, the hero of "The Trist," has been described as breaking in the door of the "obstinate and maliceful" Hermit, only to find a "dragon of scaly and prodigious demeanour . . . which sate in guard before a palace of gold." The monster shrieks while being destroyed, thereby providing another grim sound to parallel the noises made by Madeleine in approaching her cowardly and homicidal brother.

This Gothic interlude—too well known to need detailed presentation—has surely seemed less interesting than the earlier portions of the fascinating tale of the neurasthenic dilettante, Roderick Usher with his "wild" guitar music, morbid painting, and general ambience of decadence. Professor Mabbott alone seems even to have bothered to detect the origin of Sir Launcelot Canning, "author" of "The Mad Trist." His note is characteristically brief and much to the point: "The Mad Trist's author, Sir Launcelot Canning, is surely a relative of Chatterton's mythical authors."[3] Given the context of a Gothic castle, "the dark deeds" of an insane English nobleman, and

a narrative of "uncouth and unimaginable prolixity," I find
rather fruitful this hint concerning the "William Canynge" of
Thomas Chatterton's "Thomas Rowley" poems. The source is
by no means to be limited to this one author, however, for it
is fairly obvious that Poe, an idolator of Tennyson, derived the
first part of his "buried" pseudonym from Tennyson's reference to Sir Lancelot, the gallant but blemished knight of the
Round Table, mentioned early in "The Lady of Shalott." Even
more astonishing is the fact that the name Poe used for the
author of this tale within a tale was used once again—this
time more directly as the pseudonym for Edgar Allan Poe in
his *Stylus* prospectus of 1843; within the prospectus he included a motto of three lines of verse on the subject of criticism, which was signed by "Launcelot Canning." If my conclu-
sions are correct, the two lines of verse in the narrative of "The
Mad Trist" and the three lines about magazine critics in his
prospectus must join the canon of Poe's poetry. More important than this addition is the need to explain fully the content
of those three lines in terms of the derivation of the imagery
and also of the titles of *The Penn* magazine and *The Stylus*.
For that inquiry we shall have to consider the reputation of
the Renaissance writer named Paulus Jovius or Paolo Giovio.

First, let us take note of Launcelot Canning in "The Fall of
the House of Usher." The period of the enframing story is contemporary, *vide* the reference to Von Weber's last waltz or
even the *Vert Vert* of Jean Baptiste Louis Gresset (1709–1777).[4]
The "Mad Trist" episode is deliberately "uncouth" in its *mise-
en-scène* and in its language. In this it is similar to Thomas
Chatterton's fraudulent medieval manuscripts. Of course, Poe
does not go to the length of ransacking Bailey's and Walker's
dictionaries for archaic terms, as did the "wonderful boy" for
his works. He merely remembers several of the obsolete terms
read in Scott and other historical novelists, changes spellings as
in "trist" for *tryst* in the title,[5] and gives us a veneer of medievalism which does not interfere with immediate comprehen-
sion.[6] On one page we have "maliceful," "uplifted his mace

outright," "alarumed," "sore enraged," and "sate" for *sat*, on the next, "pesty breath," "withal so piercing," "had fain to close," and finally "in sooth tarried not" (3.293–295). The quality of the language is shown also in the couplet that should be printed in any edition of Poe's complete poems, since Poe is undoubtedly the "romancer" named Canning. It is inscribed on the brass shield on the wall, to be read by the knight who has broken down the hermit's door:

> Who entereth herein, a conqueror hath bin;
> Who slayeth the dragon, the shield he shall win;

It is not difficult to prove Poe's awareness of the unhappy story of Thomas Chatterton, source of "Master Canynge" and Poe's "Sir Launcelot Canning." I believe that Poe also knew a somewhat less familiar sequel to Chatterton's unhappy story —that which involved the insidious Sir Herbert Croft, who profited enormously from the precious letters owned by Chatterton's family and who engaged in a celebrated literary controversy with Robert Southey. Chatterton, born at Bristol in 1752, son of the sexton of St. Mary Redcliffe's, derived notions about medievalism from the parchments which his father brought home from the muniment room of the church; medievalism was a stream which flowed freely, at that period, in the same channels as the sources of *The Castle of Otranto*. Horace Walpole, the author of this prototype of Gothic tales, had almost been beguiled by Chatterton's history of painting, purportedly composed by a fifteenth-century monk, Thomas Rowley, for his Bristol patron, William Canynge. After a prolific period of unremunerated hack work, the destitute Chatterton took arsenic when he was not yet eighteen years old. The outlines of his unhappy life were known to the American writer; Poe, after his virtually stillborn *Tamerlane and Other Poems* of 1827, liked to consider himself an unappreciated boy genius.

Poe's single reference to Chatterton in the collected works confirms this knowledge. It occurs in his review of the *Poetical*

Remains of the Late Lucretia Maria Davidson in *Graham's Magazine* of December, 1841. The two Davidson sisters, Lucretia Maria (1808–1825) and Margaret (1823–1838), of Plattsburg, New York, had become internationally famous for their precocious verse publications and their early death from tuberculosis.[7] Clearly they had many things in common with Chatterton, including Robert Southey's admiration. This is mentioned by Poe in his review of Washington Irving's *Biography and Remains of the Late Margaret Davidson,* in *Graham's* of August, 1841.[8] Four months later, Poe speaks again of her previously praised "Lenore" and of Lucretia's long poem *Amir Khan.*[9] As for Southey and Chatterton, Poe's reference is this:

> Partly through the Professor [Professor Morse's preface to Lucretia's poem *Amir Khan*], yet no doubt partly through their own merits, the poems found their way to the laureate, Southey, who, after his peculiar fashion, and not unmindful of his previous *furores* in the case of Kirke White, Chatterton, and others of precocious ability, or at least celebrity, thought proper to *review* them in the *Quarterly.*[10]

Apparently Poe knew that Southey had engaged in a verbal battle with Sir Herbert Croft, who had profited greatly from the epistolary novel into which he incorporated letters written by Chatterton to his mother and sister. The book exploited the growing interest in the dead poet even in its title: *Love and Madness; in a Series of Letters which contains the original account of Chatterton* (London, 1786).[11] The surrounding text consisted almost entirely of the letters exchanged between a "Mr. H." and "Miss R.," which tell of their trysts for four years and of his murdering her when she refuses to marry him. Croft, the so-called author, had managed to secure, probably from Kearsley, his publisher, the real letters of Mr. James Hackman, who had murdered Miss Reay, his inamorata, the mistress of the Earl of Sandwich; and this affair too was only thinly veiled in the sensational novel. The book reached nine editions and was widely known by the pithy title *Love and Madness.*[12]

Southey, in his reformistic mood of the late 1790's, admiring Chatterton as did the early romantics in general, became indignant when he discovered how Croft had cheated the impecunious and ailing mother and sister of Chatterton; he had promised them support in return for the use of their precious documents but paid them a total of eleven pounds, one shilling and sixpence. Announcing his projected volumes of Chatterton's works, Southey sent a letter to the *Monthly Magazine*, denouncing Croft. He even printed the letter as a handbill.[13] Croft, from abroad—or so he claimed to be—sent irate letters to the Tory *Gentleman's Magazine*, full of *ad hominem* arguments against Southey as a Jacobin.[14] With these he sought to distract the readers from his own obvious venality in the affair. Southey exposed his lies and trickery in a final letter to the *Monthly Magazine* of April, 1800.[15] Southey's publication in 1803 of the three volumes realized a goodly sum for the relief of Chatterton's family.[16] Poe must have heard about this famous controversy, as his reference above shows, and taken note of the title of Croft's book. In *Love and Madness* allusions to William Canynge might have suggested the Canning part of the pseudonym[17] (although Poe's source here could have been Chatterton directly), while the rendezvous and the dementia of "Mr. H." might have furnished "The Mad Trist" title.

There are two indications in Poe's works that he had dipped into Croft's stock of arcane learning. One of the letters of *Love and Madness* deals with the derivation of *The Life . . . of Robinson Crusoe* from Alexander Selkirk's "strange sequestration at Juan Fernandez." Croft (or Mr. Hackman) says: "It is mentioned, I believe, in Walter's account of Anson's Voyage (which, by the way, was not written by Walter, but by Robins),"[18] that is, Benjamin Robins (1707–1751). This is an allusion to the *Voyage Round the World* of Lord George Anson, British admiral (1697–1792), written by his chaplain, Richard Walter, and published in 1748. On doubtful grounds Benjamin Robins was given credit for a share in this popular

work.[19] Poe's "Marginalia" paragraph about far-fetched attribu-
tions is in the December, 1844 issue of the *Democratic Review:*

> For my part I agree with Joshua Barnes: nobody but Sol-
> omon could have written the Iliad. The catalogue of ships
> was the work of Robins. [Harrison, 16.37]

Poe derived his information about Joshua Barnes from H. N.
Coleridge's *Greek Classic Poets.* His interest in Robins, I believe, was stimulated by Croft.[20] The second indication of Poe's
knowledge of the novel concerns his discussion of "palpable
plagiarism":

> Goldsmith's celebrated lines
>> Man wants but little here below
>> Nor wants that little long.
> are stolen from Young; who has
>> Man wants but little, nor that little long.
>>   [Harrison, 14.47–48 and 16.76]

This is a point made in *Love and Madness.*[21]

"Sir Launcelot" presents very little difficulty, I feel. Poe's
admiration for Tennyson was frequently expressed, and it is
easy to prove his fondness for "The Lady of Shalott," which
had appeared in Tennyson's *Poems* of 1833.[22] (Tennyson's next
reference to Sir Launcelot was to be in his "Morte d'Arthur"
and "Sir Launcelot and Queen Guinevere," published in
1842.[23]) Poe's pseudonym in the "Usher" of 1839 derives from
"The Lady of Shalott," the third section of which tells of the
knight who fatally awakens the girl. (Incidentally, there are
marked resemblances here to the knight in "Eldorado."[24]) Poe's
awareness of the early volume is shown through charges of
plagiarism incurred by his 1827 volume, which he counters
with his headnote of 1845: "Private reasons . . . which have
reference to . . . the date of Tennyson's first poems—have
induced me . . . to re-publish these, the crude compositions of
my earliest boyhood" (Harrison, 7.xlix). It is to this charge also
that Poe alludes in a letter to Lowell, in which he shows his
knowledge of the dates of Tennyson's early poetry.[25] In his

Drake-Halleck review of April, 1836, Poe had referred to Tennyson with an implied familiarity with his works and also in a context of medieval knight errantry.[26] Clearly, he knew the 1833 volume of poetry well. As for Poe's specific knowledge of Sir Lancelot from "The Lady of Shalott," there are three references to the poem, all of which come after 1839 but which indicate a long-standing acquaintance with the poem; these references are in August, 1843, December, 1844, and June, 1845.[27] Without doubt Poe was deeply aware of this lyrical and medieval early poem by Tennyson, and, I think, borrowed the name, Sir Lancelot, in an archaic spelling employed by Tennyson himself in 1842 at the first printing of "Sir Launcelot and Queen Guinevere."

In continuing our pursuit of Sir Launcelot Canning we must follow Poe into one of the most complicated and deeply worn paths that he ever trod—his attempt to found a magazine for whose editorial policy he would be solely responsible and which would guarantee him a sizable income such as was enjoyed by Thomas W. White of the *Messenger* or George R. Graham of *Graham's Magazine* (an income that he felt reflected then the labors of Edgar Allan Poe more than of any other person on the staff). But Poe's ambitions were not primarily materialistic or egotistic, save in the sense that he wished to become a cultural force in a nation that sadly needed one. Of course, the New England literati expressed their own viewpoint, which Poe variously derided as moralistic or puritanical, provincial, and transcendental—that of the "Frogpond," as he often called it—while New York literary aspirations were expressed, rather badly he thought, through *The Knickerbocker* of the detested Lewis Gaylord Clark. The Philadelphia magazines had yielded to frilly prettiness or the "namby-pamby" style, as he termed it more than once,[28] and the *Southern Literary Messenger* had gone to ruin since his departure. While serving under the unappreciative and crass theatrical man William Burton, Poe cherished the ideal of having his own organ with which to lead "the literary community."[29] To see how constant was this effort to secure the necessary financial backing through a patron and through subscribers, glance into the indices of any biography of Poe under the headings *"The Penn"* and *"The Stylus."* Poe called control of a powerful magazine "the one great purpose of my literary life." Unhappily, it was never fulfilled, even when he had the *Broadway Journal,* the moribund relic of Charles F. Briggs, in his own hands in 1845.[30]

Perhaps I should explain why this long and tangled series of false starts and almost successful journeys, as with Thomas Cottrell Clarke in 1843 and Edward N. H. Patterson of Oquawka, Ohio, in 1848, should involve the study of "Launcelot Canning." The answer lies in one of the many forms of the printed prospectus for the magazine, that of March 4, 1843, on which appears a motto concerning the type of literary criticism that was to be a major feature of *The Stylus.* The three lines of poetry, which deserve a place in the Poe canon, are signed "Launcelot Canning." It is found in Quinn's reprint of portions of this prospectus but not in any of Poe's collected works.[31] This omission may have caused Poe students to overlook the fact that the author of "The Mad Trist," now deprived of his sobriquet "Sir," is the author of the motto statement on *The Stylus:*

> —unbending that all men
> Of thy firm Truth may say—"Lo! this is writ
> With the antique *iron pen.*"
> Launcelot Canning

This motto is pregnant with implications for Poe's critical opinions and literary efforts throughout the rest of his career.

First I must indicate the way in which the "pen" or "Penn" magazine became the "Stylus," as far as the prospectus of the journal and Poe's glowing plans were concerned. Poe must have been revolving in his mind the founding of his own magazine soon after his departure from the *Messenger* in January, 1837, but his abject poverty made this simply a fantasy. During his unsatisfactory association, as a subordinate, with William E. Burton of the *Gentleman's* Magazine, July, 1839 to June, 1840, the fantasy came to assume body and substance. In a letter of June, 1840, recriminating Burton for his plans (inadequately concealed) to sell the journal to free himself for the stage, Poe avows his own magazine plans more definitely than before: "Had I not firmly believed it your design to give up your Journal, with a view of attending to the Theatre, I should [never] have dreamed of attempting one of my own" (Ostrom, 1.132). I cite this to explain Poe's rather rapid production of a prospectus for *The Penn* magazine in the *Saturday Courier* of June 13, 1840. Strangely enough, although there was to be a succession of modified and revised prospectuses, this first is the only form of Poe's fundamental position on magazine publication which has been widely available in entirety to the students of Poe.[32] Since the country and, as usual, Poe were in the midst of a financial depression, the would-be proprietor became an associate of Graham on the reorganized *Gentleman's Magazine* sold by Burton; he postponed but did not abandon the publication of *The Penn*.

By 1842, after he was separated from *Graham's Magazine*, Poe revived his plan for *The Penn*.[33] On February 3, 1842, he wrote to F. W. Thomas that "The project of the new Magazine still . . . occupies my thoughts" and expresses his belief that it "might even play an important part in the politics of the day, like Blackwood" (Ostrom, 1.192). This notion represents an expansion of the critical and literary purpose he had previously entertained. On July 6, 1842 (Ostrom, 1.208) and October 5 (1.216) he still thinks of the magazine as *The Penn*. Moreover, up to September 27, 1842, Poe has not had a new prospectus printed (Ostrom, 1.214).

When Thomas Cottrell Clarke, publisher of the weekly *Saturday Museum* of Philadelphia, offered to patronize Poe's new magazine, the name was changed to *The Stylus*, since *The Penn* was a too local pun on Pennsylvania plus editor's pen. A new prospectus was printed by February 23, 1843, when Poe used one of the broadsides as writing paper for his letter to Frederick W. Thomas (Ostrom, 1.223–225). The same letter alludes to the prospectus as being "on the outside" of Clarke's *Saturday Museum*. Quinn has covered adequately the propaganda campaign conducted by the *Museum*, beginning with Poe's front-page biography in the issue of February 25, 1843, reprinted in the March 4 issue. Poe also mentions to Thomas his having to supply all the literary material for the first year under his own name and "pseudonyms." His being represented, in a sense, as "Launcelot Canning" in the advance notice of the magazine is significant.

I know of no study *per se* of the pseudonyms used by Poe for his various personae throughout his anxious and unhappy life. If ever there lived a sensitive being with reason to wish himself possessed of another form, it was Poe, especially after he found himself cut off from the benefits that he had expected as a member of John Allan's family. From that early period he must frequently have thought of himself under the guise of other names and other personalities. The pseudonyms that he used fall into three groups: the names that he used as incognitos; those which he signed to tales or poems as the author, which were not intrinsic to the action of the fiction itself; and, third, those in which he became the named character through the device of autobiographical narrative. Of the first group, the earliest was Henri Le Rennet, used in 1827.[34] Upon entering the United States Army on May 26, 1827, Poe gave the pseudonym of Edgar A. Perry, as well as the false age of twenty-two. As Quinn observes, since "minors were at that time accepted, it is evident that Poe intended to disappear."[35]

Perhaps the development of his creative gifts through the ensuing years after his return from Fort Moultrie enabled Poe to represent himself in the many narrators, for whatever motivations of catharsis or sublimation one may impute to the creative act. Only in 1844 do we find "a seedy looking gentleman" giving his name as Thaddeus Perley to Mr. Gabriel Harrison, tobacconist and president of the White Eagle Political

Club. When he returned a few weeks later for a second "hand-out" of tobacco, he also wrote a campaign song for the club called "The White Eagle"—an act for which he accepted a bag of coffee.[36] "Edward S. T. Grey," the next one of Poe's pseudonyms, was used first in a disguised note sent to Mrs. Helen Whitman on September 5, 1848 (Ostrom, 2.367); and finally in a plan to have Maria Clemm send her future mail "direct to Phila. For fear I should not get the letter, sign no name & address it to E. S. T. Grey Esqre" (Ostrom, 2.461).[37]

As for his first-person narratives—the scope of his imaginative role-playing appears throughout his varied "autobiographies." It is worthy of note, perhaps, that Poe, uncertain about his place in the family of John Allan, should so often have given no name at all to the narrator, as in the "Ms. Found in a Bottle" or "The Assignation" or "The Tell-Tale Heart," an omission which helps to universalize each of these tales. Often the names are brief or generalized or, occasionally, humorous. The narrator of "Berenice" is Egeus (Shakespeare's?); of "Lionizing," Robert Jones; of "William Wilson," the character of that name; of "How to Write a Blackwood Article," Signora Psyche Zenobia; of "Why the Little Frenchman," Sir Pathrick O'Grandison; of "The Spectacles," Adolphus Simpson, né Napoleon Bonaparte Froissart; of "The Literary Life," Thingum Bob, Esquire; of "The Cask of Amontillado," Montresor; of "Mellonta Tauta," Pundita, of "The Business Man," Peter Pendulum, changed to Peter Proffit; of *The Narrative*, Arthur Gordon Pym, significantly of Edgarton, Nantucket, and of "The Journal," Julius Rodman.

Of the pseudonyms which Poe gave to his writings, aside from the last two autobiographical travels ("Pym" and "Rodman"), there are only two or three before "Launcelot Canning," although one name was to be applied to five tales. The first was attached to a satire, "The Atlantis, a Southern World —or a wonderful Continent discovered," by Peter Prospero, published in the *Baltimore American Museum*, serially, September, 1838, to June, 1839. Although it has not been collected by Harrison, I believe that A. H. Quinn is correct in his attribution, as I have shown elsewhere.[38] The name Peter Prospero (like that of Peter Proffit in "The Business Man") has a mocking irrelevancy to Poe and also a touch of whimsy in its combination of the humdrum "Peter" with the Italian "Prospero," perhaps reminiscent of the prince in "The Masque of the Red Death." This stylistic discrepancy between forename and family name can be found in Launcelot and Canning.

Early in 1845, Poe published "The Raven," under the curious pseudonym of "Quarles."[39] I scarcely think that he ignored Francis Quarles, whose name occurs in his 1836 review of S. C. Hall's *The Book of Gems* (Harrison, 9.91); there may be a small measure of fitness in the fact that Quarles published in 1620 his paraphrase of the book of Jonah, entitled *Feast of Wormes,* and in 1635 his more famous *Emblems.* I doubt that the pseudonym was derived from the word for controversies (quarrels) in which Poe was so often embroiled. As for the possibility that this pseudonym led to its extension as Quarles Quickens, satire on Charles Dickens, I leave that exploded theory to the multifold pages of Mary Phillips.[40] Later in the year 1845, Poe signed "Lyttleton Barry" to five of his early tales when he reprinted them in the *Broadway Journal.*[41] In these two words are implied many possibilities of literary and personal meaning, just as in Launcelot Canning. There is, first of all, George Lord Lyttleton (1709–1773), to whose celebrated *Dialogues of the Dead* Poe alludes in the "Pinakidia" of 1836 (14.56). "Barry" could easily have been suggested by the popular Barry Cornwall, pseudonym of Bryan Waller Procter (1787–1874), poet, dramatist, etc., whom Poe mentions four times.[42] But I think that a more important author—at least in Poe's day—suggests the two names, Bulwer Lytton himself, who loomed so important in Poe's criticism and also in his creative works.[43] The similarity of initials and the near correspondence of syllables manifest Poe at his word-play methods.[44]

It is fitting that in 1843 Poe should have dropped the "Sir" part of the pseudonym used in "The Fall of the House of

Usher," when he attached the name to a motto sounding the trumpet call of "firm Truth" in criticism, rather than the minor strains of Gothic melodrama. Yet the archaic quality of Canning, from William Canynge, is carried over a bit in the phrase "With the antique *iron pen*" of the verses. Since the lines occur in the never completely reprinted prospectus to *The Stylus* of 1843, I shall briefly postpone discussion until the reader can see how they fit into the total text, taken from the Philadelphia *Saturday Museum* of March 4, 1843:[45]

Prospectus of the Stylus:
A Monthly Journal of General Literature
TO BE EDITED BY

E D G A R   A .   P O E
And Published, in the City of Philadelphia, by
C L A R K E   &   P O E

——————— unbending that all men
Of thy firm TRUTH may say—"Lo! this is writ
With the antique *iron pen*."
Launcelot Canning

1   *To the Public.*—The Prospectus of a Monthly Journal to have been called "THE PENN MAGAZINE," has already been partially circulated. Circumstances, in which the public have no interest, induced a suspension of the project, which is now, under the best auspices, resumed, with no other modification than that of the title. "The Penn Magazine," it has been thought; and "THE STYLUS" has been finally adopted.

2   It has become obvious, indeed, to even the most unthinking, that the period has at length arrived when a journal of the character here proposed, is demanded and will be sustained. The late movements on the great question of International Copy-Right, are but an index of the universal *disgust* excited by what is quaintly termed the cheap literature of the day:—as if that which is utterly worthless in itself can be cheap at any price under the sun.

3   "The Stylus" will include about one hundred royal octavo

pages, in single column, per month; forming two thick volumes per year. In its mechanical appearance—in its typography, paper and binding—it will far surpass all American journals of its kind. Engravings, when used, will be in the highest style of Art, but are promised only in obvious illustration of the text, and in strict keeping with the Magazine character. Upon application to the proprietors, by any agent of repute who may desire the work, or by any other individual who may feel interested, a specimen sheet will be forwarded. As, for many reasons, it is inexpedient to commence a journal of this kind at any other period than the beginning or middle of the year, the first number of "The Stylus" will not be regularly issued until the first of July, 1843. In the meantime, to insure its perfect and permanent success, no means will be left untried which long experience, untiring energy, and the amplest capital, can supply. The price will be *Five Dollars* per annum, or *Three Dollars* per single volume, in advance. Letters which concern only the Editorial management may be addressed to Edgar A. Poe, individually; all others to Clarke & Poe.

4   The necessity for any very rigid definition of the literary character or aims of "The Stylus," is, in some measure, obviated by the general knowledge, on the part of the public, of the editor's connexion, formerly, with the two most successful periodicals in the country—"The Southern Literary Messenger," and "Graham's Magazine." Having no proprietary right, however, in either of these journals; his objects, too, being, in many respects, at variance with those of their very worthy owners; he found it not only impossible to effect anything, on the score of taste, for the mechanical appearance of the works, but exceedingly difficult, also, to stamp, upon their internal character, that *individuality* which he believes essential to the full success of all similar publications. In regard to their extensive and permanant influence, it appears to him that continuity, definitiveness, and a marked certainty of purpose, are requisites of vital importance; and he cannot help thinking that these requisites are attainable, only where a single mind has at least *the general* direction of the enterprise. Experience, in a word, has distinctly shown

him—what, indeed, might have been demonstrated *à priori* —that in founding a Magazine wherein his interest should be not merely editorial, lies his sole chance of carrying out to completion whatever peculiar intentions he may have entertained.

5   In many important points, then, the new journal will differ widely from either of those named. It will endeavor to be at the same time more varied and more *unique*;—more vigorous, more pungent, more original, more individual, and more independent. It will discuss not only the Belles-Lettres, but, very thoroughly, the Fine Arts, with the Drama; and, more in brief, will give, each month, a Retrospect of our Political History. It will enlist the loftiest talent, but employ it not always in the loftiest—at least not always in the most pompous or Puritanical way. It will aim at affording a fair and not dishonorable field for the *true* intellect of the land, without reference to the mere prestige of celebrated names. It will support the general interests of the Republic of Letters, and insist upon regarding the world at large as the sole proper audience for the author. It will resist the dictation of Foreign Reviews. It will eschew the stilted dulness of our own Quarterlies, and while it *may*, if necessary, be no less learned, will deem it wiser to be less anonymous, and difficult to be more dishonest, than they.

6   An important feature of the work, and one which will be introduced in the opening number, will be a series of *Critical* and *Biographical Sketches of American Writers*. These Sketches will be accompanied with full length and characteristic portraits; will include every person of literary note in America; and will investigate carefully and with rigorous impartiality, the individual claims of each.

7   It shall, in fact, be the *chief purpose* of "The Stylus," to become known as a journal wherein may be found, at all times, upon all subjects within its legitimate reach, a sincere and a fearless opinion. It shall be a leading object to assert in precept, and to maintain in practice, the rights, while, in effect, it demonstrates the advantages, of an absolutely independent criticism;—a criticism self-sustained; guiding itself only by the purest rules of Art; analyzing and urging these

rules as it applies them, holding itself aloof from all personal bias; and acknowledging no fear, save that of outraging
the Right.

CLARK & POE

8   N.B. Those friends of the Proprietors, throughout the
     country, who may feel disposed to support "The Stylus," will
     confer an important favor by sending in their names *at once.*
9   The provision in respect to payment *"in advance,"* is
     intended only as a general rule, and has reference to the
     Magazine *when established.* In the commencement, the sub-
     scription money will not be demanded until the issue of the
     second number.

C & P

Certainly no great creative effort was needed for the versi-
fied motto. Yet it should be placed unequivocally in the canon
of Poe's poetry, along with Poe's examples of dactylics and
hexameters in "The Rationale of Verse," which have been left
out of every edition of his poetry thus far (Harrison, 14.228
and 265). As for "Canning's" metrics, one wonders what verse
form Poe was implying for the poem of which this is supposed
to be a part, since the first line, printed as though the end of
one, contains three iambic feet, which correspond with those
of the third line (an anapest substituting for an iambus in the
first foot). The second line is scarcely reconcilable with the
others, since it starts with three feet of iambic trimeter and
then veers into feet lacking the first unstressed syllable before
the resumption of the iambic pattern ("Lo! this is writ). It is
what Poe too loosely called "catalectic" (14.244). Perhaps Poe
showed that he felt the lines to be weak when he dropped the
motto from two other versions of the prospectus, printed in
1848 (although there may have been another cause in that he
provided a Latin motto plus a picture for the title page, as we
shall see). The idea of the lines is close to the prospectuses that
he had prepared, all of which stress his resolution as sole editor
of the newly founded magazine to deliver an "honest and fear-

less opinion" (paragraph 3 in 1840) or "a sincere and a fearless opinion" (in 1843 and 1848). Poe was conscious, of course, of being called the tomahawk critic, and commentators often try to vindicate his unsparing slashing of weak authors like Norman Leslie or Thomas Ward ("Flaccus") as well as his sentimental sparing of literary ladies whose sole merits lay in their good intentions and femininity.[46]

In view of the picture, however, that he drew later for the title page of *The Stylus*, with a prominent place given to "truth," it is important to realize that Poe earnestly thought of his role in criticism as a *vates*, drawing his dicta from some aesthetic height and gifted with a sense of first principles as absolute and immanent as those of the New England moralists or Puritans, as he sneeringly called them in the prospectus. Appropriately he capitalizes every letter of "Truth," for his sense of truth as a critic is fundamentally derived from the aesthetic empyrean. Throughout the prospectus he promises that he will be unsparing or, as he says in the motto, "unbending"; the new journal will try to be "more vigorous, more pungent, more original, more individual and more independent" (paragraph 5). It will offer "a fair field" for the *"true* [Poe's italics] intellect of the land." Compared with such quarterlies as the *North American Review The Stylus* will find it "difficult" to be as "dishonest" (5, last sentence). In its "Critical and Biographical sketches of American Writers" (basis of the "Literati" sketches), it will present with "rigorous impartiality" the "claims of each" (6). It will be "aloof from all personal bias," and will fear only "outraging the Right," another capital concept, if we may pun in using a favorite Poe adjective (7). Poe wished to establish a "vision of Literary Order" or a "Republic of Letters," but one fears that a functioning *Stylus* would only have established a none-too-benevolent autocracy, ruled absolutely by the caustic critic Edgar Allan Poe; witness his narrow or narrowing concept of the beautiful in "The Philosophy of Composition" (Harrison, 14.201) or "The Poetic Principle" (14.290).[47] Nevertheless, Poe vigorously maintained this estimate of his own peculiar ability to convey truth, interpreted a little in the Keatsian strain.

Another key phrase in Poe's motto, the "antique iron pen," needs explanation, although of course it obviously refers both to the title of the magazine and to the objectivity of the managing editor. This is explained by Poe in his second sentence: "'The Penn Magazine,' it has been thought, was a name somewhat too local in its suggestions, and THE STYLUS has been finally adopted." Launcelot Canning, of course, did not originate the phrase "iron pen," which was, to be sure, "antique" in itself, being found in the Old Testament, Jeremiah 17:1: "Written with a pen of iron, and with the point of a diamond [Scriptum est stylo ferreo in unque adamantino]."[48] I believe that Poe combined the biblical reference with one which he picked up from Wallace's novel *Stanley*, from which he had borrowed many erudite references.[49] The basic source, as I shall prove, was Paolo Giovio, known as Paulus Jovius (1483–1552) of Como, Florence, Rome, and other places. His Latin *Lives of Illustrious Men* (*Elogia virorum illustrium*) of 1546 and *History of His Own Times* (*Pauli Jovii historiarum sui temporis*) of 1550 won fame and fortune for him; he had the papal patrons Leo X and Clement VII, and the royal patrons Francis I and Charles V. The well-known fact about this wealthy, venal man was that he wrote history and biography to please his benefactors. All the commentaries concur in associating him with a saying that he had two pens, one of gold and the other of iron, depending upon the payment or favors received. In view of Poe's attributing the statement in Latin directly to Jovius (see below), I have sought the original source but with little success. Michaud refers the idea to his letters, but my perusal of those collected has not revealed the statement.[50] The *Grand Dictionnaire Universel* implies that this was said of Jovius by Brantôme, the chatty annalist, but that source has not yielded it.[51] Pierre Bayle in his *Dictionnaire Historique et critique* asserts that "some said that he prided himself on having" the two pens for princes who had been generous to him or parsimonious.[52]

Alexander Chalmers cautiously writes that he "is said to have
asserted that he had two pens, the one of iron and the other of
gold, which he made use of alternately, as occasion required."[53]
Apparently, it is the less cautious or the epitomizing sources,
such as Joseph Thomas, which attribute it directly to him.[54]
The ambiguous derivation seems to be this: "The old story that
he said he kept a golden and an iron pen, to use according as
people paid him, condenses the truth in epigram."[55] It is
impossible to determine whose epigram it originally was.

Wallace's inept comparison of the independent pens of Pope
and Jovius led to Poe's allusion, printed in the "Marginalia"
of the *Messenger*, July, 1849:

> Paulus Jovius, living in those benighted times when dia-
> mond-pointed styluses were as yet unknown, thought proper,
> nevertheless, to speak of his goosequill as *"aliquando ferreus,
> aureus aliquando"*—intending, of course, a mere figure of
> speech; and from the class of modern authors who use really
> nothing to write with but steel and gold, some, no doubt,
> will let their pens, *vice versâ*, descend to posterity under
> the designation of "anserine"—of course, intending always
> a mere figure of speech. [Harrison, 16.168]

Poe's comment on Jovius's phrase shows either an unlikely
ignorance of Jeremiah or a deliberate warping of the point of
"adamantine" in order to make a pun on the goose quill and
"goose heads" of authors. I doubt that Poe was ignorant of
Byron's words on the subject, at the very beginning of *English
Bards and Scotch Reviewers*, a work which he knew well:

> Oh! Nature's noblest gift—my grey-goose quill!
> Slave of my thoughts, obedient to my will,
> Torn from thy parent bird to form a pen,
> That mighty instrument of little men![56]

The bimetallic standard of Jovius obviously made a strong
impression on Poe. When he was finally successful in securing
another backer of his magazine after the Clarke fiasco in 1843,
in the person of E. H. N. Patterson, owner of the Oquawka,

Illinois, *Spectator,* in May, 1849, he sent the man a title page "designed by myself about a year ago" (Ostrom, 2.443). On it appears a motto in Latin purporting to be the words of Paulus Jovius, although somewhat differently arranged from Poe's "Marginalia" citation: "Aureus aliquando STYLUS, ferreus aliquando."

At the same time, in January and again in April, 1848, Poe revised the prospectus in his final search for subscribers and a patron. The January version of this "critical work" by Poe was printed in 1934 by Robertson, but it has been apparently ignored by students of Poe.[57] The final version of the prospectus, dated April, 1848, originally contained in a letter of February 29, 1848, is owned by the Lilly Library of Indiana University. I reprint the text of this presumably unique copy below.[58] The revised prospectus does not include the 1843 motto by "Launcelot Canning." In a way, it has received a substitute in the motto now assigned to the title page of the "forthcoming" magazine as designed by Poe himself. Poe apparently had a strong sense of the epitomizing force of a good motto. This is seen in his changing the mottoes of works that he reprinted, or in his adding them to many tales when reprinted in the *Broadway Journal.* In critical references too he evinces this sense, as when he says about the detested *North American Review:* "As I see no motto on its title-page, let me recommend it one" (Harrison, 16.145) or when he discusses the overlong poetic mottoes heading the verses of Mrs. Hemans and Mrs. Sigourney (8.125–126). In addition to the change concerning the motto, the last prospectus for Poe's "dream" shows many changes of content, chiefly in a shift away from criticism as the sole purpose of *The Stylus.*

THE

STYLUS

*A Monthly Journal of Literature Proper,
the Fine Arts and the Drama.*

TO BE EDITED BY

EDGAR A. POE

1   *To the Public.*—Since resigning the conduct of the Southern Literary Messenger at the beginning of its third year, and
more especially since retiring from the editorship of Graham's Magazine soon after the commencement of its second,
I have had always in view the establishment of a monthly
journal which should retain one or two of the chief features
of the work first mentioned, abandoning or greatly modify-
ing its general character;—but not until now have I felt at
liberty to attempt the execution of the design.

2   I shall be pardoned for speaking more directly of the two
magazines in question. Having in neither of them any proprietary right; the objects of their worthy owners, too, being
at variance with my own; I found it not only impossible to
effect anything, on the score of taste, for their mechanical
appearance, but difficult to stamp upon them internally that
individuality which I believed essential to their success. In
regard to the permanent influence of such publications, it
appears to me that continuity and a marked certainty of
purpose are requisites of vital importance; but attainable
only where one mind alone has at least the general control. Experience, to be brief, has shown me that in founding
a journal of my own, lies my sole chance of carrying out
to completion whatever peculiar intentions I may have
entertained.

3   These intentions are now as heretofore. It shall be the
chief purpose of the magazine proposed, to become known
as one wherein may be found at all times, on all topics
within its legitimate reach, a sincere and a fearless opinion.
It shall be a leading object to assert in precept and to maintain in practice the rights, while in effect it demonstrates
the advantages, of an absolutely independent criticism:—
a criticism self-sustained; guiding itself only by intelligible
laws of art; analyzing these laws as it applies them; holding
itself aloof from all personal bias, and acknowledging no
fear save that of outraging the Right.

4   There is no design, however, to make the journal a critical
one solely, or even very especially. It will aim at something
more than the usual magazine variety, and at affording a
fair field for the *true* talent of the land, without reference
to the mere *prestige* of name or the advantages of worldly

position. But since the efficiency of the work must in great
measure depend upon its definitiveness, The Stylus will
limit itself strictly to *Literature Proper, the Fine Arts and
the Drama.*

5   In regard to what is going on, within the limits assigned,
throughout the civilized world, it will be a principal object
of the magazine to keep its readers really *au courant.* For
this end, accurate arrangements have been made [at] London, Paris, Rome and Vienna. The most distinguished of
American scholars has agreed to superint[end the] department of classical letters. At *all* points the most effective
aid is secured.

6   In the matter of mechanical execution it is proposed to
surpass *by very much* the ordinary magazine style[. The]
Stylus will include about 100 royal octavo pages per month;
forming two thick volumes per year. The pap[er will] be of
superior texture; the type bold and clear. The price will be
Five Dollars per annum, in advance[. The] provision in
respect to advance payment, however, is meant only as a
general rule and in reference to the m[agazine] when established. In the commencement, the subscription will not be
considered *due* until the issue of th[e third] number.

Edgar A. Poe

New York City, April, 1848

SUBSCRIBERS.   RESIDENCE.

A comparison of the three prospectuses reveals many interesting shifts in Poe's thought about the role of the magazine
in national culture and the role of criticism.[59] From the two
additional prospectuses printed above, it appears evident that
Poe has gone back to *The Penn* prospectus for the major part
of his 1848 version. The first paragraphs in both are the same
save that *Graham's Magazine* is now added to the *Messenger*
as his "points of departure" in editing (see paragraph 4 of
1843). Slight changes in wording occur in paragraphs 2 and 3.
The 1840 "purest rules of Art" now become "intelligible laws
of art," and there is no return to the discussion of the "overdone causticity" in the critical notices and the "mellowing" of
the formerly petulant critic. At the same time, the petulance

of paragraph 2 of 1843 entirely disappears from the last prospectus. Paragraph 4 voices a concept new to *The Penn* but
not to the 1843 *Stylus,* in which the fifth paragraph speaks of
discussing "the Belles-Lettres, . . . the Fine Arts, . . . the
Drama" and of provision for a "Retrospect of our Political History." While the "fair field for the *true* talent of the land"
suggests the "Republic of Letters" (paragraph 5, 1843), mentioned in *The Penn* (without capitals), an emphasis which
Lewis Simpson finds paramount in both, the elimination of the
phrase suggests a more disillusioned Poe, less comradely in
feeling with the many literati (save for the women), who had
drawn away from him during the years.

Yet he seems to broaden the scope of the magazine—purely
critical in 1840 and called a "Monthly Journal of General
Literature" in 1843—to a true cultural organ in 1848; notice
the subtitle and the italics of the same phrase in paragraph 4
(*"Literature Proper,"* etc.). The element of political history,
included in 1843, has now disappeared, another proof perhaps
of Poe's disenchantment with that field. And yet the ideas current in the world of broad culture are now to become a regular feature, through European correspondents, while Charles
Anthon, as is clearly intended, will supervise "classical letters."[60] This feature, in a sense, counterbalances the loss of the
1843 idea, in paragraph 4, of a series of "Critical and Biographical Sketches of American Writers," to be investigated
with "rigorous impartiality." The publication of the "Literati"
papers made this less urgent, and the antagonisms and outcries
stimulated may have taught him the danger of thus passing
judgment *ex cathedra* on his fellow authors. Most important,
throughout the entire prospectus, the language is modified
from its bold, self-righteous tone in the first two versions; Poe
still insists on "one mind alone" in "general control" (paragraph 2), "a sincere and a fearless opinion," and an "independent criticism," but he eliminates all contemptuous remarks to
the "arrogance" of "organized *cliques*" (1840) or the "pompous
or Puritanical way" and "stilted dulness" of the quarterlies

(1843). Also, the aim, which was to "please" in 1840 and to "judge" in 1843, now seems a bit uncertain, as one might expect from the erratic course of Poe's life during 1847–1849. There are hints in the subtitle and in paragraphs 4 and 5 that perhaps Poe was less averse to the Utilitarian or Benthamite goal of general enlightenment as presupposing the improvement of public taste. And yet paragraphs 2 and 3 still contain the core of his opinion—that a magazine must exert a vigorous and individualized critical influence to lead to national growth and to broad effectiveness.

And this was clearly shown in the design that Poe sketched for Mr. Patterson in Oquawka, enclosing it in his letter of May 23, 1849, showing a right hand with an iron stylus writing on a tablet the Greek word for "truth," with Jovius's Latin motto underneath it and the words "Edited by Edgar A. Poe" at the very bottom.[61] (See the frontispiece illustration of this book.)

We now see clearly that the iron pen or "stylus" was derived from Paulus Jovius, whose form of utterance is slightly different from the *Messenger* citation. The iron pen, having nothing to do with the flattery of Jovius, is shown in the hand of the editor. Poe seems unaware of the venality of Jovius, in view of his identification of the motto on the title page. Although the poetic motto of "Launcelot Canning" has disappeared from the prospectus, the title page of the journal preserves and interestingly displays its essential phrase. The editor's opinion, we had been told, must be open only to truth, not to "personal bias" or "fear" of outraged dignity, and this stress is continued in the word written by the iron pen, for we can easily see the Greek word for truth, "Aletheia" ('Αλήθεια) or rather "Alethe" ('Αλήθε) since the pen has not completed the whole. Poe had delivered metaphysical and scientific truth to America the previous year in *Eureka*, and the same spirit apparently drove him in his search for a magazine that would bring an enlightening criticism to an unappreciative and uncomprehending America.

NOTES

NOTES TO CHAPTER 1

1. Poe changed the form of the title rather significantly; the first one, in *Graham's Magazine*, 20.257–259, and also in the *Literary Souvenir*, 5 (June, 1842), 172–173, clearly emphasizes the "mask" covering the face of the spectral figure who brings the plague, since this was an uncommon spelling for masquerade or masque in nineteenth-century America (see the *OED*). The subtitle serves to underscore the dreamlike and theatrical quality of the whole. Poe's collection of tales, planned for 1842, was to be called "Phantasy Pieces," a clear sign of the importance Poe attached to the "fantasy" element of this and other tales. For the publication attempt see Arthur Hobson Quinn, *Edgar Allan Poe* (New York, 1941), pp. 337–340, to which text hereafter I shall refer as "Quinn."

2. See Franz Karl Mohr, "The Influence of Eichendorff's 'Ahnung und Gegenwart' on Poe's 'Masque of the Red Death'" in *Modern Language Quarterly*, 10 (Mar., 1949), 3–15, and Joseph P. Roppolo, "Meaning and 'The Masque of the Red Death,'" in *Tulane Studies in English*, 13 (1963), 59–69. Eichendorff's novel was almost certainly unavailable to Poe for many reasons. The suggested *I Promessi Sposi*, it is now known, was not reviewed by Poe, as erroneously listed by James A. Harrison, ed., *The Complete Works of Edgar Allan Poe* (New York, 1902), 8.12, to which edition my text will refer under "Harrison."

3. Thomas Ollive Mabbott, in his *Selected Poetry and Prose of Edgar Allan Poe* (New York, 1951), p. 422, offers the following note: "The references to Victor Hugo's *Hernani* are suggestive, for the hero of that play must die when his enemy sounds a horn." I must add that there is only *one* reference in Poe's tale.

4. See Harrison, 4.250–258 and 4.319–320, for the text and variant readings.

5. For a possible source of the black draperies in *Miserrimus,* a novel which Poe admired, see chap. xi below. For sources of the ending see chap. v below.

6. For example see Régis Messac, *Influences françaises dans l'oeuvre d'Edgar Poe* (Paris, 1929), pp. 91–94, for an unsubstantiated tracing of the color scheme of the seven chambers to *Voyages et aventures des trois princes de Sarendip* by de Mailly. There is no correspondence in colors but a very malapropos correspondence of costume shadings. Una Pope-Hennessy, in *Edgar Allan Poe* (London, 1934), pp. 139–140, borrows from Messac without ascription.

7. Cambiaire, *The Influence of Edgar Allan Poe in France* (New York, 1927); Lauvrière, *Edgar Poe, sa vie et son oeuvre* (Paris, 1904); and Colling, *Edgar Poe* (Paris, 1952).

8. For a reference to Poe as fitting psychologically into Hugo's Paris of 1828, see *Revue Contemporaine,* 15 juillet 1857, p. 496, cited by Leon Lemonnier, *Poe et la critique française* (Paris, 1928), p. 28. Lemonnier's excellent studies *Poe et les poètes français* (1932) and *Poe et les conteurs français* (1947) yield no reference to Hugo.

9. Matthew Josephson, *Victor Hugo* (New York, 1942), p. 132.

10. Author's translation.

11. It appeared in the *Foreign Quarterly Review,* 1 (July, 1827), 60–97, for a discussion of which see Quinn, p. 289. For Poe's preface, see Harrison, 1.150–151.

12. It must be granted that for use in both "The Mask of the Red Death" and "The Assignation" (Harrison, 2.109–124) Poe might have recalled the grotesque décor of "the palace of that arch-brained Italian prince" with his "depraved imagination" who is mentioned by Scott in his article on p. 93.

13. Author's translation of excerpts from *Cromwell* in Victor Hugo's *Oeuvres Complètes* (Paris, 1881), 1.17–23. I find that Lewis A. Lawson, "Poe and the Grotesque," in *Poe Newsletter,* 1 (Apr., 1968), 9–10, also lists *Cromwell* and Scott's review as possible sources for Poe's concept.

14. The review is in 2.715–718, this excerpt on 716. Among many references by Poe to this journal see those in his *Letters,* ed.

John W. Ostrom (Cambridge, Mass., 1948) 1.246–247 and 253–254, and Harrison, 2.36, 13.31, 15.23–24. See also Lewis A. Lawson's article, "Poe's Conception of the Grotesque," in *Mississippi Quarterly*, 19 (1966), 200–205, asserting that Poe had read the Scott review not very long before 1835.

15. L. Petit de Julleville, *Histoire de la langue et de la littérature française* (Paris, 1899), 7.374 and 377–378 (author's translation). See also D. S. Blondheim, Introduction to *Hernani* (Boston, 1891 and 1929), pp. ix and xi. Charles Morice in *La Littérature de tout à l'heure* (Paris, 1889), made a brief comparison between Hugo and Poe for the latter's superior use of the grotesque; cited by Patrick Quinn, *The French Face of Edgar Poe* (Carbondale, Ill., 1957), pp. 41–42.

16. Láng, *Music in Western Civilization* (New York, 1941), p. 828.

17. All my citations from *Hernani* are from the translation of Mrs. Newton Crossland in Brander Matthews, *Chief European Dramatists* (Cambridge, Mass., 1944). This passage appears on pp. 401–402.

18. See the apt comment of Quinn, *The French Face of Edgar Poe*, p. 129: "The reader . . . understands that the drama is not being played out on any realistic stage."

19. Kenneth W. Hooker, *The Fortunes of Victor Hugo in England* (New York, 1938), pp. 27 and 45.

20. Much better in language and fidelity to the French are the verse excerpts, given in English, by the reviewer of *Hernani* in the *Foreign Quarterly Review*, 6 (Oct., 1830), 455–473. He too stresses the striking effect of Act V with its "voluptuous music, luster of variegated lamps" and "solitary mask clad in black" crossing the scene (p. 467).

21. Published by C. Chapple (London) and by T. Lacy, "Acting Edition of Plays," Vol. 77 (1831?). This version became almost the standard English version, being used for the Stirling edition of the two-volume *Dramas of Victor Hugo* (Boston: Cambridge University Press, n.d.; circa 1900), with no ascription to Kenney.

22. Hooker, *The Fortunes of Victor Hugo*, pp. 47–48.

23. W. Davenport Adams, *A Dictionary of the Drama* (London, 1904), p. 118. He ignores Barrymore's career in Philadelphia and shows, in his sketch of Mrs. Barrymore, that the two must have

spent several years in Boston after 1832.

24. George C. Odell, *Annals of the New York Stage* (New York, 1928), 3.556.

25. Wemyss, *Theatrical Biography* (New York, 1847), p. 254.

26. I find in *Le Figaro* of Paris, 8 (Mar. 4, 1833), 3, a mocking column on "The Psychology of the Masked Ball," evoked specifically by *Gustavus III* and *Hernani.*

27. Arthur Herman Wilson, *A History of the Philadelphia Theatre, 1835–1855* (Philadelphia, 1935), p. 672, attributes *Zanthe, or the Fatal Oath* as an adaptation, to W. Barrymore, with no mention of Kenney. There is, however, an undated printed prompter's copy of *Hernani; or, The Pledge* in the New York Public Library, bearing this subtitle: "Translated from the French of Victor Hugo. By James Kenney. As performed at the Walnut Street Theatre, Philadelphia." The printed cast of characters almost duplicates that listed for the January 28, 1835 opening performance given by Wilson, p. 131. The contemporary cover of this 72-page pamphlet has a pasted label, apparently from a playbill title: "Zanthe or the Fatal Oath." Copies must have remained in the effects of the Walnut Street Theatre, to be used for the 1842 performance.

28. *The Histrionic Mr. Poe* (Baltimore, 1949).

29. Wilson, p. 682, lists twenty presentations in 1835 and one in 1836; see p. 6 for Barrymore's being the stage manager for Wemyss in 1835. For the performance details, see Wemyss, *Theatrical Biography,* pp. 254–255.

30. Poe had long been an ardent Byronist and would know Byron's "The Waltz" with its lines: "Hot from the hands promiscuously applied, / Round the slight waist or down the glowing side, / Where were the rapture then to clasp the form / From this lewd grasp and lawless contact warm?" (11.234–237). See chap. v below.

31. Quinn, p. 274.

32. See the article on Smith in the *Dictionary of American Biography* and also the reminiscences of his son, H. Wemyss Smith, given by Edwin Wolf II, *The Library Chronicle of the Friends of the Library of the University of Pennsylvania,* 17 (1951), 90–103; see also Quinn, pp. 274–275, 301.

33. Messac, *Influences françaises,* pp. 18–19, and George E. Woodberry, *The Life of Edgar Allan Poe* (Boston, 1909), 1.179–

180; see also Woodberry and E. C. Stedman, *Works of Edgar Allan Poe* (New York, 1903), 4.289 and 291. Professor Mabbott defends the breadth and depth of Poe's reading in French, *Selected Poetry*, p. xii. For Béranger see chap. iv below.

34. "The French of Edgar Allan Poe," *American Speech*, 2 (Mar., 1927), 270–274.

35. For example, Killis Campbell, *The Mind of Poe* (Cambridge, Mass., 1933), p. 8.

36. I am inclined to agree with Messac and therefore am skeptical about Professor Mabbott's idea that the last act of *Hernani* provided a source for *Politian* in its combination of nuptials and death, since the date that he assigns to the writing of *Politian*, 1833–35, precluded Poe's seeing it on the stage or his reading any version save one in French, q.v. in *Notes and Queries*, 194 (June, 1949), 279. I see almost no correspondence between this work by Poe and *Hernani*, in any respect.

37. Concerning Dupin, Loménie writes in the *Galerie* (Paris, 1840), pp. 31–32, "He has read everything, retained everything, and knows an astonishing amount about the most varied topics. . . . He is the greatest redresser of wrongs in the world." Clearly he is the ancestor of Poe's Dupin and of Sherlock Holmes.

38. The page numbers in my text refer to the 1841 Philadelphia translation by Walsh.

39. Harrison, 16.91 and 16.400.

40. For this correction of the Harrison text I am deeply indebted to Professor Mabbott, who also suggested to me that the deprecation of *Cromwell* by Poe (Harrison, 16.66) has no reference to Hugo but to an American writer, Henry William Herbert, whose *Cromwell* Poe calls "wofully turgid" in Nov., 1841 (Harrison, 15.206). At least one commentator has misinterpreted Poe's allusion. For a fuller treatment of Hague see C. S. Brigham, "Edgar Allan Poe's Contributions to Alexander's Weekly Messenger," *Proceedings of the American Antiquarian Society*, n.s. 52 (Apr., 1942), 45–125, specifically, 118–123.

41. Campbell, ed., *Poems of Edgar Allan Poe* (Cambridge, Mass., 1917), p. 235; Harrison, 3.270.

42. *Notre-Dame de Paris*, 1832 version, edition of Paris, 1961, Book VII, chap. vi, p. 328. Textual references to the French text will apply to this edition.

43. *Notre-Dame de Paris,* Dent edition in English, no translator indicated (London, 1910), p. 264. Future English translations in this chapter will be taken from this edition.

44. Poe had tried to sell to this firm, Carey, Lea and Carey, his *Al Aaraaf* in 1829 and continued dealing with them frequently. Effingham Wilson of London also published in 1833 a translation called *Notre Dame: A Tale of the "Ancient Regime."*

45. In the first (1831) version of *Notre-Dame* it occurs at the end of Book I, chap. vi, but in the 1832 version it has been moved, intact, to Book VII, chap. iv.

46. Given by J. E. Spannuth and Thomas O. Mabbott in their reprint of the series, *Doings of Gotham* (Pottsville, Pa., 1929), p. 68. Professor Mabbott's note, p. 71, correctly attributes it to *Notre-Dame* and also refers to the second use of the comparison, discussed in my text.

47. A critical discussion of these sources is given by Quinn, p. 359.

48. See O. A. Roorbach, *Bibliotheca Americana* (New York, 1852).

49. Given by Poe in 1848 to Mrs. Whitman, who gave it to Ingram, it eventually found its way into the Huntington Library, to which my thanks are due for the response to several questions about it; they are also due to the Alderman Library of the University of Virginia and to William Doyle Hull II, for "A Canon of the Critical Works of Edgar Allan Poe" (diss., University of Virginia, 1941), in which I find my view of Poe's authorship confirmed (p. 681).

50. Poe's statement about the French "style" echoes the preface of Colburn's 1843 London edition, probably the source of the Wiley and Putnam reprint of 1845 which Poe was reviewing.

51. *Servii Grammatici Qui Feruntur in Vergilii Carmina Commentarii* (Leipzig, 1923), 1.604.

52. Harrison, 11.156–160, prints the review with a misleading date, derived from Griswold as first editor of Poe's works.

53. Discussed in my "Du Bartas and Victor Hugo in Poe's Criticism," *Mississippi Quarterly,* 22 (Fall, 1969).

54. Margaret Alterton, "Origins of Poe's Critical Theory," *University of Iowa Studies,* 2 (Apr., 1925), 93, mentions that Poe was finding principles in the drama and fine arts to improve his stan-

dards of criticism and his practice in constructing his tale of effect, but she does not cite Hugo's work.

55. See the eulogy by Baudelaire, for example, in "Notes Nouvelles sur Edgar Poe: Preface" of the *Nouvelles Histoires Extraordinaires* (Paris, 1857) or the five volumes of translations in his *Oeuvres Complètes* (Paris, 1931). It is fitting for Hugo to show a respectful admiration for Poe, in his turn; unfortunately, the record is not complete. Dec. 7, 1859, Charles Baudelaire sent to Hugo a letter, now unavailable, which a sales catalogue excerpt indicates as including a reference to Baudelaire's fear that the recent partial publication of his version of *Eureka* in the *Revue internationale* might give Hugo a poor idea of Poe and of his translator, q.v. in Baudelaire, *Oeuvres, Correspondance Générale* (Paris, 1953), 6.82. Hugo's reply is given in his *Oeuvres Complètes, Correspondance* (Paris, 1950), 2.323: "Be calm, I shall read your Poe only when you send it to me. I understand your sensitivity, since I have had prepared, for the sake of the commas, eleven proofs of *La Légende des Siècles*. The subject handled by Poe is my constant preoccupation. But I shall wait." Mary E. Phillips, *Edgar Allan Poe—The Man* (Philadelphia, 1926), 2.1606, asserts without source that Hugo called Poe "the prince of American literature," but I have not found the original statement in Hugo's writings.

NOTES TO CHAPTER 2

1. *Notre-Dame de Paris*, Book IX, chap. i., p. 413 in the Garnier edition (Paris, 1961), drawn from the 1832 revision of the 1831 work. All textual references in French in my text will be to this edition.

2. The edition used here and below for English translations is that of Dent Publishers (London, 1910), p. 337, the translator not being given. Poe was familiar with *The Hunchback of Notre-Dame*, translated by Frederic Shoberl for Bentley's "Standard Novels" (London, 1833), 2.56 for the corresponding passage, the book having been pirated in Philadelphia in 1834. My evidence is given in "Du Bartas and Victor Hugo in Poe's Criticism," *Mississippi Quarterly*, 22 (Fall, 1969).

3. James A. Harrison, ed., *The Complete Works of Edgar Allan*

Poe (New York, 1902), 5.163–176. All textual references indicated under "Harrison" are to this edition.

4. Maurice Le Breton, "Edgar Poe and Macaulay," *Revue Anglo-Américaine*, 21 (Oct., 1935), 38–42. He seems unaware of a similar discovery published by Lawrence Oliphant, "Poe and Macaulay," in a publication called by Mary E. Phillips "*T. P.'s Weekly*" of June 12, 1914, in her *Edgar Allan Poe—The Man* (Philadelphia, 1926), 2.867 and 1634, n. 2.

5. Lord Macaulay's *Essays and Lays of Ancient Rome* (London, 1886), pp. 612–613, the whole essay occupying pp. 595–658.

6. See the *Dictionary of National Biography* articles for the pertinent facts concerning William Bedloe and Titus Oates.

7. Poe records the mystic and significant omission of the final *e* of Bedloe's name in the obituary notice.

8. Observe that Poe's last use of Hugo material, in the "Marginalia" of the *Southern Literary Messenger* (July, 1849), concerns the imputed efforts of critics to imitate Macaulay—perhaps a sign of Poe's awareness of his debt to Macaulay in this "Eastern" tale and his indirect shifting of guilt by deriding American critics, *en masse*, for *their* borrowing from Macaulay.

9. The *OED* gives citations of 1550 from Skelton, 1575 from Banister, and 1609 from A. Hume for *sanguisuge*. Webster's *New International Dictionary of the English Language*, 3rd ed. (1961), p. 2011, gives *sangsue* as an ordinary English word, coming from *sanguisuga* through the French. The Funk and Wagnalls *New Standard Dictionary* (New York, 1961) gives *sangsue* as "same as sanguisuge" with no indication of extent or date of usage. The only other English dictionary with extensive citations, *The Century Dictionary* (New York, 1887), p. 5333–5334, cites only Poe's tale for its use and says: "A leech, also called sanguisuge."

10. See the *Cambridge Natural History*, eds. S. F. Harmer and A. E. Shipley (London, 1896; reprint of 1922 used), 2.392–408, chap. xiv, "Hirudinea." The *Encyclopedia Americana* (New York, 1953), 17.191–192, declares that the only terrestrial leech of the U.S.A. belongs to Macrobdella Decora, used for blood-letting. See *Grand Larousse Encyclopédique* (Paris, 1964), 9.578, on the "sangsue" and 5.904 on "Hirudinées."

11. The *Random House Dictionary of the English Language* (New York, 1966) omits the word *sangsue*.

12. I have questioned persons reared near Charlottesville, none of whom have heard the term *sangsue* applied to leeches. The following specialized dictionaries omit the term: Craigie and Hulbert, *Dictionary of American English* (Chicago, 1944); Thornton, *American Glossary* (New York, 1912); Bartlett, *Dictionary of Americanisms* (Boston, 1896); Kenyon and Knott, *Pronouncing Dictionary of American English* (Springfield, 1953); Weekley, *Etymological Dictionary of Modern English* (London, 1923).

13. *Encyclopaedia Britannica* (Chicago, 1955), 13.866.

14. The *Cambridge Natural History*, 2.408, citing Sir J. E. Tennent's *Natural History of Ceylon*.

15. They are "usually olive green to brown" according to the *Encyclopaedia Britannica*, 11th ed. (1911), 16.366.

16. Régis Messac, *Influences françaises dans l'oeuvre d'Edgar Poe* (Paris, 1929), pp. 12–19, doubts that Poe could or would read difficult or complicated French; see also G. E. Woodberry, *The Life of Edgar Allan Poe* (Boston, 1909), 1.179–180.

17. For proof that he used the Shoberl translation see the article on Du Bartas indicated in n. 2, above.

18. Thomas Ollive Mabbott, ed., *Selected Poetry and Prose of Edgar Allan Poe* (New York, 1951), p. 425.

19. There is a review of a reprint of this work in the *Broadway Journal*, 2.287–289, which is not by Poe, I think, but which indicates that the book had recently passed through his hands. For many other references to Lamb in his work see my *Dictionary of Names and Titles in Poe's Collected Works* (New York, 1968), p. 53.

20. The ending of Poe's tale, to be sure, speaks of a lapse of fifty years. It has always seemed to me to be Poe's afterthought and to have a testamentary flavor.

21. See Joseph S. Schick, *American Literature*, 6 (Mar., 1934), 18–21, for parallel passages in Poe and Headley's account. C. L. Rasor, in *Furman Studies*, 31 (Winter, 1949), 46–50, repeats Schick's "proof" and also adds as sources Balzac's *La Grande Bretèche* and Bulwer's *Last Days of Pompeii*, both of which were originally proposed by Killis Campbell, *The Mind of Poe* (Boston, 1917), pp. 170–171. It has not been noticed that Poe reviewed Headley's *Letters from Italy* in the *Broadway Journal*, 2 (Aug. 9, 1845), 75. Headley's work was the third volume in Wiley and

Putnam's "Library of American Books," the second being Poe's 1845 *Tales*.

22. The *Dictionnaire de l'Academie Française*, 8th ed. (Paris, 1935), gives the same meaning and adds that the expression is used today only figuratively for a prison.

23. Preceding this item, in Vol. 4, no. 234, I have counted six major articles on Hugo and his works in *Le Figaro* of 1829, all in Vol. 4: nos. 24, 29, 32, 38, 74, and 207; see also, no. 228.

24. For the "interchange of personality" theory see the tripartite article in *Notes and Queries*, 199 (Oct., 1954), pp. 447–449; for the "identity of victor and victim," see James W. Gargano's article in *Studies in Short Fiction*, 4 (1967), 119–126; for denial of the revenge motif, see J. Rea's article in the same journal, 4.57–69.

25. Professor Mabbott, *Selected Poetry and Prose*, p. 425, suggests the identity of Thomas Dunn English and Fortunato. For the fullest account of Poe's libel suit against English see Joseph F. Moriarty, *A Literary Tomahawking* (Passaic, 1963).

26. Mary E. Phillips, *Poe*, 2.1181.

27. Harold P. Clunn, *The Face of Paris* (London, n.d.), p. 205, and Michelin, *Guide to Paris* (1954), p. 155.

28. *La Grande Encyclopédie* (Paris, n.d.), 9.796 (author's translation). For a highly particularized description of the construction and "decorations" of the catacombs see also *Grande Dictionnaire Universelle* (Paris, 1867), 3.541–542.

29. Paul Fassy, *Les Catacombes de Paris* (Paris, 1862), frontispiece engraving from a photograph by Nadar (i.e., Félix Tournachon) entitled "Ossuaire des Catacombes." See, incidentally, Nadar's early interest in Poe's works, according to Mary E. Phillips, *Poe*, 1.656–657.

30. See the nine references to the magazine listed in my *Dictionary of Names and Titles*, p. 138, and the many uncollected items in the *Broadway Journal* which discuss the material in the "Editor's Table."

31. *Knickerbocker Magazine*, 11 (Mar., 1838), 290.

32. *Encyclopaedia Britannica*, 11th ed., 18.792; see also Michaud's article on Montrésor in *Biographie Universelle*. Edward H. Davidson in *Selected Writings of Edgar Allan Poe* (Boston, 1956), pp. 502–503 and Professor Mabbott, *Selected Poetry and Prose*, p. 425, propose a source in John Montrésor, the lover of Charlotte

Temple in Susanna Rowson's popular novel of that name, although I do not find any episode involving Montrésor's building a block-house for Charlotte, as reported in the second comment; nevertheless, as a British army engineer, Montrésor might have provided Poe with his trowel-wielding character's name. Poe mentions the novel once (Harrison, 11.40) and might have known about Montrésor (whose name is different in *Charlotte Temple*), from the fact that his name was originally given to the island later called Randall's Island, q.v. in the edition of the novel edited by Francis W. Halsey (New York, 1905), pp. liii–lxxxvi.

33. For the General see *Encyclopaedia Britannica*, 11th ed., 16.505.

34. *Notes and Queries*, 199 (Apr., 1954), 180. I assume that "Maiter-di-dauns" is "Maître de dance" and—hesitantly—suggest that "A Goose" signifies "the count à Guise," on the analogy of the duc de Guise. In this article Professor Mabbott also asserts that the story is obviously set in France, citing "Montresor" as evidence.

35. Jacob H. Adler, in *Notes and Queries*, 199 (Jan., 1954), 32–34, regards the variety of wines as a "real imperfection" and also traces Montrésor's names to the British and French source. Professor Mabbott, in the *Explicator*, 25 (Nov., 1966), item 30, notes that "Medoc" was assumed to have therapeutic value and that "De Grâve" is an obvious pun.

36. The cloak, named after the eighteenth-century duc de Roquelaure, is usually spelled with a *u*, not an *i*. Besides Poe's usage, the *OED* gives one more *i* spelling, that of Hone, *Every-day Book* of 1825. Poe uses the "roquelaure" spelling in his "Man of the Crowd," published in *Burton's*, Dec., 1840, but changes it to "roquelaire" upon reprinting the story in *Tales* (1845). In both tales his italics indicate his awareness of the French provenance of the word.

37. See, for example, Walter James, *Wine: A Brief Encyclopedia* (New York, 1960), p. 8. Poe makes the same error in "Lionizing" (Harrison, 2.39) in a passage also containing "Médoc" and "Grâve" (*sic*). I find untenable Charles W. Strele's idea that Poe's "amontillado" was a pun on an Italian word for "collected or formed into little heaps," in *Explicator*, 18 (Apr., 1960), item 43. For evidence that the name *amontillado* was applied to a fine, dry sherry in the 1840's see Richard Ford, *Gatherings from Spain* (Lon-

don, 1906), chap. xiv, which concerns the production of sherry wines; the book dates from 1846, being revised from *The Handbook for Travellers in Spain* (London, 1845).

NOTES TO CHAPTER 3

1. Arthur Hobson Quinn, *Edgar Allan Poe* (New York, 1941), p. 328, suggests a publication date of Sept. 1, 1841 for the *Gift*, since two of the following journals which reprinted the story in September mention it as "From the Gift for 1842": *Boston Notion*, 2 (Sept. 4, 1841), 1; *Roberts' Semi-Monthly Magazine*, 2 (Sept. 15, 1841), 701–703; *New York Weekly Tribune*, 1 (Sept. 18, 1841); *New York Daily Tribune* (Sept. 20, 1841); *Literary Souvenir*, 4 and 5 (Nov. 13, 1841, and July 9, 1842), 147–148, 214–215; the list comes from Arthur Hobson Quinn and Edward H. O'Neill, eds., *The Complete Poems and Stories of Edgar Allan Poe* (New York, 1946), 2.1079.

2. *Broadway Journal*, 1 (May 24, 1845), 322–324. Printed seven times, this ranks with "Mesmeric Revelation" as the work most frequently published in his lifetime.

3. Quinn, *Poe*, pp. 466 and 329.

4. For the omissions from the original version to be discussed in my text, see James A. Harrison, ed., *The Complete Works of Edgar Allan Poe* (New York, 1902), 4.312–316, "Notes," with 1845 printing on pp. 236–244. Reference to this edition of the works will be made hereafter under "Harrison."

5. Woodberry, *The Life of Edgar Allan Poe* (Boston, 1909), 1.299–300. Compare the theme of the poem and the name, "Valley of the Many-Colored Grass," to stanza 52 of "Adonais," by Shelley, whom Poe greatly admired: "The One remains, the many change and pass; / Heaven's light forever shines, Earth's shadows fly; / Life, like a dome of many-colored glass, / Stains the white radiance of Eternity, / Until Death tramples it to fragments."

6. Bonaparte, *Life and Works of Edgar Allan Poe* (English trans., London, 1949), pp. 252–253.

7. Carlson, *Introduction to Poe* (Glenview, Ill., 1967), p. 582; Hardin Craig, *Edgar Allan Poe: Representative Selections* (New

York, 1935), Introduction, p. cii. Margaret Alterton is coauthor of
the book and the notes, but not of this part of the Introduction.

8. Thomas O. Mabbott, ed., *Selected Poetry and Prose of Edgar
Allan Poe* (New York, 1951), p. 421, says of the motto: "I do not
have a reference for it."

9. *Chamber's Biographical Dictionary* (New York, 1961), p.
817. For full accounts of Lull's life and works see Armand Llinarès,
Raymond Lulle, Philosophe de l'action (Grenoble, 1963) and Juan
Saiz Barbera, *Raimundo Lulio, Genio de la filosofía y mística
española* (Madrid, 1963).

10. For a good treatment of the spurious Lull writings see Lynn
Thorndike, *History of Magic and Experimental Science* (New
York, 1923 and 1934), 2.862–873 and 4.3–64. Armand Llinarès,
"Propos de Lulle sur l'alchimie," *Bulletin Hispanique*, 68 (Jan.,
1966), 86–94, examines the few works of Lull that deal slightly
with alchemy, a study which Lull basically opposed. For lists and
descriptions of Lull's many works see Joan Avinyó, *Les Obres
Autèntiques del Beat Ramón Llull* (Barcelona, 1935), pp. 23–318,
where 239 works are described; P. Pedro Blanco Soto, *Estudios de
Bibliografía Luliana* (Madrid, 1916), pp. 33–118, and Llinarès,
Raymond Lulle, pp. 11–17, 427–453, where 280 works are listed
and 213 works systematically catalogued.

11. *Encyclopaedia Britannica*, 7th ed. (London, 1842), 13.594,
and *Edinburgh Encyclopaedia* (Philadelphia ed., 1832), 1.375.

12. I have not found the quotation in skimming through the
Opera Latina Raimundi Lulli (Palma, 1961), in five volumes, or
in the available six out of the ten volumes of *Opera* (Frankfurt,
1965 reprint of Mainz, 1737 ed.). Dr. Llinarès has kindly informed
me that the philosopher's stone context of the quotation in Hugo
and Sauval (see below in text) makes him believe the excerpt to
derive from one of the apocryphal texts, thereby confirming my
own inference. Thorndike, *History of Magic*, 4.3 and 28, asserts
that the spurious "Lull" works, especially of the fourteenth century,
"imitate his writings" and adopt tricks of his style; this factor en-
courages me to use Lull's text for an explication of this passage. We
can only wonder whether it is Ramón Lull or Raymundo de Tárrega
(Tárraga in the *Encyclopaedia Britannica*, 11th ed., 17.120–121),
or Raymundus Lullius Neophytus, or another who wrote the excerpt
under discussion.

13. The *Literary Souvenir* saw fit to republish it on July 9, 1842, but without Poe's intervention (see n. 1 above).

14. Wallace, *Stanley* (Philadelphia, 1838), 1.127 and 1.231–232. George E. Hatvary traces the passage in "Poe's Borrowings from H. B. Wallace," *American Literature*, 38 (Nov. 1966), 365–372, specifically in n. 7, last item. For Lull and nitric acid, see *Encyclopaedia Britannica*, 11th ed., 19.711.

15. Harrison, 12.61. For the Hugo sentence see *Notre-Dame de Paris*, ed. Marius-François Guyard (Paris: Garnier, 1961), p. 328. Unless otherwise specified all future references in the text are made to this edition.

16. The translator of this edition (London: Dent, 1910), p. 263, is anonymous.

17. "Ligeia," Poe's favorite tale, appeared in Sept., 1838. Professor Mabbott, *Selected Poetry*, p. 418, asserts that "Poe intended real magic." For a treatment of thaumaturgy in "Von Kempelen" see chap. x below.

18. For a discussion see Guyard's introduction to *Notre-Dame*, pp. i–xxxiii, and the studies listed in his "Bibliographie," pp. 599–600, especially those by Huard and Huguet.

19. *Notre-Dame*, pp. 100 and 567. Over sixty references to Sauval, traced by Guyard, are indicated under the title *Comptes de la Prévôté*, actually a large section of Vol. 3 of Henri Sauval's *Histoire et recherches des antiquités de la ville de Paris* (Paris, 1724).

20. The Lull passage in Sauval, given here in my translation, occurs in the section "Visions des chercheurs de pierre philosophale, touchant plusieurs figures d'Eglise," 3.56, in Book XIV, "Curiosités de divers endroits de Paris."

21. Du Cange, *Glossarium mediae et infimae Latinitatis*, new ed., ed. Leopold Faver (Graz, 1954), 7.548; see also R. F. Latham, *Revised Medieval Word-List* (London, 1965), p. 447, and for other words discussed below, pp. 108 and 197.

22. Du Cange, 2.515; see also W. H. Maigne D'Arnis, *Lexicon Manuale ad Scriptores mediae et infimae latinitatis* (Paris, 1866), p. 158. Thorndike, *History of Magic*, 4.13, indicates a medical text ascribed to Lull in fifteenth-century mss., *De conservatione humanae vitae*, the end of which praises gold-making and the *aqua permanens*. Obviously the title refers to "preserving" life.

23. Andrews, *Latin-English Lexicon* (New York, 1890), p. 105.

24. *Opera Latina Raimundi Lulli* (Palma, 1961), 3.149, 220, 332.

25. *Opera* (Frankfurt, 1965), 6.334.

26. Alterton and Craig, *Poe: Representative Selections*, p. 517.

27. Carlson, *Introduction to Poe*, p. 583.

28. Mabbott, *Selected Poetry*, p. 421.

29. My gratitude is due to Carey S. Bliss, of the Henry E. Huntington Library, who answered my queries about annotations, and to the Duke University Library, which sent me its microfilm of the Halsey copy of the *Broadway Journal*, now in the Huntington Library.

30. My thanks are due to Allen Hazen of the Columbia University Library School and George E. Hatvary, who helped me to determine the authorship.

31. See Mabbott, *Selected Poetry*, p. 416, for a more likely source in the name of Juliana Morella of the seventeenth century.

32. Paull F. Baum, "Poe's 'To Helen,'" *Modern Language Notes*, 64 (May, 1949), 289–297, argues convincingly that the major stimulus was not Jane Stanard but Mrs. Frances Allan; likewise, T. O. Mabbott, "Poe's 'To Helen,'" *Explicator*, 1 (June, 1943), no. 60. See also, Killis Campbell, ed., *Poems of Edgar Allan Poe* (Boston, 1917), pp. 199–201.

33. Cited by Caroline Ticknor, *Poe's Helen* (New York, 1916), p. 88; given also by Baum, p. 296.

34. They are best presented by Ticknor, pp. 42–48.

35. John W. Ostrom, ed., *The Letters of Edgar Allan Poe* (Cambridge, Mass., 1948), 2.385–388.

36. Cf. also Shelley's "Love's Philosophy": "All things by a law divine / In one another's being mingle: / Why not I with thine?" See also Poe's letter to John Neal, of Oct., 1829, which mentions Shelley and uses many phrases derived, without question, from the same lines of the poem (Ostrom, *Letters*, 1.32).

37. See her Sonnets II and VI to Poe, on his "glorious eyes" and on her hope that her "soul" will meet his after death, given by Ticknor, *Poe's Helen*, pp. 141 and 143; also in *Poems* by Mrs. Whitman (Boston, 1879), pp. 90–95. Quinn, *Poe*, p. 574, makes the assertion about her eyes being her best feature.

38. Written on the top margin of Vol. 2, following p. 176 and unnumbered, but succeeded by erroneous page 172, the magazine

having mistakenly started a new numbering at this point. Poe also sidelined two references to eyes in the margin of "Ligeia."

39. See his letter of Sept. 21, 1839, analyzing the tale; of July 2, 1844, to James R. Lowell; and of Jan. 2, 1846, to Duyckinck, Ostrom, *Letters*, 1.118 and 258; 2.309.

40. Quinn, *Poe*, pp. 573–574, aptly characterizes the poem thus.

41. Richard P. Benton, in *Nineteenth-Century Fiction*, 20 (Dec., 1967), 293–297, presents a thoughtful suggestion that "Eleonora" is "an allegory about the role of love in man's life . . . constructed upon a Platonic model," with the first girl representing the Uranian Venus, the second, the Dionaean Venus. Poe's elimination of the long description of Eleonora as the "Greek Venus" and his insertion of the motto show his changed emphasis, I feel.

42. The strange name "Ermengarde," given to the second woman, is important, although I cannot agree with Sam S. Baskett, "A Damsel with a Dulcimer," *Modern Language Notes*, 73 (May, 1958), 332–338, that Poe knew an Old German word *ermen*, meaning "universal" or "immense." In considering the parallel use of Scott's name "Rowena," the Saxon beauty in *Ivanhoe*, for the second bride in "Ligeia," we are led to Scott's well-known novel *The Betrothed*, the first of the *Tales of the Crusaders* (1826). There the name "Ermengarde" is that of the Lady of Baldringham, proud of her Saxon identity, who requires her great-niece Eveline, as a trial, to confront the "Bahr-geist" of Vanda in the haunted room; the situation is parallel too, in that Eveline is pledged to the Constable, although in love with his nephew, and is visited in the Conclusion by the appeased Vanda, who blesses her marriage with the nephew. Several passages on spectral appearances in chaps. xiv and xv also suggest ideas and phrases in "Eleonora," in the first version of which Ermengarde has blue eyes.

43. This is the phrase of Carlson, *Introduction to Poe*, p. 583.

44. "Morella" was published in the Apr., 1835 *Messenger;* Professor Mabbott (*Selected Poetry*, p. 417), believes that the three tales are linked through the theme of "reincarnation." Ruth Hudson, in her article on "Ligeia" in *English Studies in Honor of James Southall Wilson* (Charlottesville, 1951), pp. 35–44, recognizes the importance of Poe's changes in "Eleonora" but oversimplifies his motive. She thinks he merely wanted to avoid similarity to the preceding tales. See also the discursive treatment of the importance

of the will in Poe's tales of metempsychosis in Allen Tate's "The Forlorn Demon" in *Collected Essays* (Denver, 1959), pp. 432–454.

45. Harrison, 4.313 and 315. Baskett, pp. 332–338, finds a key to the tale in "The Poetic Principle" and regards Pyrros as equivalent to "the poet" and the girl, to "poetic creation." This is untenable, I think, despite the clear borrowing of details for the story from Coleridge. In the early tale "Ms. Found in a Bottle," Poe speaks of the narrator's pyrrhonism (Harrison, 2.1).

46. See Mary Mills Patrick, *The Greek Sceptics* (New York, 1929), pp. 63–64.

47. See Patrick, pp. 31–49; R. D. Hicks, *Stoic and Epicurean* (New York, 1910), pp. 315–317; and Léon Robin, *Pyrrhon et le Scepticisme Grec* (Paris, 1944), pp. 12–14. A good brief account is given by the *Encyclopaedia Britannica*, 11th ed., 22.696.

48. Craig, Introduction, in Alterton and Craig, *Representative Selections*, pp. cii–ciii.

49. See Emma K. Norman, "Poe's Knowledge of Latin," *American Literature*, 6 (1934), 72–77. The study, unfortunately, accepts as firsthand citations by Poe, material that he culled from compendia or intermediary sources, like the motto of "Eleonora."

NOTES TO CHAPTER 4

1. Campbell, "Poe, Stevenson, and Béranger," in *The Dial*, 57 (Nov. 16, 1909), 374–375.

2. See, e.g., Joseph Wood Krutch, *Edgar Allan Poe* (New York, 1926), pp. 96–97; Una Pope-Hennessy, *Edgar Allan Poe* (London, 1934), p. 122; Frances Winwar, *The Haunted Palace* (New York, 1959), p. 133; and David Galloway, ed., *Selected Writings of Edgar Allan Poe* (Baltimore, 1967), p. 523.

3. These are the last two lines of stanza 7 (each of eight lines) in "Le Refus. Chanson addressée au Général Sébastiani" to the air by Pierre Laujon, "Le premier du mois de janvier," cited from *Oeuvres Complètes de Pierre-Jean de Béranger* (Paris, 1840), pp. 552–553. My citations hereafter will be taken from this edition, unless otherwise indicated. For the music of his songs see *Musique*

des chansons de Béranger, 10th ed. (Paris, n.d.); "Le Refus" is no. 296 with music on p. 244.

4. These collections, called variously *chansons inédites, oeuvres, chansons,* etc., may be seen in Jules Brivois, *Bibliographie de l'oeuvre de Pierre-Jean de Béranger* (Paris, 1876); the following fall within Poe's lifetime: 1828, 1829 (5 eds.), 1830 (4 eds.), 1832, 1833 (2 eds.), 1834 (3 eds.), 1835, 1836, 1839, 1840 (2 eds.), 1841, 1843, 1844, 1847 (3 eds.). Béranger's dates are 1780–1857.

5. *Songs of Béranger,* trans. by the author of the *Exile of Idria* (London, 1837); *The Songs of Béranger,* ed. Rufus W. Griswold (Philadelphia, 1844); William Young, *Béranger: Two Hundred of His Lyrical Poems Done into English Verse* (New York, 1850). Only the last includes "Le Refus" (pp. 294–295). J.-M. Quérard, *La Littérature Française Contemporaine* (Paris, n.d.), 1.296, mentions an English translation of 1831 by Mme. Elisabeth Collins, but the British Museum *Catalogue* lists only her *Metrical Translations from the Works of Lamartine, Casimir Delavigne, Victor Hugo and Béranger* (Paris, 1850?). Quérard may refer to translations in periodicals.

6. *Béranger's Songs,* trans. Robert B. Brough (London, 1856), pp. 147–149 for "Le Refus"; *Songs from Béranger, Translated in the Original Metres,* trans. Craven Langstroth Belts (New York, 1888), pp. 179–181, "The Refusal."

7. Griswold, *Songs of Béranger,* p. iii; Young, *Béranger,* p. iii.

8. Arthur Hobson Quinn, *Edgar Allan Poe* (New York, 1941), p. 175. This volume will hereafter be cited as "Quinn."

9. Campbell, ed., *The Poems of Edgar Allan Poe* (Boston, 1917), pp. 204–205, and James A. Harrison, ed., *The Complete Works of Edgar Allan Poe* (New York, 1902), 1.156. Textual references will be made to this edition under "Harrison."

10. Young, *Béranger,* pp. 294–295. "Le Refus" is no. 160 of the 200 poems given.

11. *Oeuvres Complètes* (1840), p. 460, and "Ma Biographie" in *Oeuvres Posthumes de Béranger* (Paris, 1858), p. 437.

12. Campbell may have followed the lead of Young, whose headnote on p. 294 reads: "This ode was probably written shortly after the Revolution of July." There is also a note by Dr. G. O. Strauss in the 1856 translation by Brough, p. 188, n. 34, concerning

Béranger's refusal of Sébastiani's offer "soon after" the July Revolution.

13. Quinn, p. 180; this point is briefly presented also by Arthur H. Quinn and Edward H. O'Neill, eds., *The Complete Poems and Stories of Edgar Allan Poe* (New York, 1946), 2.1065. Poe's "lute" reference in the third stanza of "The Haunted Palace" (Apr., 1839), included in "The Fall of the House of Usher" (Sept., 1839), may have led him to use Béranger's lines after he read them in Walsh's *Sketches*.

14. *Grove's Dictionary of Music and Musicians*, 3rd. ed. (New York, 1939), 3.252–255.

15. Campbell, *Poems*, p. 207, points out the "Skylark" touch at the end.

16. Poe's poet friend Dr. T. H. Chivers, in his *Life of Poe* (New York, 1952), p. 62, furnished a similar confusion when he speaks of "Poe's soft, mellow, melodious" voice which was "musical as Apollo's Lute." Perhaps he had read "Israfel" too well. *Le Figaro,* Dec. 14, 1831, impatiently says of Béranger: "He has neither lyre nor lute nor theorbo; he is neither a bard, nor minstrel, nor weeping willow, nor victim of the divine afflatus; he has never been a martyr. . . . Ask him what he is and he will reply: a maker of songs" (author's translation).

17. Given by Harrison, 8.122–142; Mrs. Ellet's book is discussed on pp. 138–142.

18. Young, *Béranger,* p. 120; Ellet, *Poems,* pp. 112–113. Young's headnote serves to indicate the cause of Béranger's popularity among the French: "This song . . . appears to hint at the period after the restoration, when the Allied troops were still garrisoned in France."

19. Lamartine, *Oeuvres Complètes* (Paris, 1847), 2.85–90. The lines in question are on p. 89.

20. Letter to the "Editor of the Richmond 'Courier and Daily Compiler'" sometime before Sept. 2, 1836, given by John Ward Ostrom, ed., *The Letters of Edgar Allan Poe* (Cambridge, Mass., 1948), 1.101, to which future references will be made under "Ostrom."

21. See, e.g., *Oeuvres Complètes* (1840), "La Fortune," pp. 280–281.

22. See chap. i, above. My textual citations are from Walsh's translation of the *Sketches* (Philadelphia, 1841).

23. Young, *Béranger*, p. 10.

24. *Oeuvres Complètes* (1840), pp. 463–464, author's translation.

25. *Oeuvres Posthumes* (1858), "Appendice," pp. 468–470, author's translation.

26. Bagehot, *Literary Studies* (London, 1879), 2.261–298.

27. *Library of the World's Best Literature* (New York, 1896), 4.1786.

28. Lanson, *Histoire Illustrée de la Littérature Française*, 2nd. ed. (Paris, 1923), 2.278–280.

29. Pierre Moreau, *Histoire de la Littérature Française* (Paris, 1951), 8.80; L. Cazamian, *A History of French Literature* (London, 1955; ed. of 1960), pp. 317 and 367.

30. See the marked change of views in the uncollected article "Young America" in the *Broadway Journal*, 2.26–27, correctly ascribed to Poe by Perry Miller, *The Raven and the Whale* (New York, 1956), p. 135 and discussed by Claude Richard, "Poe and 'Young America,'" *Studies in Bibliography*, 21 (1968), 25–58.

31. *PMLA*, 58 (1943), 754–779, especially 775 for the Béranger excerpt.

32. See Quinn, pp. 326–327, and also C. S. Brigham, "Edgar Allan Poe's Contributions to *Alexander's Weekly Messenger*" in *Proceedings of the American Antiquarian Society*, n.s. 52 (Apr., 1942), 45–125.

33. It is printed in the *Oeuvres* (1840) as using the air, "Toto, carabo." As is customary with Poe, his quotation is individualistic, for the verses read differently: "Il dit: Moi, je m'en . . . / Il dit: Moi, je m'en . . . / Ma foi, moi, je m'en ris!" Young, *Béranger*, offers a translation on pp. 75–76.

34. In the *Oeuvres* (1840) these are on pp. 98, 277, 381, 414, 417, 482, 487, 495, 498, 555, and 579. There are ninety-one more poems in the *Oeuvres Posthumes*, with one of eight lines on p. 180 and one of sixteen on p. 210.

35. *Burton's Gentleman's Magazine*, 5 (Sept., 1839), 145–152; *Tales of the Grotesque and Arabesque* (1840), 1.75–103; and *Bentley's Miscellany*, Aug., 1840.

36. For example, see Poe's use of two Latin quotations from *Notre-Dame* for "The Island of the Fay" and "Eleonora," discussed above in chaps. i and iii.

37. My gratitude is due to William Doyle Hull II and the Alderman Library, University of Virginia, for the dissertation, "A Canon of the Critical Works of Edgar Allan Poe" (Charlottesville, 1941), which makes this correction of Harrison's error (p. 195). Régis Messac, *Influences françaises dans l'oeuvre d'Edgar Poe* (Paris, 1929), pp. 18, 60–61, notes the many references to Béranger but doubts his influence over Poe, sagely observing that something "rococo, of the First Empire" in him escaped Poe.

38. Harrison, 6.78–102, 116–138, 197–215. For a discussion of Poe's view of progress via science applied to modern industry and urbanization, see my "New York City in the Tales of Poe," in the *Journal of the Bronx Historical Society*, 2 (Jan., 1965), 16–22, and also the end of chap. vii.

39. J. B. L. Foucault in 1843 and W. Greener and W. E. Staite in 1846 improved lamp carbons; F. de Moleyns in 1841, E. A. King and J. W. Starr in 1845, and W. E. Staite in 1848 improved the wire in the incandescent lamp, q.v. in *Encyclopaedia Britannica*, 11th ed., 16.659–667, article on "Lighting: Electric." See the paragraph in the *New-York Evening Mirror* of Feb. 15, 1845, discussing Milton J. Saunders as an inventor "of the electric light," which is considered by Dr. Hull, p. 475, to be probably by Poe.

40. For this ascription of date and the printing of the most complete form of this incomplete story see T. O. Mabbott, ed., *Selected Poetry and Prose of Edgar Allan Poe* (New York, 1951), pp. 344–345 and 426. See chap. ix below, for fuller discussion.

41. *Encyclopaedia Britannica*, 11th ed., 16.641. The first lighthouse installation of this kind was in England, in 1858, only nine years later than Poe's reference.

42. *Home Journal*, no. 36 (Aug. 31, 1850), 1; Sartain's *Union Magazine*, 7 (Oct., 1850), 231–239. For discussion see Quinn, p. 607.

43. See Ostrom, 2.458 for letter of Aug., 1849; for details, including reception of the lecture, see Hervey Allen, *Israfel*, rev. ed. (New York, 1960), pp. 657, 665, 667; see also Quinn, p. 634, for Elmira Shelton's view of the lecture on Sept. 22, 1849.

NOTES TO CHAPTER 5

1. A good survey is provided by A. J. Sambrook, "A Romantic Theme: The Last Man," in *Forum for Modern Language Studies,* 2 (Jan., 1966), 25–33. Sambrook treats only French eighteenth-century and British nineteenth-century works, such as those of Volney, Mercier, John E. Reade, Robert Pollok, Campbell, Ouseley, Beddoes, John Martin (paintings), and Thomas Hood. He does not touch upon American contributions to the theme.

2. *The Knickerbocker Magazine,* 2 (Oct., 1833), 315.

3. For this summer of inspiration see the biographies of Mary Shelley by Elizabeth Nitchie, R. Glynn Grylls, and Mrs. Julian Marshall and my article on *Frankenstein* in *Comparative Literature,* 17 (Spring, 1965), 97–108.

4. For their comments and the manuscript notes of Byron see *The Poetical Works of Lord Byron* (London, 1859), pp. 563–564. The touches of the "Ancient Mariner" in "Darkness" recall the discussions of the supernatural and Byron's recitation of "Christabel," which Murray had just published at his suggestion. See Edward Dowden, *Life of Percy Bysshe Shelley* (London, 1886), 2.33–34.

5. For Eugen Köbling's view of Byron's debt to the work of de Grainville see *The Prisoner of Chillon* (Weimar, 1898). Köbling's view is summarized by Ernest H. Coleridge in *Byron's Works,* Vol. 4, *Poetry* (London, 1901), 42–43.

6. Michaud, *Biographie Universelle* (Paris, n.d.), 17.315–318.

7. The suicide is also pointed out in a review of *Le Dernier Homme, poème imité de Grainville* by Creuzé de Lesser, in the *Journal Général,* 34 (1831), 121. Another review in the *Furet de Londres,* 6, no. 262 (Apr., 1831), 141, declares that the poem helps to render de Grainville truly immortal. Jean de Palacio, "Mary Shelley and the 'Last Man,'" *Revue de Littérature Comparée,* 42 (Jan.–Mar., 1968), 37–49, discusses the works on the theme by de Grainville, Creuzé de Lesser, and Mary Shelley as well as Thomas Campbell and Thomas Hood. This illuminating article, which I read after completing the present chapter, does not follow the theme into Poe's writings.

8. *Blackwood's Edinburgh Magazine,* 19 (Mar., 1826), 284–286, and 21 (Jan., 1827), 54–57, the latter citing Hood's "Last Man" and referring to Mrs. Shelley's novel as "an abortion." For the text of Poe's "How to Write a Blackwood Article," see James A.

Harrison, ed., *The Complete Works of Edgar Allan Poe* (New York, 1902), 2.269–282. Future references will be made to this edition under "Harrison" or by volume and page numbers alone. For Poe's eight references to *Blackwood's* see my *Dictionary of Names and Titles in Poe's Collected Works* (New York, 1968), p. 110. See also Michael Allen, *Poe and the British Magazine Tradition* (New York, 1969).

9. Harrison, 4.258. For a plague passage with marked similarity of wording see the early tale "King Pest," in Harrison, 2.180: "that unearthly sovereign whose reign is over us all, whose dominions are unlimited, and whose name is 'Death.'"

10. *Dunciad,* Book IV, lines 654–656. It is mentioned by Harry Levin, *The Power of Blackness* (New York, 1958), p. 150.

11. For Poe's reading in the *Dunciad,* see my *Dictionary,* p. 123. See also Poe's letter of 1835, in John W. Ostrom, ed., *The Letters of Edgar Allan Poe* (Cambridge, Mass., 1948), 1.78.

12. For specific echoes of "Darkness" in *Al Aaraaf* and in "The City in the Sea," see the notes by Killis Campbell to Poe's *Poems* (New York, 1962; reprint of 1917 ed.), pp. 192 and 208. See Campbell, "Poe's Reading," *University of Texas Studies in English,* no. 5 (1925), p. 168, for thirty-three references to Byron; also his *The Mind of Poe* (Cambridge, Mass., 1933), pp. 150–152. See also my chap. vi for this topic.

13. Byron, *Works* (1859 ed.), p. 119.

14. The ending of this tale as well as the whole *mise-en-scène* admirably illustrates the central thesis of N. Bryllion Fagin's *The Histrionic Mr. Poe* (Baltimore, 1949). For Prospero as the man of taste who creates effects of beauty, see Kermit Vanderbilt, "Art and Nature in 'The Masque of the Red Death,'" *Nineteenth-Century Fiction,* 22 (Mar., 1968), 379–389.

15. *The French Face of Edgar Poe* (Carbondale, Ill., 1957), p. 129.

16. See chapter vi for the influence of Byron's death on the sonnet. See also R. S. Forsythe, "Poe's 'Nevermore': A Note," *American Literature,* 7 (Jan., 1936), 439–452.

17. *Mary Shelley's Letters,* ed. F. L. Jones (Norman, Okla., 1944), 1.212, letter of Jan. 7, 1823.

18. *The Letters of Percy Bysshe Shelley* (Oxford, 1964), 2.471.

19. *Mary Shelley's Journal,* ed. F. L. Jones (Norman, 1947), p. 193.

20. For the correspondence of characters to the two men see Elizabeth Nitchie, *Mary Shelley* (New Brunswick, 1953), pp. 150–152, and R. Glynn Grylls, *Mary Shelley* (London, 1938), p. 186. The theme of loneliness and alienation is central also to *Frankenstein*.

21. Mary Shelley, *The Last Man* (London, 1826), 2.187, 195, 207.

22. According to Hugh J. Luke, Jr., ed., *The Last Man* (Lincoln, Nebr., 1965), p. xx, the publication of her novel was in February, 1826, but Godwin gives it as January 23, and his accuracy is unimpeachable. He is reading *Omegarius* on January 10, 12, and 13. My textual citations to *The Last Man* are from Luke's convenient edition. Godwin's journal was consulted through the courtesy of Lord Abinger and, subsequently, in microfilm, through the courtesy of The Carl H. Pforzheimer Library.

23. *The Literary Magnet or Monthly Journal of the Belles Lettres*, n.s. 1 (Jan., 1826), p. 56, "Chit-Chat, Literary and Miscellaneous," says that Mrs. Shelley, authoress of "that monstrous literary abortion Frankenstein," is about to produce *The Last Man* and it asks why the novel entitled *Omegarius* should not have spared her the trouble.

24. For the 1823 date see the *OED* and L. Fabian Hirst, *The Conquest of Plague* (Oxford, 1953), p. 32. Hirst, p. 33, notes that the blotches or "tokens" of dark red or purple color were more common in older outbreaks of plague than in the modern epidemics. For description of the plague boils, see W. E. Jennings, *A Manual of Plague* (London, 1903), pp. 74, 83, and 87; James Leasor, *The Plague and the Fire* (London, 1962), pp. 49, 127, and 136; and Francis A. Gasquet, *The Black Death*, 2nd ed. (London, 1908), p. 31. Gasquet's point about an average "five month's course" for the disease reminds us that Prospero and his courtiers have been "secluded" for this period of time. James Cantlie, *Plague* (London, 1900), p. 34, is firm in his statement that there is no characteristic skin rash in plague.

25. See Grylls, *Mary Shelley*, p. 105, for the travels of Mary and Shelley in 1818. Verney may be derived from Voltaire's residence at Ferney, which they had visited in 1816.

26. Jennings, p. 66, notes that the most virulent cases take a few hours; likewise, Hirst, p. 34, referring to Defoe.

27. Poe abandons his usual first-person method to make annihilation universal.

28. A common source for Mrs. Shelley and for Poe, the *Decameron,* tells of the quick death of hogs which rooted among the rags of a victim, in "Day the First." See Gasquet, *The Black Death,* pp. 28–32, for the widespread fatality of the 1348 epidemic in Florence and the rest of Italy. Both of Poe's references to Boccaccio (Harrison, 8.228 and 8.235) indicate his knowledge of the *Decameron,* which may have provided him with a general setting, while such works as *The Last Man* furnished details and phrases.

29. See Gerald Gerber, "Additional Sources for the 'Masque of the Red Death,'" *American Literature,* 37 (Mar., 1965), 52–54, for attributing to Poe a knowledge of two works mentioned in *The Canons of Good Breeding,* a book being very facetiously reviewed by Poe (Harrison, 10.45–49). Mrs. Hemans's "The Revellers," I find, presents a rather general treatment of the carefree dance of pleasure before the coming of death, *not* through plague, although she does mention "a wilder strain" of music (not the waltz), q.v. in her *Poetical Works* (Philadelphia, 1841), p. 264. Poe mentions many of her works, but never this one. Yet it may have made its contribution to his tale.

30. See, for example, the article, "History of the Skeleton of Death," in Isaac Disraeli's *Curiosities of Literature* (New York, 1865), 4.95–105, a book well known to Poe (see notes to chap. vi below). Disraeli speaks of a costumed Death, as a "horrid Harlequin . . . in a sort of masquerade" (p. 100), and yet too few are the corroborating details to render this a likely source for the Mary Shelley and Poe pieces.

31. See chap. i, n. 30 for an excerpt. For the English scorn of the new dance see *Grove's Dictionary of Music and Musicians* (New York, 1929), 5.624. Poe's use of a modern dance in an obviously Renaissance setting was more strikingly discordant before he dropped from the 1845 version Prospero's sentence, "Uncase the varlet" (4.319).

32. It was published separately in the Apr., 1839 issue of the *American Museum of Science, Literature and the Arts,* while "The Fall of the House of Usher" appeared in Sept. in *Burton's Gentleman's Magazine* (see Harrison, 3.341).

33. Both were published in London in 1825. While Cooke's light

opera (probably seen by Mrs. Shelley) adheres to Weber's libretto, Dimond, in his prefatory "advertisement," claims that he went back to *The Arabian Nights' Entertainments* for his text.

34. T. O. Mabbott, ed., *Selected Poetry and Prose of Edgar Allan Poe* (New York, 1951), p. 418; Kenneth Graham, *Selected Tales of Edgar Allan Poe* (New York, 1951), p. 418 and Eric W. Carlson, *Introduction to Poe* (Glenview, Ill., 1967), p. 578.

35. No. 5 of the *Danses* is the "Last Waltz," written in 1822, q.v. in *Grove's Dictionary of Music* (New York, 1939), 4.362.

36. Percy Scholes, *Oxford Companion to Music*, 9th ed. (London, 1956), p. 654; see also *Grove's Dictionary*, 5th ed. (New York, 1955), 7.118–119, for the correction concerning *"Gedanke."*

37. The Karr variations are in the Columbia University Music Library and those by Berr and by Herz are in the New York Public Library Music Collection. In *Masterpieces of Piano Music*, ed. Albert E. Wier (New York, n.d.), p. 47, "Weber's Last Thought," subtitled "Dernière Pensée Musicale," is still attributed to C. M. von Weber.

38. *Religio Medici* (London, 1950), pp. 70–73.

39. *Mary Shelley's Journal*, pp. 40 and 219.

40. Shelley, *Letters*, 1.341.

41. *Hydriotaphia* (New York, 1951), p. 177. For Poe's reference see Harrison, 10.189.

42. Forrest, *Biblical Allusions in Poe* (New York, 1928), especially p. 161; Killis Campbell, "Poe's Knowledge of the Bible," *Studies in Philology*, 27 (July, 1930), 546–551, and also his "Poe's Reading," *University of Texas Studies in English*, no. 5 (1925), p. 193. I consider the biblical elements in Poe's "Shadow," in *Studies in Short Fiction*, 6 (Fall, 1968).

43. Arthur Hobson Quinn, *Edgar Allan Poe* (New York, 1941), p. 187, correctly, I think, assigns details in "King Pest" and "The Masque of the Red Death" to the cholera plague in Baltimore in 1831, but errs in saying that Poe escaped it, for he left New York for Baltimore early in the year. For confirmation see John Ward Ostrom, ed., *The Letters of Edgar Allan Poe* (Cambridge, Mass., 1948), 1.45–47, for letters of Poe from Baltimore dated May 6, Oct. 16, and Nov. 18, 1831.

44. Quinn, p. 138.

45. Quinn, pp. 225–226.

46. *Graham's Magazine*, 18 (Jan., 1841), 48. Professor Mabbott kindly confirmed this as undoubtedly Poe's. William Doyle Hull II, "A Canon of the Critical Works of Edgar Allan Poe" (diss., University of Virginia, 1941), p. 310, is noncommittal about authorship of the item and then rejects it (p. 348).

47. *French Writers* (Philadelphia, 1841), 2.339.

48. *Graham's Magazine*, 19 (Sept., 1841), 144. This is confirmed as Poe's by Professor Mabbott and by Dr. Hull, p. 348.

49. Edwin Wolf II, "Horace Wemyss Smith's Recollections of Poe," in *The Library Chronicle of the Friends of the Library of the University of Pennsylvania*, 17 (Spring-Summer, 1951), 90–103, specifically p. 93.

NOTES TO CHAPTER 6

1. *Al Aaraaf* (Baltimore, 1829), p. 17; the facsimile reprint, ed. Thomas Ollive Mabbott (New York, 1933), has been used for this and all subsequent references.

2. My text is that of James A. Harrison, ed., *The Complete Works of Edgar Allan Poe* (New York, 1902), 7.80. Hereafter all references to this edition will be made under "Harrison."

3. For a collation of the various printings, see Floyd Stovall, ed., *The Poems of Edgar Allan Poe* (Charlottesville, 1965), p. 253. The two printings in the Philadelphia *Saturday Museum*, Feb. 25 and Mar. 4, 1843, are mentioned only by Stovall; John Robertson, *Bibliography of the Writings of Edgar A. Poe* (San Francisco, 1934), p. 12, and Heartman and Canny, *A Bibliography of Edgar Allan Poe* (Hattiesburg, Miss., 1943), p. 248.

4. For the 1840 copy sent to Stoddard, who had apparently requested Poe's autograph, see J. H. Whitty, ed., *Complete Poems of Edgar Allan Poe* (Boston, 1911), p. 218; it is discussed also in *The Letters of Edgar Allan Poe*, ed. John W. Ostrom (Cambridge, Mass., 1948), 2.486, and given in Ostrom's 1966 supplement, 2.692–693. For the relations of Stoddard and Poe see chap. xi of my text.

5. Professor Mabbott has helpfully furnished me with relevant excerpts from the manuscript, including Poe's inexplicable refer-

ence to the sonnet as "so obvious an imitation" of one of "the more obscure classics"—perhaps a deliberate mystification by Poe. For large excerpts of the manuscript, see Mary E. Phillips, *Edgar Allan Poe—The Man* (Philadelphia, 1926), 2.961–967.

6. There is a slight similarity in situation and language to Wordsworth's "Solitary Reaper." Killis Campbell, *The Mind of Poe* (Cambridge, Mass., 1933), traces a couplet in "The Valley of Unrest" (*Poems*, 1831) to Wordsworth's poem.

7. Killis Campbell, ed., *Poems of Edgar Allan Poe* (Boston, 1917), p. 235, notes its uncertain date and lack of Poe's customary revisions in all printings.

8. J. Lemprière, *A Classical Dictionary* (London, n.d.), p. 727, gives *Odyssey* I, 246; *Aeneid* III, 270; *Heroides et Amores* I, x, 87; Pliny IV, chap. 12 (erroneous for 19), as well as references by Livy, Strabo, Mela, and Pausanias. None of them are as relevant as the first three. For discussion of Zacynthos as eponymous ancestor of the Zantians see Robert Graves, *The Greek Myths* (New York, 1955), 2.261 and 345.

9. For these facts about Zante and Santa Maura see *Encyclopaedia Britannica*, 11th ed., 28.956 and 24.189. In *Memoirs on the Ionian Islands* by General Guillaume de Vaudoncourt, trans. William Walton (London, 1816), p. 395, I find "Cape Dukato." In "The First Evening" of the recently published *Evenings in Greece* (1826), Thomas Moore, one of Poe's favorite authors, has a long section of footnoted flower references, much like those in *Al Aaraaf*, with references to Leucadia, Sappho, Santa Maura, and, even more significantly, to "those bramble flowers, that breathe / Their odour into Zante's wines" (Moore, *The Poetical Works* [London, 1854], 5.8).

10. *Al Aaraaf*, p. 28. For a discussion of the confusing syntax of this passage, see Margaret Alterton and Hardin Craig, *Edgar Allan Poe: Representative Selections* (New York, 1935), p. 487, in which Killis Campbell is held to regard Zante as "a spirit representing the hyacinth," thereby driving Poe's etymological error to a new extreme.

11. C. D. Yonge, *An English-Greek Lexicon* (New York, 1886), p. 602.

12. On Poe's Greek see the deprecatory letter from Charles F. Briggs to Lowell of Aug. 21, 1845, in George Woodberry, *The Life*

of *Edgar Allan Poe* (Boston, 1909), 2.146. Woodberry speaks of his Greek, Spanish, and Italian as "the merest smattering" (1.131) but mentions his regular attendance at classes in those languages (1.32).

13. George H. Green, "Poe's Notes to *Al Aaraaf*," *Aberystwyth Studies,* 14 (1936), 1–34, specifically p. 7.

14. *Georgics* IV, 336–338. The line "Nesaee Spioque Thaliaque Cymodoceque," being omitted from Codices Mediceus, Palatinus, Romanus, and Gudianus, may not have appeared in any text used by Poe, but it is to be found in *Aeneid* V, 826; also in V (803 and 808) occur two instances of Xanthus, the river in Asia Minor. This, known as the Scamander, could change to yellow the hair of bathers.

15. In "To Helen," we find two key adjectives of the type found in Zante: The Nicéan barks carry the "way-worn wanderer" over a "perfumed sea" and Helen has "hyacinth hair."

16. Quinn, *Edgar Allan Poe* (New York, 1941), p. 157, notes Poe's spelling of "Archaian" for "Achaian" in 1829, an apparent misprint which is given twice.

17. Harrison, 1.345.

18. No one believes the romantic tale; see Quinn, p. 118, and Woodberry, *Life of Poe,* 1.73, who speaks of the travels of Poe's brother.

19. R. H. Stoddard, ed., *Poems by Edgar Allan Poe* (New York, 1875), pp. 34–35.

20. Quinn, p. 104.

21. Frances Winwar, *The Haunted Palace* (New York, 1959), p. 80.

22. Hervey Allen, *Israfel,* 3rd printing (New York, 1960), p. 146, n. 249.

23. Note D, *The Poetical Works of Lord Byron* (London, 1859), p. 765.

24. These and other details can be found in Leslie Marchand, *Byron* (New York, 1957), 3.1091–1146.

25. *Ibid.,* 3.1120, n. 1.7.

26. *Ibid.,* 3.1213.

27. See, for example, Count Pietro Gamba, *Narrative of Lord Byron's Last Journey to Greece* (London, 1825) and William Parry, *The Last Days of Lord Byron* (London, 1825). For details in

Thomas Moore, see *The Works of Lord Byron* (London, 1832), 6.220.

28. Letter to Thomas W. White, of Apr. 30, 1835, given by Whitty, *Complete Poems*, pp. xxviii–xxix.

29. Mary E. Phillips, *Poe*, 1.284, speaks of the early copies of "The Dream" made by Poe.

30. Campbell, *Poems*, p. 235.

31. Campbell, *Poems*, p. 77, gives the rejected stanza and links the two poems in his article in *The Nation*, 88 (Mar. 11, 1909), 248–249. Quinn, *Poe*, p. 93, considers the connection between his love for Sarah Elmira and the passion in these poems as either doubtful or merely that of a "dramatized" emotion.

32. Roy Basler, "Byronism in Poe's 'To One in Paradise,'" *American Literature*, 9 (1937), 232–236, postulates that the item was jotted down between 1830 and 1834, although published to accompany an illustration of Byron and Mary Chaworth in the *Columbian Magazine* of Dec., 1844.

33. For Byron's text, see *Works* (1859), p. 54; for Poe's article see Harrison, 14.150–152; and for Lady Trevanion, see Marchand, *Byron*, 1.11.

34. *The Life and Letters of Fitz-Greene Halleck*, ed. James Grant Wilson (New York, 1869), pp. 396–397 and 430–431. See also indexed material on Halleck in Quinn, *Poe*.

35. For the complete article, "The Culprit Fay, and Other Poems Together with Halleck's 'Alnwick Castle, with Other Poems,'" see Harrison, 8.275–318.

36. Marchand, *Byron*, 3.1103, 1114–1115.

37. *Ibid.*, 3.1235.

38. Notice the quite gratuitous connection made by Poe between "Alnwick Castle" and *Don Juan* (Harrison, 8.310).

39. Quinn, *Poe*, p. 124.

40. Marchand, *Byron*, 1.554.

41. Woodberry, *Life of Poe*, 1.64.

42. Quinn, *Poe*, pp. 124–125, 160.

43. I agree with Professor Mabbot that this is a more likely source than the "Ianthe" of Shelley's *Queen Mab*, which Poe cited in his Drake-Halleck review of 1836. Charles W. Kent, in Harrison, 7.279, calls *Al Aaraaf* "Queen-Mablike."

44. See n. 31 above for *The Nation*. See also Killis Campbell,

"Poe's Reading," University of *Texas Studies in English*, no. 5 (1925), 165–190, especially 168–169. Poe referred to Byron thirty-three times. For echoes of Byron in the poems see Campbell, *Poems*, pp. 178, 185, 186, 188, 192, and *The Mind of Poe*, pp. 150–152. For other comments, see Quinn, *Poe*, p. 104, and Joseph Wood Krutch, *Edgar Allan Poe* (New York, 1926), p. 65; John H. Ingram, *Edgar Allan Poe* (London, 1880), 1.38–42, 59, 250; 2.188–190, 273; and Haldeen Braddy, *Glorious Incense* (Washington, 1933), p. 36.

45. Ostrom, *Letters*, 1.20.

46. *Ibid.*, 1.19.

47. Quinn, *Poe*, p. 162.

48. See n. 31 above. The "misty clime" of the speaker recalls Byron rather than Poe.

49. Campbell, "Poe's Reading," p. 168. Richard P. Benton, in *Nineteenth-Century Fiction*, 18 (1963), 193–197, shows that Poe borrowed the characters of "The Assignation" from Byron's affair with the Countess Guiccioli and the art lore from Byron's Folinjo letter to Murray, as recorded in Moore's *Letters and Journals of Lord Byron* (1830).

50. See Arthur H. Quinn and Edward H. O'Neill, eds., *The Complete Poems and Stories of Edgar Allan Poe* (New York, 1946), 2.1066–67 for variant titles.

51. Woodberry, *Life of Poe*, 1.64, deplores his pretentious show of learning and quotations, begun with this line from Chateaubriand, which Woodberry traces verbatim in his edition of Poe's works (New York, 1914), 10.176–177. See Harrison, 7.198, for a mere reference to the locus in Chateaubriand.

52. Only George H. Green has traced these allusions (see n. 13 above).

53. François Chateaubriand, *Itinéraire de Paris à Jerusalem*, in *Oeuvres Complètes* (Paris, 1859), 5.117. Other editions that I have checked contain the italics. Poe could have seen editions of 1811 (two), 1812, and 1822.

54. Chateaubriand, *Itinéraire*, ed. Emile Malakis (Baltimore, 1946), 1.163.

55. *Ibid.*, 1.108. Malakis cites a later edition of this work.

56. De Vere, *Picturesque Sketches* (London, 1850), pp. 27 and 30.

57. Robertson, *Commentary on the Bibliography of Edgar A. Poe* (San Francisco, 1934), 2.163. He further deprecates the sonnet as "not dream-inspired but an intellectual conception."

58. The splitting of *fior* into two syllables is noted by G. Tusiani, *Sonettisti Americani* (Chicago, 1954), pp. 28–29, according to Frances Winwar, *The Haunted Palace*, p. 120.

59. Quinn, *Poe*, p. 124.

60. Although Chateaubriand mentions only "l'hyacinthe" in his allusion to the origin of the name, a possible source for his statement speaks of the flower of "jacinte" as the origin: Coronelle, *Description géographique et historique de la Morée* (Paris, 1686; 2nd ed., 1687)—given by Malakis, *Itinéraire*, 1.163n.

61. Earl L. Griggs, "Five Sources of Edgar Allan Poe's 'Pinakidia,'" *American Literature*, (May, 1929), 196–199.

62. See, e.g., Hervey Allen, *Israfel*, p. 282, for the notice in the *Saturday Visiter* of Oct. 19, 1833, signed by Kennedy, Latrobe, and Miller, the judges, concerning the "varied and curious learning" of the Tales of the Folio Club.

63. See, e.g., Professor Mabbott's item, given in my chap. x, n. 2.

64. Professor Griggs used a four-volume set of the *Curiosities* printed in New York, 1864, identical with my set of 1865, used below. In fact, there were two series, the first originating in 1791 and often revised, at least into the 1820's, and a second series, issued in 1823. In the 1840's these volumes, usually six in number, were merged into one set, printed consecutively. Poe knew especially well the first series, which had reached a sixth edition by 1817.

65. *Curiosities of Literature* (New York, 1865), 2.277, the whole article being 2.260–279; in the 1817 edition, 2.481–511.

66. See Andrews, *Latin-English Lexicon* (New York, 1870), p. 1047.

67. *Q. Horatii Flacci, Carminum Libri IV*, ed. T. E. Page (London, 1909), p. 103.

68. *The Complete Works of Horace* (New York, 1936), p. 272.

69. In a note for *Carminum Libri IV*, 3.15.15, p. 353, Page offers a better explanation than Disraeli for the extension of *purpureus* in meaning, as in "purpureus rosae": The ancient *purpura* had "the deep colour . . . of clotted blood" or a "peculiar sheen or

brilliancy." Hence, Vergil's *Aeneid* VI, 614, "lumine purpureo."

70. *Carminum,* 3.28.15, p. 98.

71. Citations are indicated in my *Dictionary of Names and Titles in Poe's Collected Works* (New York, 1968), p. 46.

72. For the life and associations of Hewitt, see *DAB*, 8.606–607 and *Recollections of Poe by John Hill Hewitt,* ed. Richard B. Harwell (Atlanta, 1949), both of which will be used for my text. Hewitt provides material in his *Shadows on the Wall* (Baltimore, 1877).

73. Given by Harwell, *Recollections,* p. 22. Hewitt reprinted this part of the article in *Shadows,* pp. 42–43. See also Quinn, *Poe,* p. 165.

74. See *Shadows,* pp. 39–41; Hervey Allen, *Israfel,* p. 284, is in error in giving 1833 as the date when Wilmer yielded the editorship to Hewitt, for he had assumed it in 1832 before the contest, hence the pseudonym.

75. Hewitt, in *Shadows,* pp. 154–155, offers the events of both 1829 and 1833 as causes of Poe's hostility. The date (1833) of the fist fight is revealed in Hewitt's letter of 1885, given by V. Starrett, "A Poe Mystery Uncovered," *Saturday Review of Literature,* 26, (May 1, 1943), 4–5, 25. His reprint of the *Minerva* review of *Al Aaraaf* shows how much of it was reprinted, verbatim, in *Shadows on the Wall.*

76. Poe's "A Decided Loss," as it appeared in the Philadelphia *Saturday Courier,* Nov. 10, 1832, 2.1 (columns 1 and 2), is printed in facsimile by John G. Varner, *Edgar Allan Poe and the Philadelphia Saturday Courier* (Charlottesville, 1933), pp. 38–49, the passage being on pp. 41–42. Had Hewitt known about his inclusion in the tale, he would not have printed "Serenade" by "E. A. Poe," in the Apr. 20, 1833 *Visiter,* or the possible Poe poems by "Tamerlane," entitled "To —" and "Fanny," all three of which are ascribed by John C. French in "Poe and the *Baltimore Saturday Visiter,*" *Modern Language Notes,* 33 (May, 1918), 257–267.

77. Harrison, 2.155 and 2.357.

78. Grandjean appears also in "The Angel of the Odd" of Oct., 1844, in connection with false hair, for which reason Varner, p. vi, supposes him to be a wigmaker. Professor Mabbott has identified him for me as Auguste Grandjean, New York "hair treatment expert."

79. The favor, mentioned by Hewitt, *Shadows*, p. 43, is specified by Harwell, *Recollections*, p. 19, as the loan of a half dollar—an indication of Poe's desperate straits in Washington. This is the only point at which Hewitt's antagonism to Poe is tempered.

80. In 1839, according to the *DAB*.

81. Ostrom, *Letters*, 1.201.

82. Hewitt reprinted it next to Poe's "Coliseum" in *Shadows*, 157–159, with a resentful remark: "The first may be found in every edition of Poe's poems; the second in the *only* edition of my poetic works, published about thirty-five years ago." He alludes to *Miscellaneous Poems* (Baltimore, 1838), pp. 74–76.

83. *Shadows*, p. 42, taken from his 1829 review.

84. Palmer C. Holt, "Notes on Poe's 'To Science,' 'To Helen,' and 'Ulalume,'" *Bulletin of the New York Public Library*, 63 (Nov., 1959), 568–570, effectively proves that Poe's "To Science" derives from a translation of Bernardin de St. Pierre's *Studies in Nature*, not from Keats's *Lamia* as claimed by Margaret Alterton, *Representative Selections*, p. 479. For traces of *Endymion* and "The Eve of St. Agnes" in Poe's works see Marvin B. Perry, Jr., "Keats and Poe," in *English Studies in Honor of James Southall Wilson* (Charlottesville, 1951), pp. 45–52.

85. Allen, *Israfel*, pp. 106 and 141; Frances Winwar, *The Haunted Palace*, p. 81.

86. Poe's review of *Ballads and Other Poems* of Longfellow, first printed in *Graham's*, Mar., 1842, given in Harrison, 11.64–85, specifically, p. 76.

87. Quinn, *Poe*, p. 429, and Ostrom, *Letters*, 1.257–258.

NOTES TO CHAPTER 7

1. Carter Boyd, in "Poe's Debt to Charles Brockden Brown," *Prairie Schooner*, 27 (1953), 190–196, mentions Forgues's article in the *Revue*, but he is in error about its being the fashion to trace literary ancestry to Godwin as well as to Hoffman. For French criticism, see Patrick F. Quinn, *The French Face of Edgar Poe* (Carbondale, Ill., 1957) and Arthur H. Quinn, *Edgar Allan Poe* (New York, 1941), pp. 516–519. The latter merely comments that Forgues

placed Poe's tales "for the first time in the great succession of English fiction," without noting Godwin's role.

2. For Poe's statement see *The Complete Works of Edgar Allan Poe*, ed. James A. Harrison (New York, 1902), 16.145; this edition will be used and cited hereafter under "Harrison" or by volume and page number alone. For the "encouragement" see Arthur H. Quinn, Introduction, *The Complete Poems and Stories of Edgar Allan Poe* (New York, 1958), pp. 11–12, although he gives no evidence of Poe's awareness of the reviews in 1846.

3. E. D. Forgues, "Les Contes d'Edgar Poe," *Revue des Deux Mondes*, Ser. 5. Vol. 16 (Oct., 1846), 341–366. Poe himself underscored the comparison of his own work with that of Godwin and Brown in the biographical article for which he provided the material in the *Saturday Museum* of Philadelphia, 1 (Mar. 4, 1843), 1. Among the many laudations of his writings he includes the following:

> Professor John Frost says: "William Wilson, by Mr. Poe, reminds us of Godwin and Brockden Brown. . . . We like to see the evidences of . . . careful and elaborate handling in the execution, not less than of grand and striking effect in the *tout ensemble*." [col. 4, lower half]

For Professor Frost see Poe's "Autography" sketch in *Graham's Magazine*, 19 (Dec., 1841), 285 (Harrison, 15.242–243). My thanks are due to Dean Walter Sedelow and Donna Setzer of the University of North Carolina for sending me the page, xeroxed, of the very rare *Saturday Museum*.

4. *Edinburgh Review*, 107 (Apr., 1858), 426.

5. See William Dunlap, *Life of Charles Brockden Brown* (Philadelphia, 1815), 1.107 and 2.15, and *Cyclopaedia of American Literature*, ed. Evert Duyckinck (Detroit, 1882), 1.612, for the letter from Brown to his brother on the "transcendent merits" of *Caleb Williams*. For Poe's references to Brown see Harrison, 11.206, 12.224, and 16.41. See also Quinn, *Poe*, p. 359, for *Edgar Huntly* as source of "The Pit and the Pendulum." See Ostrom, ed., *Letters of Edgar Allan Poe* (Cambridge, Mass., 1948), 1.117, concerning Poe's intention to devote an article in the *Examiner and Hesperian* of 1839 to C. B. Brown.

6. References to four of these have been made by René Wellek and Austin Warren, *Theory of Literature* (New York, 1949), p.

335, n. 9; Killis Campbell, "Poe's Reading," in *University of Texas Studies in English*, no. 5 (1925), p. 181; Killis Campbell, *The Mind of Poe* (Cambridge, Mass., 1933), p. 15, n. 3. Woodberry, *The Life of Edgar Allan Poe* (Boston, 1909), 1.174, mentions that "he praises with enthusiasm Godwin" and others. The only comment of any length is that of Gerald Grubb, "Dickens and Poe," *Nineteenth-Century Fiction*, 5 (1950), 1–22, specifically, p. 19.

7. The Larousse *Grand Dictionnaire Universel du XIXe Siècle* (1870), 7.1342, remarks that Godwin's death "made more noise in France than in his own country." See also the adulation in *Biographie Universelle et Portative des Contemporains* (Paris, 1834), 2.1900–1902, and *Nouvelle Biographie Générale* (Paris, 1857), 20.934–937.

8. Harrison, 2.154. Poe is quoting *Mandeville* (London, 1817), 3.48.

9. See Harrison, 8.92–94, for Poe's review. After the 1835 American reprint of *Lives of the Necromancers* came those of 1847 and 1876; it was reviewed by the *New-York Mirror*, 13 (Aug. 29, 1835), 70–71; *The Knickerbocker*, 6 (Nov., 1835), 477–478; *Atkinson's Casket*, no. 12 (Dec., 1835), p. 715; *The Southern Rose*, 3 (May 30, 1835), 155–156; and, in the 1847 edition, by *The Literary World*, 2 (Aug., 1847), 91–92. At Griswold's death his library contained only the *Necromancers* and *Caleb Williams* as representatives of Godwin's writings, according to the *Catalogue of the Entire Private Library of the late Rev. Rufus W. Griswold* (New York, 1859).

10. Harrison, 14.6, 20, 23, 31; Brewster, *Letters on Natural Magic* (New York, 1832), pp. 248–255. In his preface Godwin indirectly suggests the comparison between his own and Brewster's book: "The work I have written is not a treatise of natural magic." Among the many reviews of Godwin's work that I have seen, the only other one to compare Godwin and Brewster is that in the *Irish Monthly Magazine of Politics and Literature*, 3 (July, 1834), 408–420. For Poe's use of Brewster see also W. K. Wimsatt, Jr., "Poe and the Chess Automaton," *American Literature*, 11 (May, 1939), 138–151.

11. See Harrison, 8.xvi, on Poe's "curious verbal analysis." Poe was able to read *St. Leon* in the Baltimore Athenaeum library, which he used during his long sojourns in Baltimore, according to Killis Campbell, "Poe's Reading," q.v. in n. 6. The Peabody Institute

has generously lent me the *Catalogue* (1827) showing *St. Leon* (Alexandria, 1801) as included.

12. For Godwin's stress on clear style, see my *Education and Enlightenment in the Works of William Godwin* (New York, 1962), pp. 101–102, 114, 194–195.

13. It is made perhaps indirectly, however, in Robert Spiller, *et al.*, *Literary History of the United States* (New York, 1949), 1.276, in a mention of Bird as showing common traits with Cooper and Simms; Simms may be viewed as a member of the Godwin school of fiction.

14. Occasionally, but rarely, the critics might object to the "tautology of reflections" of the hero, as did the reviewer of *Deloraine*, in the *Metropolitan Magazine*, 5 (1833), 114.

15. Ford K. Brown, *William Godwin* (London, 1926), p. 87: "*Caleb Williams* was thought to have influenced the style and method of Bulwer-Lytton, Ainsworth, and Dickens." Ainsworth's biographers—Ellis, Elwin, Joline, and Blanchard—omit Godwin in favor of Monk Lewis, Mrs. Radcliffe, and Maturin—wrongly, I think.

16. S. M. Ellis, *William Harrison Ainsworth and His Friends* (London, 1911), 1.121–122.

17. Malcolm Elwin, *The London Mercury*, 26 (Aug., 1932), 358, "Like Dickens he had the vaguest notion of a plot." A. H. Joline, *At the Library Table* (Boston, 1910), p. 122, "No power to portray character or to analyze motives; his genius was purely descriptive." However, S. M. Ellis says: "*Guy Fawkes* is one of Ainsworth's best romances: very carefully written, the original scheme laid down skilfully . . . it is also the most psychical. . . . There is indeed a very considerable power of analysis of character, not as a rule a prominent feature of Ainsworth's work" (*William Harrison Ainsworth*, 1.397).

18. Grubb, "Dickens and Poe," *Nineteenth-Century Fiction*, 5 (1950), 1–22, 101–120, 209–221.

19. Grubb, p. 19; Hervey Allen, *Israfel* (New York, 1927), 2.528.

20. *Literary Gazette*, no. 828 (Dec. 1, 1832), pp. 759–760; for the friendship of the two see Una Pope-Hennessy, *Charles Dickens* (London, 1947), p. 134 and Edgar Johnson, *Charles Dickens* (New York, 1952), 1.104.

21. *Museum of Foreign Literature*, 22 (Mar., 1833), 403–405.

22. Quinn, *Poe*, pp. 417–418, verifies the fact that Poe's letter to Mrs. Hale of May 31, 1844, concerned "A Chapter of Suggestions," for the annual *The Opal*, of 1845, published late in 1844; see also Ostrom, *Letters*, 1.255.

23. For the three quotations see *Ellen Middleton*, Tauchnitz ed. (Berne, 1846), pp. 104, 299, 334. For Shelley's remark see his review of *Mandeville* in *Shelley's Prose* (Albuquerque, 1954), p. 311.

24. See Pauline M. Craven, *Lady Georgiana Fullerton, Sa Vie et ses oeuvres*. 5th ed. (Paris, 1889), pp. 39–48 and 104–106.

25. See J. Lasley Dameron, "Poe's Reading of the British Periodicals, *Mississippi Quarterly*, 18 (1965), 19–25, for a related topic.

26. See the *New-York Mirror*, no. 10, whole no. 36 (June 14, 1845), p. 159 for a description of the two art works. Ideas and phrases from this editorial are liberally and literally borrowed by Poe in his article on the "Ivory Christ," in the *Broadway Journal* (2.214), signed "P" but not collected by Harrison.

27. *Ettore Fieramosca* (New York, 1845), pp. 33–34, 76–77, 96, 197, and 273–274, the last being three paragraphs at the end concerning the use of history by a novelist. In the *Broadway Journal*, 2.109, is an uncollected editorial by Poe (initialled in the Halsey copy), giving a devastatingly sarcastic and intemperate rejoinder to a recent *New-York Mirror* defense of Lester's book against Poe's charge of lack of "autorial comment."

28. The language and references of the text and William Doyle Hull II, "A Canon of the Critical Works of Edgar Allan Poe" (diss., University of Virginia, 1941), p. 691, all confirm this as Poe's. The markings by Poe are also proof. My thanks are due to the Huntington Library for answering my queries about the markings in the Halsey copy and to the Duke University Library for a microfilm of the Huntington Library copy.

29. *A First Gallery*, 2nd ed. (Edinburgh, 1851), pp. 20–24. The sequel to it, *Modern Literature and Literary Men, Being a Second Gallery of Literary Portraits*, of 1849, with a New York edition of 1850, continues its praise of Godwin and predicts immortality for three of his novels (New York, 1850), pp. 251–255 and 261.

30. Ostrom, *Letters*, 1.253–254; see also the same charge made earlier, 1.246–247.

31. *Ibid.*, 1.258.

32. *Fleetwood* (London, 1832), pp. viii–ix.

33. Ostrom, 2.329, letter of Aug. 9, 1846, to Philip P. Cooke.

34. *Fleetwood* (1832), p. x. See also Godwin's preface to the 1831 edition of *St. Leon,* p. vi, concerning his growing belief that "the present race of readers" are interested in the previous "train of thoughts" of an author.

35. Ostrom, *Letters,* 2.316.

36. *Ibid.,* 1.256.

NOTES TO CHAPTER 8

1. See Killis Campbell, "Contemporary Opinion of Poe," *PMLA,* 36 (June, 1921), 142–166.

2. See Mary E. Phillips, *Edgar Allan Poe—The Man* (Philadelphia, 1926), 2.1370–1371, for the silhouette of Poe as a "literary Mohawk" with a tomahawk, which together with satirical verses appeared in *Holden's Dollar Magazine,* 3 (Jan., 1849), 22. See W. H. Auden, *Edgar Allan Poe: Selected Prose and Poetry* (New York, 1950), Introduction, for Poe's polemical attitude and his need to deal with so much third-rate writing.

3. Edmund Wilson, "Poe at Home and Abroad," reprinted from *The Shores of Light* (New York, 1952), in Eric W. Carlson, *The Recognition of Edgar Allan Poe* (Ann Arbor, 1966), pp. 142–151, specifically, p. 149.

4. Reprinted from the *Southern Literary Messenger,* June, 1836, in James A. Harrison, ed., *The Complete Works of Edgar Allan Poe* (New York, 1902), 9.46. Textual references to this edition will be made hereafter under "Harrison" or simply by volume and page number.

5. The faulty punctuation of the original statement in *Graham's Magazine* obscures this tripartite division, as I show in "Byron, Poe, and Miss Matilda," *Names,* 16 (Dec., 1968), 390–414.

6. Harrison, 12.248. For a fuller treatment of this theme see chap. xi.

7. Given in David K. Jackson, *Poe and the Southern Literary Messenger* (Richmond, 1934), p. 98.

8. Harrison, 8.74–75; *Messenger,* 2.46–47. The correct dates for the original editions are 1833 for the *Recollections* and 1835 for the

Tales, despite the incorrect dating in the memoirs of Lady Dacre's descendant, Gertrude Lyster, *A Family Chronicle* (London, 1908), p. 75.

9. *The Cambridge Bibliography of English Literature* (Cambridge, 1940), 3.229, is the only source that I have found which says that Lady Dacre both edited and revised Mrs. Sullivan's two works; this is contradicted by the *Quarterly Review,* 49 (Apr., 1833), 228–240.

10. Harrison, 8.74. The London *Athenaeum* also had trouble deciding upon the author and, in its second notice of the book, no. 272 (Jan. 12, 1833), p. 17, declared: "We are not without some suspicion that Lady Dacre had more to do with the composition of these volumes than the title page indicates. . . . We may, however, be mistaken." This notice, reprinted entire in the *New-York Mirror,* 10 (May 4, 1833), 350, if seen by Poe, may have influenced his opinion in this matter.

11. *Quarterly Review,* 49.231.

12. Lyster, *A Family Chronicle,* pp. 79–81. Lady Dacre also feared, with justice, that the *Quarterly* would attack her daughter's book (see n. 30 below).

13. Roorbach, *Bibliotheca Americana* (1852), asserts that Harper and Bros. published the *Recollections* as well as the *Tales* "by Lady Dacre," but gives no date. British novels were usually pirated here within a few months. The *New-York Mirror* of May 4, 1833, writes: "As this popular work is shortly to issue from the American Press, we reprint the Athenaeum notice." The book probably appeared in 1833, although I have found no reviews of this edition in American journals for 1833–1834. I assume that Poe saw the American reprint.

14. Lyster, *A Family Chronicle,* p. 19. The last forty-five pages of Foscolo's *Essays on Petrarch* were devoted to her translations, highly praised by *Blackwood's Edinburgh Magazine,* 13 (May, 1823), 579–588, the review of Foscolo's work, specifically p. 584; see also "Loves of the Poets," *Blackwood's,* 26 (Sept., 1829), 524–530, specifically, p. 530 for praise of Lady Dacre's translations.

15. *The Works of Lord Byron,* ed. R. E. Prothero (London, 1904), Vol. 10 of the set and Vol. 3 of the *Letters,* pp. 196–197. For a favorable reference by Byron to "Mrs. Wilmot" as poet, see Vol. 9 (*Letters,* Vol. 2), 332. Her children's play was *Frogs and Bulls: A Lilliputian Piece in Three Acts* (London, 1838).

16. T. O. Mabbott, *Notes and Queries*, 163 (Dec. 17, 1932), 441, and William Doyle Hull II, "A Canon of the Critical Works of Edgar Allan Poe" (diss., University of Virginia, 1941), p. 390. For the opportunity to use the latter, I am grateful to Dr. Hull and the Alderman Library, University of Virginia.

17. Spiller, Thorp, *et al.*, *Literary History of the United States* (New York, 1949), "Bibliography," 3.451, attributes *Ned Myers* to Cooper. Robert Spiller, *Fenimore Cooper* (New York, 1931), pp. 297–298, speaks of it as "his last book" for the Carey firm in 1843. James Grossman, *James Fenimore Cooper* (New York, 1949), p. 184, excludes the book from the Cooper canon on the basis of style, a view adopted by Donald A. Ringe, *Cooper* (New York, 1962), p. 162, n. 10.

18. Poe's knowledge of *The Pilot* may have led to his calling Pym's boat "The Ariel," the name used by Cooper in *The Pilot*.

19. *Broadway Journal*, 1.81. My gratitude is due to the Duke University Library for sending me its microfilm of the Halsey copy of the *Broadway Journal*, now in the Huntington Library, showing Poe's initial to indicate his authorship of this article.

20. *Tales of the Peerage* had even more success, being reissued in 1849 and 1854 as Bentley's "Standard Novel No. 117" and by Darton and Company in 1859 as "The Parlour Library, No. 190." The fragile, cheap paper of mid-Victorian novels may be one reason why few copies of Mrs. Sullivan's novels can be found today.

21. Both editions are listed in the British Museum *Catalogue*, the first as Vol. 112 of Duncombe's edition of plays, the second as Vol. 134 of Lacy's "Acting Edition of Plays." The only other play by Burton given here is *The Court Fool* with a questioned publication date of 1883. W. Davenport Adams, *A Dictionary of the Drama* (Philadelphia, 1904), p. 232, lists several other apparent farces by Burton, in addition to *The Court Fool*, with no dates: *Forty Winks, Ladies' Man, Player's Progress, Silver King.*

22. William L. Keese, *William E. Burton, Actor, Author, and Manager* (New York, 1885), pp. 7 and 115.

23 Adams, *Dictionary of the Drama*, p. 453, hints at more than these two adaptations, for he speaks of "several plays founded" on this "tale" from *Recollections of a Chaperon* but gives only those by Burton and Buckstone.

24. See Keese, *Burton*, p.8.

25. George C. D. Odell, *Annals of the New York Stage* (New York, 1928), 3.677. The entire series lists no further New York performances.

26. For Burton's career, especially in Philadelphia, see F. C. Wemyss, *Twenty-six Years of the Life of an Actor and Manager* (New York, 1847). For the Philadelphia productions see Arthur H. Wilson, *A History of the Philadelphia Theatre, 1835–1855* (Philadelphia, 1935), p. 571.

27. See Edwin Wolf II, "Horace Wemyss Smith's Recollections of Poe" in *The Library Chronicle: Friends of the Library of the University of Pennsylvania,* 17 (Spring-Summer, 1951), 90–103.

28. A. H. Quinn, *Edgar Allan Poe* (New York, 1941), pp. 274–275. Note that Quinn, p. 277, mentions Burton's "one successful play, *Ellen Wareham,*" without noting its being an adaptation or Poe's interest in the novel. Frances Winwar, *The Haunted Palace* (New York, 1959), p. 199, writes about Burton: "Fancying himself a litterateur as well as an actor-manager and playwright, he had recently produced a successful play, *Ellen Wareham,* in which he combined his talents."

29. *Recollections of a Chaperon: Ellen Wareham* (London, 1853), pp. 322 and 357.

30. Harrison, 8.74. In contrast to Poe's high praise for the tale, the *Quarterly Review* satirized the naive snobbery of *Ellen Wareham.* It says, for example, "Mrs. Sullivan has the art, however, to heighten this apparently superlative distress by some additional touches of extraordinary merit." Ellen is saved from an ignominious journey to the courtroom in a hired "hack chaise" by the kind loan of Lord Besville's carriage (*Quarterly Review,* 49.239–240).

31. Harrison, 8.229–234. See John W. Ostrom, ed., *Letters of Edgar Allan Poe* (Cambridge, Mass., 1948), 1.100–102, for Poe's letter of 1836 to the editor of the *Richmond Courier* giving proof of the clemency of his critiques. Yet Poe himself referred to the "somewhat overdone causticity" of his *Messenger* articles in the "Prospectus of the Penn Magazine," given by Quinn, *Poe,* p. 307.

32. Edward H. Davidson, *Poe: A Critical Study* (Cambridge, Mass., 1957), p. 112. For Poe's praise of *Conti* in Oct., 1836, see Harrison, 9.195.

NOTES TO CHAPTER 9

1. The poem, minus the third stanza, is cited from Poe's *The Raven and Other Poems* (New York, 1845) as reprinted by James A. Harrison, ed., *The Complete Works of Edgar Allan Poe* (New York, 1902), 7.21. This edition is indicated hereafter under "Harrison."

2. See Harrison, 7.155–156 for the following significant variations: 1827 version—line 1, "In youth's spring"; line 18, "poison'd wave"; line 21, "dark imagining"; 1829 version (Boston), p. 64—for 1845 lines 9–12: "And the black wind murmur'd by, / In a dirge of melody— / My infant spirit would awake / To the terror of the lone lake."

3. This is the 1831 version, in Harrison, 7.176. In 1845 the word *deep* is dropped and the reference to "graves" is intensified in "There open fanes and gaping graves / Yawn level with the luminous waves."

4. Both in the title and in the "sinking towers" there is a suggestion of a submerged or submerging city, as in Shelley's stormy "West Wind Ode," with its "old palaces and towers . . . / All overgrown with azure moss and flowers"; compare Poe's second stanza (Harrison, 7.49). Killis Campbell in his edition of Poe's *Poems* (Boston, 1917), p. 209, finds a similarity only in Shelley's "Lines Written among the Euganean Hills," line 49. Louise Pound in two discussions of this poem by Poe in *American Literature*, 6 (1934), 22–27 and 8 (1936), 70–71, assumes an engulfed city.

5. I agree with Killis Campbell, *The Mind of Poe* (Cambridge, Mass., 1932), p. 155, in finding Wordsworth's "Solitary Reaper" in the Hebrides reference, but see below in my text for the possibility that Poe may have seen the misty and desolate isles of the lower Hebrides, such as Egg, Staffa, and Muck.

6. All dictionaries consulted agree with the *OED* in calling the *simoom* or *simoon* (the source perhaps of Poe's confusion) "a hot, dry, suffocating sand wind which sweeps across the African and Asiatic deserts."

7. See Sidney Kaplan on the Tsalalians in his fine Introduction to *The Narrative of Arthur Gordon Pym* (New York, 1960).

8. Arthur H. Quinn, *Edgar Allan Poe* (New York, 1941), pp. 745–746 and 213, discredits Latrobe's inclusion of the "Descent"

among the six prize tales of 1833. My future references to this book will be made as "Quinn" or "Quinn, *Poe*."

9. This is an early instance of the "illimitable dominion" through the plague of King Death, which so powerfully concludes the later tale, "The Masque of the Red Death," as presented in chap. v.

10. Woodberry, in the appendix to his *Life of Edgar Allan Poe* (Boston, 1909), 2.397–399, prints all but the first 200 words of the fragment with the comment that it is "very clearly written, without alteration or erasure, on three narrow strips of blue paper such as Poe used in other MSS. of 1845." If this fact dates the composition, the references to lighthouse material in the 1845 *Broadway Journal*, below, are particularly apposite. T. O. Mabbott prints the whole fragment, including the missing words, in *Selected Poetry and Prose of Edgar Allan Poe* (New York, 1951), pp. 344–345; Mabbott says, however: "The handwriting seems to me to indicate that it was written very late in the author's life" (p. 426). In *Notes and Queries*, 182 (Apr. 25, 1942), 226–227, he asserts that Poe's death must have prevented its being completed.

11. T. O. Mabbott says that an encyclopaedia account seen by Poe must have suggested the tale. Brewster's *Edinburgh Encyclopaedia* (Philadelphia ed., 1832) gives a long, descriptive account of lighthouses with plates of the Eddystone and Bell-Rock structures, 12.48–66 and plate 347; Poe took material from this work for his "Maelstrom" details, as Woodberry shows, *Works of Edgar Allan Poe* (New York, 1903), 4.289–294, and for his Maelzel exposure, as W. K. Wimsatt, Jr., shows in *American Literature*, 11 (May, 1939), 138–151. Poe's tale, dated as 1796, suggests the South Rock lighthouse in Ireland, also of 1796, and secured by iron in the walls, as described by the *Edinburgh Encyclopaedia*, 12.63–64.

12. D. Alan Stevenson, *The World's Lighthouses before 1820* (London, 1919), p. 182, notes the establishment by Act of Congress of lighthouses in 1798 in Hatteras, Ocracoke, and Cape Cod.

13. George R. Putnam, *Lighthouses and Lightships* (Boston, 1933), pp. 92–93 and 98–99, speaks of a ninety-foot-high building at Cape Hatteras in 1798; when rebuilt in 1870 it was 193 feet. He also speaks of those on other dangerous capes along the way to Charleston.

14. See the *Encyclopaedia Britannica*, 14th ed. (1929), 13.628; also Putnam, p. 180, on caissons for lighthouses.

15. See W. H. McCormick, *Modern Book of Lighthouses* (London, 1936), p. 63, and *New International Encyclopaedia* (New York, 1915), 14.130.

16. See Floyd Stovall, "Poe's Debt to Coleridge," *University of Texas Studies in English*, 10 (July, 1930), 70–127. Darrel Abel, "A Key to the House of Usher," *The University of Toronto Quarterly*, 18 (Jan., 1949), 176–186, discusses the tarn as "a symbol of Death-in-Life."

17. Harrison, 2.80 and 2.338. When Poe revised this section of the piece for his 1840 *Tales*, he extended this "lake" passage. The hero's name has several variant spellings.

18. Quinn, *Poe*, pp. 745–746.

19. The name, used by Camoëns in the *Lusiads*, is a Portuguese variant of a Bantu word, and Poe was not confusing the geographical name with the work by Voltaire to which he alluded elsewhere (2.278–279), although his placing it in Libya is arbitrary.

20. See F. De Wolfe Miller, "The Basis for Poe's 'The Island of the Fay,' " *American Literature*, 14 (1942), 135–140. I have failed to discover the original work by John Martin. I suspect that the title, "The Island of the Fay," is Poe's addition, since the paddling figure shows no wings; he may also have requested Sartain to add this figure and some vague wisps on the island itself.

21. Woodberry, *Life of Poe*, 1.236.

22. See Perry Miller, *The Raven and the Whale* (New York, 1956), pp. 71–117 and Claude Richard, "Poe and 'Young America,' " *Studies in Bibliography*, 21 (1968), 25–58.

23. This idea is the basis of a plate article on Harper's Ferry in the May, 1842 *Graham's Magazine*, which I consider to be Poe's, although unsigned. For validation, see my article in *American Literature*, 40 (May, 1968), 164–178.

24. For a good account of what Poe must have observed there, see Cornelius Weygandt, *Philadelphia Folks* (New York, 1938), pp. 292–294, and also Francis B. Brandt, *The Wissahickon Valley Within the City of Philadelphia* (Philadelphia, 1927), pp. 109–111.

25. Quinn, *Poe*, pp. 395–397, and Hervey Allen, *Israfel* (New York, 1926; 1960 ed.), pp. 404–406.

26. For Lippard, see Joseph Jackson, *A Bibliography of the Books of George Lippard* (Pennsylvania Historical Society, n.p., 1930)

and Ellis P. Oberholtzer, *The Literary History of Philadelphia* (Philadelphia, 1906), pp. 254–257. Of Lippard's many works, see especially *Rose of Wissahickon, or the 4th of July, 1776* (Philadelphia, 1847), Prologue, pp. 3–9. In the *Broadway Journal* (1.363) is Poe's uncollected review of the *Quaker City*, by Lippard, called "a genius."

27. Cornelius Weygandt, *The Wissahickon Hills* (Philadelphia, 1940), pp. 31–32, reports it as being signed by B. Matthias when it was reprinted in *The Philadelphia Book or Specimens of Metropolitan Literature*, published in 1836.

28. Quinn, *Poe*, p. 397. An elk is an unlikely pet for patients, being a large dangerous animal, as indicated by Olaus J. Murie, *The Elk of North America* (Harrisburg, 1951), pp. 69, 263–264, and 308.

29. John W. Ostrom, ed., *The Letters of Edgar Allan Poe* (Cambridge, Mass., 1948), 2.356, hereafter cited in my text as "Ostrom."

30. Quinn, *Poe*, p. 358, n. 21, cites R. V. Costello and W. K. Wimsatt, Jr., on the baselessness of Poe's assumption.

31. Poe was perhaps assuming the pseudonym of "William Landor," i.e., Horace Binney Wallace, from whose essays and novel *Stanley* he borrowed many scraps of erudition for his own columns, q.v. in George E. Hatvary's "Poe's Borrowings from H. B. Wallace," *American Literature*, 38 (Nov., 1966), 365–372.

32. Agnes Bondurant, *Poe's Richmond* (Richmond, 1942), pp. 202–203, and H. Allen, *Israfel*, pp. 27–28 and 78–80.

33. Quinn, *Poe*, pp. 65–68; H. Allen, *Israfel*, pp. 55–56, and Mary E. Phillips, *Edgar Allan Poe—the Man* (Philadelphia, 1926), 1.122–132.

34. See *Muniments of the Royal Burgh of Irvine* (Edinburgh, 1891), 2.163, for a discussion of the early use and abuse of this old structure.

35. See, for example, Arnold F. McJannet, *The Royal Burgh of Irvine* (Glasgow, 1938), pp. 223–224. This book was kindly shown me by the Irvine Clerk of Records, in the summer of 1968. See J. H. Whitty, "Poe in England and Scotland," *Bookman* (Sept., 1916), pp. 14–21, for a good account of this period and for photographs of Irvine.

36. H. Allen, *Israfel*, pp. 58–59.

37. This illuminating little leaflet, citing the Boston and Charles-

ton papers of the period, was published in Columbia, South Carolina, 1940, and reproduced *in toto* in the Charleston *News and Courier* of Jan. 5, 1941. I am grateful to Professor Davis's daughter, Sarah Davis Burns, for a copy of the first and to the editor of the paper for the second.

38. H. Allen, *Israfel*, pp. 170–183. See also the article by Charles Lee Lewis, "Edgar Allan Poe and the Sea," in the *Southern Literary Messenger*, 3 (Jan., 1941), 5–10, consulted after this chapter was completed, which traces several sea references in Poe's works to show "the fascination which the sea had for Poe"; he does not specify the nature of the fascination.

39. See "Washington Irving's Letters to Mary Kennedy," by S. T. Williams and Leonard B. Beach, in *American Literature*, 6 (Mar., 1934), 44–65, specifically p. 53. Irving also compares the romantic prospect of the Harper's Ferry gorge to the Hudson at West Point, as does Poe in his Harper's Ferry plate article (see n. 23 above).

40. See Mary E. Phillips's detailed account of Poe's stay at the Brennan farm, *Poe*, 2.882–898; transit to the lower city, she says, was made "by omnibus and ferry-boat," a trip taken at least twice by Virginia who "loved the water" (p. 898). Her detailed map of Poe's New York City residence (p. 892) shows the farm on 84th Street, contradicting the "87th Street" location (p. 883). See also Quinn, *Poe*, p. 414.

41. Phillips, *Poe*, 2.909, and Woodberry, *Life of Poe*, 2.114.

42. Edward Wagenknecht, *Edgar Allan Poe* (New York, 1963), p. 62, mentions Sarah Miller's 1909 account of Poe's rowing to the islands south of Blackwell's "for his afternoon swim."

43. Republished by Jacob E. Spannuth and T. O. Mabbott (Pottsville, Pa., 1929). I discuss Poe's regret in "New York City in the Tales of Poe," *Journal of the Bronx County Historical Society*, 2 (Jan., 1965), 16–22.

44. Sarah Helen Whitman, *Edgar Poe and His Critics* (New York, 1860), p. 32.

45. John Sartain, *The Reminiscences of a Very Old Man* (New York, 1899), 2.207–212.

46. See Quinn, *Poe*, p. 640; also Wagenknecht's brief discussion, *Poe*, p. 229, and my discussion at the end of chap. xi.

47. For example, Marie Bonaparte, *The Life and Works of Edgar Allan Poe*, trans. John Rodker (London, 1949), p. 37, writes, con-

cerning "The Lake": "For Poe, this lake would seem to have been the symbol of his dead mother which lured him on and beckoned him to return and once more merge in her."

48. See, for example, Gaston Bachelard (who admittedly takes his cue from Marie Bonaparte), in *L'Eau et les rêves* (Paris, 1942; reprinted 1947), chap. ii, "L'eau dans la rêverie d'Edgar Poe," pp. 63–96. He presents as basic Poe themes the following: "water is an invitation to die": rivers can be identified with blood; and water represents rain and, in turn, tears from the sky.

NOTES TO CHAPTER 10

1. Among Poe's biographers this tale has received attention only from Mary E. Phillips, *Edgar Allan Poe—The Man* (Philadelphia, 1926), 2.1392–1394.

2. "Von Kempelen" appeared in *The Flag of Our Union*, 4 (Apr. 14, 1849), 2, but was printed from Griswold's edition by James A. Harrison, ed., *The Complete Works of Edgar Allan Poe* (New York, 1902), 6.245–254, with corrections of the spelling of "Humphrey" and "lieden" (for "Flätplatz" see my text, below). My references will be made to the text of Harrison under "Harrison." For the gold rush in "Eldorado" see Killis Campbell, ed., *Poems of Edgar Allan Poe* (Boston, 1917), p. 286, and Oral S. Coad, *Modern Language Notes*, 59 (Jan., 1944), 59–61; T. O. Mabbott, *Modern Language Notes*, 60 (May, 1945), 312–314, also gives other sources, such as Moore's *Epicurean* and Disraeli's reprint of "Tom-a-Bedlam's Song"; see also n. 62 below.

3. John Ward Ostrom, ed., *The Letters of Edgar Allan Poe* (Cambridge, Mass., 1948), 2.417–419. All references to this work will be made under "Ostrom." A fragment of this statement is quoted by Mary Phillips, 2.1393.

4. Ostrom, 2.427; cited also by Hervey Allen, *Israfel* (New York, 1934—reprint of 1926 ed.), pp. 637–638.

5. In "Diddling Considered as One of the Exact Sciences" (Harrison, 5.211), first printed on Oct. 14, 1843, as "Raising the Wind. . . ." Note also his early advice on literary hoaxing in "How to Write a Blackwood's Article" and the tricks recommended in "The Business Man."

6. See Poe's note, added to "Hans Pfaall" in 1840, on "verisimilitude" and his "attempt to give plausibility by scientific detail" (Harrison, 2.103–108).

7. For sources and also criticism of Poe's method of "half-citation" see James O. Bailey, "Sources of Poe's *Arthur Gordon Pym*, 'Hans Pfaall,' and Other Pieces," *PMLA*, 57 (June, 1942), 513–535.

8. For sources other than those given by Bailey, see Keith Huntress, "Another Source for . . . 'Pym,'" *American Literature*, 16 (Mar., 1944), 19–24; R. L. Rhea, "Some Observations on Poe's Origins," *University of Texas Studies in English*, no. 5 (1930), pp. 135–146; and D. M. McKeithan, "Two Sources of Poe's *Pym*," *University of Texas Studies in English*, no. 13 (1933), pp. 116–137.

9. W. K. Wimsatt, Jr., "A Further Note on Poe's Balloon Hoax," *American Literature*, 22 (Jan., 1951), 491–492.

10. Published in London, 1836; Poe used the New York reprint of 1837, q.v., in Harold H. Scudder, "Poe's 'Balloon Hoax,'" *American Literature*, 21 (May, 1949), 179–190.

11. See Ronald S. Wilkinson, "Poe's 'Balloon-Hoax' Once More," *American Literature*, 32 (Nov., 1960), 313–317. For Poe's self-congratulatory account in the *Columbia Spy*, see Arthur Hobson Quinn, *Edgar Allan Poe* (New York, 1941), p. 410. I find that T. N. Weissbuch, "Edgar Allan Poe: Hoaxer in the American Tradition," *New-York Historical Society Quarterly*, 45 (July, 1961), 291–309, takes up some of this material, with less stress on Poe's descriptive use of borrowed data.

12. See Sidney E. Lind, "Poe and Mesmerism," *PMLA*, 62 (Dec., 1947), 107–194.

13. In *Notes and Queries*, 183 (Nov., 1942), 311–312, Professor Mabbott reports that the London pamphlet bore an introduction expressing belief in the hoax, but fails to give the wording. The rare book division of the Columbia University Library has a copy of this threepenny pamphlet of sixteen pages, published by Short and Company in 1846. The full title, printed with a variety of capitals on the cover reads:

Mesmerism "In Articulo Mortis." An Astounding and Horrifying Narrative, Shewing the Extraordinary Power of Mesmerism in Arresting the Progress of Death. By Edgar A. Poe, Esq. of New York.

On the reverse (p. 2), appears this "Advertisement":

The following astonishing narrative first appeared in the American Magazine, a work of some standing in the United States, where the case has excited the most intense interest.

The effects of the mesmeric influence, in this case, were so astounding, so contrary to all past experience, that no one could have possibly anticipated the final result. The Narrative, though only a plain recital of facts, is of so extraordinary a nature as almost to surpass belief. It is only necessary to add, that credence is given to it in America, where the occurrence took place.

14. According to Professor Mabbott, *Selected Poetry and Prose of Edgar Allan Poe* (New York, 1951), p. 425, "nobody took it seriously."

15. Bratislava, prominent medieval city of Slovakia, formerly the capital of Hungary, was usually given the German spelling of Pressburg, as in the *Encyclopaedia Britannica*, 11th ed., 22.299. However, I find Presburg in *Chambers's Encyclopaedia* (Philadelphia ed., 1895), 8.390.

16. Wimsatt, *American Literature*, 11 (May, 1939), 138–151, and George Woodberry, *Life of Edgar Allan Poe* (Boston, 1909), 1.178. Professor Wimsatt implies that Brewster wrote the account in the *Edinburgh Encyclopaedia;* however, Poe accuses Brewster, his real source of knowledge, of plagiarizing the account. Though he was unaware of it, Poe was correct, for the articles on "Androides" and "Automata" were written by William Dalyell. Poe's high respect for Brewster is indicated by his many references to this scientist, q.v. in my *Dictionary of Names and Titles in Poe's Collected Works* (New York, 1968), p. 13.

17. *Nouvelle Biographie Générale* (Paris, 1863), 32.643, gives the price as $500,000, while Michaud's *Biographie Universelle* (Paris, 1861), 24.13, gives it as $400,000. See both works for the great fame and prestige of Wolfgang von Kempelen in his day.

18. Harrison, 2.27. Mabbott, *Selected Poetry and Prose*, p. 416, says that Morella "presumably 'majored' " in black magic at Pressburg, renowned for the "science."

19. *The Dial,* 4 (Jan., 1844), 408.

20. It appears on p. 14 (misnumbered as 41) and p. 15.

21. *Deutsche Schnellpost*, 3 (July 2, 1845), 198. The New York Historical Society has the most complete set of this periodical, which it graciously allowed me to xerox for collation of texts.

22. See Harrison, 16.181, 186–187, and 299 for praise of Humboldt and 16.183 for his preface about the "poem."

23. Poe's obvious authorship of the items in the "Miscellany" is noted by Killis Campbell, "Bibliographical Notes on Poe," *The Nation*, 89 (1909), 623–624.

24. My text for this item is A. H. Quinn and E. H. O'Neill, eds., *The Complete Poems and Stories of Edgar Allan Poe* (New York, 1946), 2.705, since they use the text of *The Flag of Our Union*, 4 (Apr. 14, 1849), 2, which neither Griswold nor Harrison knew. Collation of the texts of Harrison and Quinn reveals that Poe's erroneous "Humphrey" and "lieden" of the first printing were corrected by Harrison (see 6.297) as being obviously wrong; Griswold's apparent change from Poe's "Flatzplatz" to "Flätplatz" was preserved by Harrison.

25. There is a hint of the same universal fate in "The Colloquy of Monos and Una" (Harrison, 4.205). Quinn, *Poe*, p. 187, surmises that the 1833 shower of meteors in Baltimore or Halley's comet of 1835 chiefly inspired "The Conversation." Poe disparages Arago in a tone caught up from Walsh's *Sketches of Conspicuous Living Characters in France*, reviewed in Apr., 1841 (Harrison, 10.134, 136, 138). Poe undoubtedly knew the rather flippant review by his colleague Briggs, in the *Broadway Journal* of Mar. 29, 1845 (1.194), of Arago's *Popular Lectures on Astronomy*.

26. John W. Wayland, *The Pathfinder of the Seas* (Richmond, 1930) and Charles Lee Lewis, *Matthew Fontaine Maury: Pathfinder of the Seas* (Annapolis, 1927). For other accounts see Diana Fontaine Maury Corbin, *A Life of Matthew Fontaine Maury* (London, 1888), Jaqueline Caskie, *Life and Letters of Matthew Fontaine Maury* (Richmond, 1928), and Patricia Jahns, *Matthew Fontaine Maury and Joseph Henry* (New York, 1961). There is available no complete or thorough life of the founder of oceanography, so far as I know.

27. *Dictionary of American Biography*, 12.429. See also Diana Corbin, chap. v, pp. 53–73, and J. Caskie, p. 27.

28. Harrison, 9.50. Of all the accounts of Maury, only that of Lewis (n. 26 above) alludes to Poe's review of his book (p. 28) and none mentions the "Von Kempelen" reference. A thorough search of Maury's papers might reveal material concerning Poe, especially in connection with his editorship of the *Messenger* in 1843.

29. For Maury's "Harry Bluff" papers, see Diana Corbin, *Life*, chap. iv, 40–52, and Lewis, *Maury*, pp. 34–41.

30. Lewis, pp. 51–65. See Patricia Jahns, *Maury and Henry*, p. 102, for the effect of the charts on travel to the gold fields. He was known to be influenced by ideas in the *Cosmos* of Humboldt, so admired by Poe; in turn Humboldt was to send him a highly flattering public letter for his contributions to science in 1855 (see J. Caskie, *Life*, pp. 52–53).

31. The printings for this and other tales are listed in Quinn and O'Neill, *Complete Poems and Stories*, 2.1073–1074, as well as in the chapter by John C. Wyllie in *Humanistic Studies in Honor of John Calvin Metcalf* (Charlottesville, 1941), pp. 322–338.

32. In fact, no major biography mentions him at all. If Poe had contributed to the *Messenger* during the first eight months of 1843, the period when Maury was editor, a direct contact could be established; Heartman and Canny, *A Bibliography of First Printings of the Writings of Edgar Allan Poe* (Hattiesburg, 1943), p. 261, list two doubtful items as reviews by Poe, under Jan. and Dec., the second being a treatment of Cooper's *Ned Myers*. See also William Doyle Hull II, "Canon of the Critical Works of Edgar Allan Poe" (diss., University of Virginia, 1941), p. 187, for the assertion that Poe contributed nothing between 1837 and 1845. Poe's use of the old title "Lieutenant" for Maury in the tale also argues against any active acquaintance of the two men.

33. The sentence, to which Professor Mabbott first called my attention, was added to the text after the edition of 1817; see the 12th edition (London, 1841), p. 104. Poe's knowledge of Disraeli's work is proved in the twenty-five items indicated in Earl L. Griggs, "Five Sources of . . . Poe's 'Pinakidia,'" *American Literature*, 1 (May, 1929), 196–199. See also n. 2 above.

34. For the *Zanoni* review, wrongly collected by Harrison, 11.115–123, see Poe's disclaimer in Ostrom, 1.202.

35. The use of the Athenaeum Library is asserted by Killis Campbell, "Poe's Reading," *University of Texas Studies in English*, no. 5 (1925), pp. 166–196, n. 7. The Peabody Institute graciously sent me the *Athenaeum Catalogue* (Baltimore, 1827), listing Davy's *Elements*.

36. Thomas Hall, "Poe's Use of a Source," *Poe Newsletter*, 1 (Oct., 1968), 28.

37. Another Davy reference by Poe appears in the *Broadway Journal* of June 7, 1845 (1.363)—Poe's review of *Lives of Men of Letters and Science who flourished in the time of George III* by Brougham. Although uncollected by Harrison, this item is confirmed by Hull, "Canon of the Critical Works," p. 614, as "probably" by Poe.

38. *Broadway Journal*, 2.375. This item is confirmed by the attribution to Poe in Hull, "Canon of the Critical Works," p. 689.

39. *North American Review*, 60 (1845), 156–195. Significantly, all but two pages are devoted to Draper's work.

40. *New-York Mirror*, 1, no. 17 (Feb. 1, 1845), 268. Hull, pp. 455–456, reports its appearance in the *Daily Mirror* of Jan. 20, 1845, 1.268. The item has not been collected. See Allen, *Israfel*, pp. 494–495, for Poe's employment as a "mechanical paragraphist."

41. Thomas O. Mabbott, "Letters from Eveleth to Poe," in the *New York Public Library Bulletin*, 26 (Mar., 1922), 174–191, and James Southall Wilson, "The Letters of Edgar A. Poe to George W. Eveleth," in *Alumni Bulletin*, University of Virginia, 3rd Series, 17 (Jan., 1924), 35–56. See Ostrom's note, 2.517.

42. For the letter see Harrison, 17.346–347. Wilson, p. 38. See also John Carl Miller, *J. H. Ingram's Poe Collection at the University of Virginia* (Charlottesville, 1960), p. 37, item #119: a letter of Mrs. Whitman to Ingram, in 1874, accusing Griswold of having "fabricated the letter." Poe knew that Eveleth was a Marylander, she asserts, but none of Poe's letters, sent to Eveleth in Brunswick or Phillips, Maine, mentions this idea.

43. Preface to *Eureka* (Harrison, 16.183) and Quinn, *Poe*, p. 541.

44. Mabbott, "Letters from Eveleth," pp. 190–191.

45. For the letter see Wilson, p. 56 and Ostrom, 2.449; for the *Eureka* reference see Harrison, 16.189–197, where, however, "Hog" is introduced as "the Ettrick shepherd," i.e., James Hogg, and seems not to allude to Draper at all.

46. Mabbott, "Letters from Eveleth," p. 180.

47. For Draper's position and contributions see Donald Fleming, *John William Draper and the Religion of Science* (Philadelphia, 1950), especially chap. iv, "The American Davy." At New York University, as professor of chemistry and botany, he helped to found the medical school in 1841. By 1847 he had edited or produced four widely circulated texts in science.

48. See Ernest Marchand, "Poe as a Social Critic," in *American Literature*, 6 (Mar., 1934), 28–34; Margaret Alterton and Hardin Craig, *Edgar Allan Poe: Representative Selections* (New York, 1935), pp. lxvii–lxxii; Killis Campbell, "Poe's Treatment of the Negro and Negro Dialect," *University of Texas Studies in English*, no. 16 (1936), pp. 107–114; and Sidney Kaplan, "Introduction," to *The Narrative of Arthur Gordon Pym* (New York, 1960).

49. See Edith Birkhead, *The Tale of Terror* (London, 1931), chap. vi, "Godwin and the Rosicrucian Novel," pp. 100–127. By 1849 the following editions of *St. Leon* had been printed: London –1799, 1800, 1816, 1831, 1839, 1849; Dublin–1800; Paris–1799, 1800; Hamburg–1800; Alexandria, Virginia–1801, 1802.

50. See *St. Leon* (London, 1831), pp. 214–247, 250–253, 400, 415, 449–478.

51. *Lives of the Necromancers* (London, 1834), pp. 29, 31, 35–36, 277–278, 283–284. As an indication of the early association of the Rosicrucian group with gold-making see Gabriel Naudé's *Instruction. . . sur la vérité des frères de la Rose-Croix*, 1623, in *Dictionnaire Infernel* (Brussels, 1845), p. 378. For Poe's general admiration of Godwin, see chap. vii above.

52. They are specified in my *Dictionary of Names and Titles*, p. 106.

53. See *DAB*, 17.161–162.

54. Feb. 11, 1848. Quinn, *Poe*, pp. 539–541, also gives a paragraph from the *Home Journal*, reprinted by the *Courier*.

55. Poe's error of "lieden" for *leiden*, as printed in the *Flag of Our Union*, 4 (Apr. 14, 1849), 2, is retained by Griswold and corrected by Harrison, as indicated in Harrison, 6.297, and reprinted in Quinn and O'Neill, *Complete Poems and Stories*, 2.704.

56. Ostrom, 2.433; see also, 2.450.

57. Quinn and O'Neill, *Complete Poems and Stories*, 2.1071, show the previous printings.

58. See, for example, the episode involving the daguerreotype taken in Providence, Nov. 8, 1848, and the picture itself in Hervey Allen, *Israfel*, pp. 622–623.

59. See Allen, *Israfel*, pp. 618–629, and Quinn, *Poe*, pp. 572–587. Quinn denies any marked deterioration in Poe at this period, pp. 568–571.

60. Only Mary E. Phillips, *Poe*, 2.1393–1394, connects the event

and the story. She comments that the "six years" might easily have been six weeks since he left the Providence hostelry, but her conjecture of a real Von Kempelen bound for California seems untenable.

61. By coincidence Sarah Helen Whitman used the words, "public notoriety," for the affair in a letter that she wrote to Griswold on Dec. 12, 1849, given by H. P. Vincent, *American Literature,* 13 (May, 1941), 162–167.

62. There is a peculiar fitness in Poe's writing in the prefatory "Letter to B—" in his West Point *Poems* of 1831: "Delicacy is the poet's own kingdom—his *El Dorado*" (Harrison, 7.xxxix). Eldorado is used for a dream world of soothing death also in "Dream-Land" of 1844, which Poe called one of his "best" poems in a letter to Lowell (Ostrom, 1.258).

NOTES TO CHAPTER 11

1. This chapter was aided by travel grants from the American Philosophical Society and the American Council of Learned Societies and by the kind permission of Lord Abinger to consult his Godwin manuscripts at Bures. *Notes and Queries,* 1st ser., 5 (Apr. 10, 1852), 354, indicates that the original inscription was "Miserimus," renewed after 1820 with a corrected spelling.

2. The *DNB* article on Thomas Morris refers to sonnets on "Miserrimus" published by Edwin Lees in 1828 and by Henry Martin in *Sonnets and Miscellaneous Pieces* (Birmingham, 1830), q.v. in n. 4 below. Lees edited the *Worcestershire Miscellany* (1829), but I have been unable to find the publication in which his sonnet appeared. There is no indication that Wordsworth or Reynolds ever knew about these two sonnets.

3. See *The Letters of William and Dorothy Wordsworth* (Oxford, 1939), 3.283–284, 293–294, 337, and 344; this text is hereafter indicated in my chapter as *"Letters."* Wordsworth apparently had a keen interest in epitaphs; see his "Essay upon Epitaphs," published in Coleridge's *Friend,* of Feb., 1810, and many poems, such as "Epitaphs, Translated from Chibrera" (1810), "Rob Roy's Grave" (1803), "Cenotaph" (1824), "Epitaph in the Chapel-Yard

of Langdale" (1824), "Elegiac Musings" (1830), "A Place of Burial" (1831), "By a Best Husband Guided" (1835), and "Inscription for a Monument" (1843).

4. *The Keepsake of 1829* (London, 1828), p. 156. Because the publication date antedates that in the title, most editors wrongly attribute this sonnet to 1829; e.g., *Poetical Works* (Oxford, 1946), 3.48, and *The Shorter Poems of William Wordsworth* (London, 1907), p. 509. The first edition of the collected poetical works (Longman *et al.*, London, 1832), 2.197, wrongly printed a capital *h* for "he" in line 10, an error preserved in all subsequent editions, with marked injury to the meaning. Not having found a single example of Henry Martin's book of 1830 in the United States (see n. 2 above), I offer my transcription from the British Museum copy. The phrase "wretched one" and Martin's note, on p. 69, specifying Thomas Morris as "Miserrimus" suggest that he is tacitly correcting Wordsworth's misconception of 1828.

Miserrimus / An Inscription in Worcester Cathedral
"Miserrimus!" What language, wretched one!
   Could for thy fate wake deeper sympathy?
   Bitter thy cup! thy stern fidelity,—
That would no other as thy sovereign own
Than him thy country banished from her throne;
   To whom thou, in thy youth's sincerity,
   Hadst vowed allegiance; what availed it thee?—
"Miserrimus!" replies thy burial stone.—
"Miserrimus!" yea, 't was thy lot to groan
   Full three score years in scorn and penury;
Twice did the Stewart's meteor flash relume
Thy dying hope,—'t was but to deepen gloom;
   Yet never did thy conscious heart bemoan
That thou hadst sacred kept thine oath's integrity.
                        [p. 16]

5. In 1826, Aug. 23; in 1827, Feb. 26 and 29, Mar. 1, Apr. 7, June 30, Sept. 9; in 1829, June 7, Sept. 29, Nov. 18 and 22; in 1830, Jan. 10, Feb. 9 and 10; in 1831, Mar. 12, 16, and 23; May 26, Sept. 13, and Oct. 12; in 1832, Sept. 28, Dec. 18 and 26; in 1833, Jan. 3 and 6, June 3–15, reading Reynolds's second novel,

Coquette, meeting him July 6 and 16 and Aug. 16; in 1834, Godwin lists for Sept. 6: "Miserrimus, pp. 201."

6. *The Court Journal,* no. 193 (Jan. 5, 1833), p. 13; *The Metropolitan Magazine,* 6 (Apr., 1833), 84. See also the laudatory review in *The London Literary Gazette,* no. 829 (Dec. 8, 1832), pp. 803–804. Brief excerpts from other British journals are furnished in the 1836 American edition, pp. 1 and 11, presumably copied from the first 1833 London edition. Richard R. Madden, *The Literary Life and Correspondence of the Countess of Blessington* (New York, 1855), 2.338, indicates that Reynolds owed his literary celebrity to *Miserrimus.*

7. *The Gentleman's Magazine,* 103 (Mar., 1833), 245. In the same note to *Miserrimus,* Reynolds indicates his debt for the idea to Wordsworth, a fact recorded also in *Notes and Queries,* 5th ser., 11 (May 31, 1879), 432.

8. *The Parricide* (Philadelphia, 1836), pp. 3–6.

9. For Poe's references see James A. Harrison, ed., *The Complete Works of Edgar Allan Poe* (New York, 1902), 16.62–63, and 13.91–95; to this edition future references in the text will be made as "Harrison" or merely by volume and page numbers. The *DNB* alone indicates this reissue of *The Parricide,* by G. W. M. Reynolds, without date; neither the British Museum *Catalogue* nor the *English Catalogue* lists it. In the copy owned by the New York Public Library, the preface is dated 1847, with an obscured title-page date, but the first printing of this production of the *Reynolds's Miscellany* office may have been earlier.

10. For the publication dates of both in 1849 and 1850 see Harrison, 7.218–219 and 222.

11. *Martin Faber* (New York, 1837), "Advertisement," pp. v–xii. It should be possible to check on the question of the derivation of *Martin Faber* now that a copy of the Nov., 1829 issue of the *Pleiades and Southern Literary Gazette* containing the short story has at last been found; the discovery and announcement of its forthcoming publication in the centennial edition of Simms's works are given as a postscript in John C. Guilds, "William Gilmore Simms and the *Southern Literary Gazette,*" *Studies in Bibliography,* 21 (1968), 59–62.

12. R. W. Griswold, *Passages from the Correspondence* (Cam-

bridge, Mass., 1898, p. 81; see also *The Letters of William Gilmore Simms* (Columbia, S. C., 1953), 2.223.

13. Griswold, *The Literati, Marginalia, Suggestions, and Essays* (New York 1850, p. xxxiii. But see Griswold's high praise of Laughton Osborn's *Confessions of a Poet* in his *Prose Writers of America,* 4th ed., (Philadelphia, 1852), p. 32.

14. Harrison, 16.151–152. Griswold also overlooked Poe's truly extravagant praise of Osborn's attack on his critics in Mar., 1849 (Harrison, 13.165–168).

15. The letter was given by George E. Woodberry in *The Life of Edgar Allan Poe* (Boston, 1909), 2.345–347.

16. In his biography of Poe, Woodberry does not follow his own suggestion made in *The Works of Edgar Allan Poe* (Chicago, 1905), 5.355–356 ("Notes"), in which he asserts: "J. N. Reynolds was an acquaintance of Poe." The hint is taken up by Mary E. Phillips, *Edgar Allan Poe* (Philadelphia, 1926), 2.1505; as a possibility by Arthur H. Quinn, *Edgar Allan Poe* (New York, 1941, p. 640; by Frances Winwar, *The Haunted Palace* (New York, 1959), p. 376; and by Hervey Allen, *Israfel* (2nd printing, New York, 1934), pp. 337 and 674.

17. Aubrey Starke, "Poe's Friend Reynolds," *American Literature,* 11 (May, 1939), 152–159; and Robert F. Almy, "J. N. Reynolds: a Brief Biography," *Colophon,* n.s. 2 (Winter, 1937), 227–245.

18. See Robert L. Rhea's "Some Observations on Poe's Origins," *University of Texas Studies in English,* no. 10 (July, 1930), pp. 135–146, which shows some parallels with the speech but chiefly with Morrell's *Narrative of Four Voyages.* For "Another Source" see K. Huntress, *American Literature,* 16 (Mar., 1944), 19–24. For Poe's references see Harrison, 3.167–170.

19. The 1843 item was not collected by Harrison; perhaps for that reason John W. Ostrom in *The Letters of Edgar Allan Poe* (Cambridge, 1948), 1.272–273, believed that the two-page "review of Reynolds" mentioned in Poe's 1845 letter to George R. Graham was not published. It appeared in *Graham's Magazine,* 23 (Sept., 1843), 164–165, to which I was led through the gracious suggestion of Thomas O. Mabbott. Starke refers to it, although Almy either missed the item or saw no reason to mention it. The *Columbia Spy* item is collected in *Doings of Gotham,* ed. T. O. Mabbott (Pottsville, Penn., 1929), pp. 49–50.

20. Given by Harrison, 1.332. He also cites the examination made by Mr. Spencer in the *New York Herald,* Mar. 27, 1881, of Dr. Moran's account of the death in the same paper on Oct. 28, 1875, 1.328–332. Moran's account is given in the *Works of Edgar Allan Poe* (New York, 1884), 1.cxvi–cxxiv.

21. Street addresses are given, and something might be gained from tracing proximity to the hospital. Most of the names are those of humble artisans and shopkeepers out of the social class of Neilson Poe. Moran eliminates all mention of Reynolds, including the death call, in his *Official Account of His Death* of 1885. For Henry R. Reynolds see Edward Wagenknecht, *Edgar Allan Poe* (New York, 1963), p. 229, n. 7.

22. For the whole course of Poe's relations with Griswold see Killis Campbell, *The Mind of Poe* (New York, 1962, reprint), pp. 63–98, and Quinn, *Poe,* chap. xx, pp. 642–695.

23. *Harper's New Monthly Magazine,* 45 (Sept., 1872), 557–568, specifically, p. 565. The later addition to the story is in Stoddard's *Recollections, Personal and Literary* (New York, 1903), p. 151.

24. Stoddard, *Recollections,* pp. 146–151, and also told in his memoir in *Select Works of Edgar Allan Poe* (New York, 1880), pp. cxii–cxv. See Woodberry, *Life of Poe,* 2.446–447, for other articles on Poe by Stoddard.

25. "Edgar Allan Poe," *The National Magazine,* 2 (Mar., 1853), 193–200.

26. *Ibid.,* p. 200. For Stoddard's habit of concluding critical surveys of authors' accomplishments with a poem see his "stories of unhappy lives," as his preface calls the articles in *Under the Evening Lamp* (New York, 1892), pp. 45, 89, 104, 117, 133, 148, 163, 199, 212, 224, 243, and 283.

27. Stoddard, *The King's Ball* (New York, 1863), p. 71, seems to be deriving a situation and language from the Worcester Cathedral gravestone; the dying King Felix, sinful and penitent, talks to his son:

> Speak kindly of me after I am gone,
> And see my name be graven on the stone,
> "Infelix," mind, not "Felix,"—that would be
> A cruel, lying epitaph for me.

28. *Songs of Summer* (Boston, 1867), pp. 145–146, and *Poems of Richard Henry Stoddard* (New York, 1880), pp. 126–127.

29. In Stoddard's *Poems* (Boston, 1852), for echoes of Keats see "To a Nightingale," pp. 119–120; "The South," pp. 74–76; and "Ode," pp. 33–36; and in *Poems* (New York, 1880), see "Hymn to Flora," pp. 11–17, and "Autumn," pp. 127–129.

30. *Recollections*, pp. 145, 152, and 154.

31. Oliver Leigh, *Edgar Allan Poe* (Chicago, 1906), p. 54.

32. *The Poe Cult* (New York, 1909), pp. 135–139.

33. *Edgar Poe and His Critics*, 2nd ed. (Providence, 1885), p. 18.

34. *The Life of Poe* (London, 1880), 2.294. *Scribner's Monthly*, 14 (Oct., 1877), 859–860, in a review of William F. Gill's *Life of Poe* cites the Englishman James Hannay's reference to Stoddard as a "pious scribbler" for his "Miserrimus" contumely.

35. This fact is given in Woodberry, *Life of Poe*, 2.448.

36. See *The Works of Poe* (1884), 1.cxxx–clv.

NOTES TO CHAPTER 12

1. Edward H. Davidson, ed., *Selected Writings of Edgar Allan Poe* (Boston, 1956), p. 500; see also Eric W. Carlson, ed., *Introduction to Poe* (Glenview, Ill, 1967), p. 574: "undoubtedly Poe's greatest story."

2. The text for the tale is that of James A. Harrison, ed., *The Complete Works of Edgar Allan Poe* (New York, 1902), 3.273–297; to this edition all references will be made under "Harrison" or simply by volume and page numbers. For the various works cited by Poe, chiefly on p. 287, see the annotations in my *Dictionary of Names and Titles in Poe's Collected Works* (New York, 1968), under each title as given originally by Poe.

3. Thomas Ollive Mabbott, ed., *Selected Poetry and Prose of Edgar Allan Poe* (New York, 1952), p. 419.

4. Professor Mabbott's note, p. 418, that all the recherché works cited by Poe "concern in one way or another the idea that spirit is present even in inanimate things, and that the world, or macrocosm, has relations to the microcosm, man" is rather questionable in application to *Vert Vert* (for Poe's "*Vertvert*"); this is the tale of a

parrot from a convent, which learns profane language and is then punished, reformed, and finally killed with kindness.

5. Although Poe was a very careless speller, I assume that he deliberately changed "tryst" to "trist" for its "uncouth effect," without necessarily knowing that it was indeed an obsolete form of the word.

6. For other instances of this "veneer" see "King Pest" (Harrison, 2.168–184; "Uncase the varlet" in the early form of "The Masque of the Red Death" (4.319); and several phrases in "Politian" (7.59–79).

7. E.g., I find a long article in the Paris *Figaro*, 5, no. 16 (Jan., 1830), 1–2, on Lucretia Maria Davidson's "melancholy genius" and "rare, native gifts."

8. Harrison, 10.174–178, specifically, p. 174.

9. Harrison, 10.223. Perhaps Poe derived his phrase "the napthaline river" (Harrison, 7.112) from a similar phrase in *Amir Khan* (New York, 1829), p. 9.

10. Harrison, 10.221–226. Poe's information about Southey's frenzied defense of Chatterton's family, here mentioned, does not come from the prefaces to the two works on the Davidson sisters which Poe reviewed in Aug. and Dec., 1841.

11. The second edition, published also in 1786, contains 341 pages, of which pp. 140–276 are devoted to Letter 51, drawn from the Chatterton manuscript papers.

12. My facts are taken from Gilbert Burgess, *The Loveletters of Mr. H and Miss R* (Chicago, 1895), Introduction, pp. v–xvi.

13. Robert Southey, *Monthly Magazine*, 8 (Nov., 1799), 770–772.

14. Sir Herbert Croft, *Gentleman's Magazine*, 70 (Feb., 1800), 99–104; 70 (Mar., 1800), 222–226; 70 (Apr., 1800), 322–325.

15. *Monthly Magazine*, 9 (Apr., 1800), 253.

16. Joseph Cottle, *Reminiscences of Samuel Taylor Coleridge* (New York, 1847), pp. 109–111, specifies £300 as the sum. The *Monthly Magazine* 15 (July, 1803), 636, briefly reviews the work and tells of Southey's generous aims.

17. Croft, *Love and Madness*, 2nd ed., pp. 154 and 188.

18. *Ibid.*, p. 37.

19. *Encyclopaedia Britannica*, 11th ed., 2.84.

20. For Poe's use of Coleridge's book, see Palmer C. Holt, *Ameri-*

can Literature, 34 (Mar., 1962), 8–30, but Holt misses the point that Robins was falsely credited with Anson's *Voyage;* the "catalogue" of ships is in Homer, not in the modern work, to which Holt makes, I believe, an irrelevant reference.

21. Croft, *Love and Madness,* p. 252.

22. *Poems* (London, 1833), pp. 8–19.

23. *Poems* (London, 1842), pp. 4–18 and 206–208. Poe must have known the Ticknor reprint (Boston, 1842 and 1843).

24. For the identification of Poe himself as the knight of "Eldorado" see chap. x. Ideas which are parallel in both Poe and Tennyson's "Lady of Shalott," Part III, are the "bold" knight, his singing a song, contrasting imagery of "sunshine" and night or "shadow," an unspecified mission, and a similar pattern of rhyme.

25. John Ward Ostrom, ed., *The Letters of Edgar Allan Poe* (Cambridge, Mass., 1948), 1.253; future references to this work will be made under "Ostrom."

26. Harrison, 8.309. Similarly, see Poe's review of Bryant's poems in the Jan., 1837 *Messenger* (Harrison, 9.304), and of Longfellow's *Voices in the Night* (Harrison, 10.78–80).

27. Harrison, 11.175–176, 16.28, and 12.180–184.

28. E.g., see his letter to F. W. Thomas of May 25, 1842, thus designating *Graham's* (Ostrom, 1.197); also his letter of Aug. 7, 1849, to Patterson (Ostrom, 2.457).

29. Lewis P. Simpson, "Touching 'The Stylus': Notes on Poe's Vision of Literary Order," *Louisiana State University Studies in American Literature,* no. 8 (1960), pp. 33–48 and 164–165.

30. For a very brief account of Poe's efforts on behalf of the two projected magazines, see Bernard Kogan, *Southern Literary Messenger,* 2 (Aug., 1940), 442–445.

31. Arthur H. Quinn, *Edgar Allan Poe* (New York, 1941), pp. 375–376. Floyd Stovall, ed., *The Poems of Edgar Alan Poe* (Charlottesville, 1965), makes no mention of the motto.

32. It is printed by George E. Woodberry, *Life of Edgar Allan Poe* (Boston, 1909), 1.271–275, with the date of Jan. 1. 1841. Except for minor aspects of spelling, punctuation, and one paragraph indentation, it is identical with the reprint in Quinn, *Poe,* pp. 306–308, taken from the *Philadelphia Saturday Courier,* 10 (June 13, 1840), 2. Hervey Allen, *Israfel* (New York, 1926; reprint of 1934), pp. 375–376 reprints Woodberry's text.

33. See Poe's letters to J. E. Snodgrass and F. W. Thomas in the fall of 1841 on Graham's financing *The Penn* (Ostrom, 1.183–185).

34. Mary E. Phillips, *Edgar Allan Poe—The Man* (Philadelphia, 1926), 1.292–293; Allen, *Israfel*, p. 163; Quinn, *Poe*, p. 116.

35. Quinn, *Poe* p. 119.

36. The anecdote is given by Gabriel Harrison, actor-artist and, at that time, storekeeper, in the *New York Times*, Mar. 4, 1899, p. 144, from which account Allen, *Israfel*, pp. 500–501, gives it. Mary E. Phillips, *Poe*, 2.927 and 2.1645, cites an earlier account by Harrison in the *Brooklyn Eagle* of Nov. 18, 1875, Vol. XXXVI, no. 273, in which she spells as "Thaddeus K. Peasley," Harrison's designation of "Peasly," which differs from the "Perley" of his second article. In the *Brooklyn Eagle*, Harrison mentions a correspondence of "The White Eagle" with the "The Star-Spangled Banner" in "measure and time." Professor Mabbott, I recall, once suggested that "Perley" came from Poe's knowledge of Horne Tooke's *Diversions of Purley*, mentioned early (Harrison, 9.105).

37. In his headnote to Wilmer's "Recollections of Edgar A. Poe," given in *Merlin, Baltimore, 1827; together with Recollections of Edgar A. Poe by Lambert A. Wilmer* (New York, 1941), p. 28, Professor Mabbott traces E. S. T. Grey to Disraeli's *Vivian Grey*, one of Poe's favorite novels.

38. Quinn, *Poe*, pp. 757–761; see my note on the subject in *The Scriblerian*, 1 (Apr., 1969), 30–31.

39. *The American Review. A Whig Journal of Politics, Literature and Science*, 1 (Feb., 1845), 143–145. For the accompanying headnote see Harrison, 7.210–211. Only this printing bore the name "Quarles."

40. Phillips, *Poe*, 1.718–738.

41. For a listing, see my *Dictionary*, p. 8.

42. Harrison, 12.36, 158, 177; and 15.64.

43. See the Poe *Dictionary* entries under Bulwer, p. 15, and my tracing of "Tell-Tale Heart" to a Bulwer tale, *American Notes and Queries*, 4 (Sept., 1965), 7–9.

44. For further sources in Bulwer of Poe's tales, see Killis Campbell, *The Mind of Poe* (Cambridge, Mass., 1933), pp. 162–163 and 170. Since the pseudonym was used for the tales as a kind of set when republished in the 1845 *Broadway Journal*, it is also possible that Poe was mindful of "The Luck of Barry Lyndon," a series pub-

lished in the 1844 *Fraser's Magazine* by Thackeray under the pseudonym of editor "Fitz-Boodle."

45. My text is that of the *Saturday Museum,* Vol. I, no. 13 (Mar. 4, 1843). I wish to express my gratitude to Dean Walter A. Sedelow of the Library School of the University of North Carolina, Chapel Hill, for providing me with a facsimile reproduction of page 1, containing the long biography of Poe, and of the prospectus of *The Stylus* on p. 3. Dudley Hutcherson, "The Philadelphia *Saturday Museum* Text of Poe's Poems," *American Literature,* 5 (Mar., 1933), 36–48, unaware of the North Carolina holding, mentions using the copy in the University of Virginia—the only other complete issue known—for his discussion of the text of the many poems cited by Poe in the biography. Hutcherson observes that this sketch was first printed on Feb. 25, 1843 (see also Ostrom, 1.223). Since the top of column 3 alludes to the prospectus on "another page" it is clear that it was printed at least once in February and once in March. Donna Setzer, of the University of North Carolina Library, has kindly searched the Mar. 18 and Apr. 1 issues, to report no trace of the prospectus. Having probably used the University of Virginia copy, Quinn printed portions of the prospectus of 1843, with a few liberties of wording and punctuation, chiefly in italics (*Poe,* pp. 375–376). He reduces the seven paragraphs of the body to five, the most serious omissions being paragraph 2 and paragraph 4; the less important paragraphs of the postscript are also omitted.

46. See, e.g., Sidney P. Moss, *Poe's Literary Battles* (Durham, 1963); see also Mary E. Phillips, *Poe,* 2.1370–1371 for the reproduction of F. O. C. Darley's silhouette of Poe as "our literary Mohawk," illustrating the satire "A Mirror for Authors" by "Motley Manners" in the Jan., 1849 issue of *Holden's Dollar Magazine.*

47. Lewis P. Simpson, in "Touching the Stylus," earnestly presents Poe's claim to defend the budding "republic of letters," and only in his final two paragraphs does he doubt Poe's temperamental fitness and America's cultural readiness for such an organ.

48. It was also known as a classical Latin phrase; see Christy, *Roman Maxims and Phrases of All Ages* (New York, 1903), 2.119: "He writes with an iron pen" (given only in English translation).

49. Horace Binney Wallace, *Stanley* (Philadelphia, 1838), 1.51: " 'It was the stern sincerity of an honest freedom,' said I, 'the consciousness that he battled singly for the right—that with a magic

transformation made the pen of Pope, as Paulus Jovius said of his own, sometimes a pen of gold and sometimes a pen of iron. . . . Buying no voices and leaguing with no confederates, he stretched forth his hand in the name of Truth, and with that name he wrought his miracles.' " See my text below for Poe's use of the hand image and chap. ix, n. 31 above for Poe's debt to Wallace.

50. Michaud, *Biographie Universelle* (Paris, 1856), 16. 515, says that he frankly admits his two pens, and as for his venality, "Il ne se défend pas lui-même dans ses lettres."

51. *Grand Dictionnaire Universel du XIXᵉ Siècle* (Paris, n.d.), 9.1058, in connection with his loss under Henry II of a pension given him by Francis I, states that "he did not fear to avow immediately that he had two pens," etc. The source given—Brantôme's *Les Vies des Grands Capitaines du Siècle Dernier*—does not seem to show it.

52. Bayle, *Dictionnaire, Historique et critique* (reprint of Paris, 1820), 8.398–408, specifically, p. 401; however, Bayle's stated source, de Thou, *Histoire Universelle*, speaks only of Jovius's crass partiality.

53. Alexander Chalmers, *The General Biographical Dictionary* (London, 1815), 19.170–172.

54. Thomas, *Universal Pronouncing Dictionary of Biography and Mythology*, 5th ed. (Philadelphia, 1930), p. 1121.

55. *Encyclopaedia Britannica*, 11th ed., 15.527.

56. *English Bards*, lines 6–9. Byron had borrowed the "gray goose-quill" from Pope's *Epistle to Dr. Arbuthnot*—not Poe's source, I believe. Poe was probably also unfamiliar with Alfred de Vigny's lines in *Livre Moderne: L'Esprit pur*, I: "Si l'orgueil prend ton coeur quand le peuple me nomme, / Que de mes livres seuls te vienne ta fierté. / J'ai mis sur le cimier doré du gentilhomme / Une plume de fer qui n'est pas sans beauté" (1837). These seem to reflect Jovius's statement.

57. See John W. Robertson, *Commentary on the Bibliography of Edgar A. Poe* (San Francisco: Russian Hill Private Press, 1934), page facing 277. Robertson notes, at the bottom, that his facsimile reprint is "from a unique copy formerly in the possession of the author." Presumably Mary Phillips, 2.1252, without giving the provenance of the document, alludes to this copy in her brief citations.

58. My gratitude is owed to David A. Randall and Josiah Q. Bennett of the Lilly Library of Indiana University for a facsimile copy of the Apr. version, sent by Poe on Feb. 29, 1848, in a letter. The lower right-hand corner has been torn and remargined, as my bracketed completions indicate.

59. There were at least four prospectus versions and probably others for *The Penn* magazine, as noted above. Since those of Jan. and Apr., 1848, are very similar, I regard them all as consisting basically of three versions. The differences of the Jan., 1848 text from that of Apr. are given below according to the paragraphs in Robertson's reprint:

2—the extensive and permanent influence
2—a journal wherein my interest should not be merely editorial, lies
7—by very much [in italics in Apr.]
7—Engravings, when used, will be of the highest order of art, but are promised only in obvious illustration of the text. [not in the Apr. version]
7—per annum, or *Three Dollars* per single volume, in advance
8—Business letters should be addressed to Edgar A. Poe & Co; all others to
9—January, 1848
lower right-hand corner—COPIES [not in Apr. version]

60. Mary Phillips, 2.1252, confirms me in this assumption concerning Anthon.

61. The title page, used as my frontispiece, is given by Eugene Field in *Some Letters of Edgar Allan Poe to E. H. N. Patterson* (Chicago, 1898), opposite p. 16, with this note on p. 22: "This drawing, an exact facsimile of which appears in its proper place, is made with black ink upon pink paper. The vignette, clipped from the prospectus of the *Stylus* (. . . 1843), is pasted upon the sheet." This is manifestly in error, as Poe's letter of May 23, 1849, indicates (Ostrom, 2.443). Field does not indicate the provenance of his page. Mary Phillips, *Poe*, 2.1405, reprints the page from Field's work. The same design, with printing alterations only, seems to be included by Allen, *Israfel*, facing p. 588, with an attribution: "Courtesy W. Van R. Whitall, Esq., of Pelham, New York."

INDEX

A Selective Listing of Names and Titles